CONTEMPORARY'S

MATH SKILLS THAT WORK

A Functional Approach for Life and Work

BOOK TWO

ROBERT MITCHELL

Project Editors
Ellen Frechette
Kathy Osmus

CONTEMPORARY BOOKS
CHICAGO

Photo Credits
Page viii: © Camerique, Inc. Page 32: © C. C. Cain.
Page 70: © Jim Whitmer. Page 106: © Norman Mosallem,
Tony Stone Worldwide. Page 140: © H. Armstrong Roberts.
Page 160: © Camerique, Inc.

Published by Contemporary Books, Inc.
180 North Michigan Avenue, Chicago, Illinois 60601
Manufactured in the United States of America
International Standard Book Number: 0-8092-4123-4

Published simultaneously in Canada by
Fitzhenry & Whiteside
91 Granton Drive
Richmond Hill, Ontario L4B 2N5
Canada

Editorial Director
Caren Van Slyke

Editorial
Karen Schenkenfelder
Cliff Wirt
Lisa Black
Lynn McEwan
Lisa Dillman

Editorial Assistant
Erica Pochis

Editorial Production Manager
Norma Fioretti

Production Assistant
Marina Micari

Cover Design
Georgene Sainati

Illustrator
Cliff Hayes

Art & Production
Carolyn Hopp

Typography
Impressions, Inc.
Madison, Wisconsin

Cover photo © Walter Hodges/Westlight

CONTENTS

To the Instructor

The Functional Approach to Math

Students often ask, "Why study math?" This is a fair question and one that is often difficult to answer convincingly in the classroom. As an instructor, you know that a student's perspective is quite different from your own. While you may see math as relevant in everyday life, many of your students regard math as something they'll never use again!

Part of our goal as math educators is to show why math is important and to do this in a way that draws students to the subject. We often ask ourselves, "How can I help my students form positive attitudes about math?"

Perhaps the best way to do this is to "make math real" by drawing on resources from your students' own experiences, resources familiar in their roles as family members, consumers, and employees. Emphasizing adult experiences is the cornerstone of the functional approach to math.

As a starting point, help adult students realize that recipes, rent payments, grocery bills, restaurant checks, phone and utility bills, checkbooks, charge cards, and dozens of other similar items are all mathematically rich topics. By using these familiar items as focal points, you can lay a groundwork of confidence and experience. Building upon these resources, you can give attention to higher-level computation and problem-solving skills as student interest and skill level increase. The functional approach to math prepares adults to use mathematics where they'll most likely need it: at home, in the marketplace, and at work.

About *Math Skills That Work*

The two *Math Skills That Work* books are designed to address the functional needs of adult students. Each book in this adult math-literacy series contains complete computation instruction and a core of functional activities interwoven for high-interest reading. The functional activities center around marketplace, workplace, and home experiences most relevant to adults. These activities are designed to pique the interest of your students and provide points for discussion, such as students' personal and classroom experiences or local newspaper ads. Special activity pages called "In Your Life" and "On the Job" highlight topics that are of particular interest and relevance to adult learners.

Each *Math Skills That Work* book can be used in independent study or in group instruction. While *Book One* covers whole numbers, money, and basic measurement topics, *Book Two* covers decimals, fractions, percents, and data analysis.

Estimation and Calculators

Another aspect of the functional approach to math is the recognition that, in today's world, most math is done either mentally or by calculator. *Math Skills That Work* responds by addressing the two math tools adults will use most often in everyday life: **estimation** and **calculators.** Throughout each book, instruction in estimation and calculator use is integrated into computation problems and functional activities. Additional activities are provided to help students learn when estimation is a reasonable alternative to computing an exact answer.

It is noteworthy that estimation is especially important when students use calculators. For example, an estimate of the quotient $588 ÷ 21 is $600 ÷ 20 = $30. The estimate $30 tells students whether they pressed the correct calculator keys when dividing. A calculator answer of $28 would be reasonable (and correct) while a calculator answer of $280 would alert students to keying errors.

The *Math Skills That Work* series is designed so that you, the instructor, can emphasize computation, estimation, and calculator use at your own level of comfort and at each student's level of ability. Whenever possible, it is recommended that each student learn all three of these important skills. Ideally, students can practice estimation and calculator skills in designated exercises and get additional practice by using these tools to check answers to selected computation problems.

To the Student

Welcome to *Math Skills That Work, Book Two*

This book is designed to provide you with the skills needed for work with decimals, fractions, percents, measurement, and data analysis. You'll also learn to apply these skills where you're most likely to need them: at home and on the job.

Each unit of this book has a number of features designed to make your study more enjoyable. Among these features are:

- short activities based on home, consumer, and workplace situations
- "In Your Life" activities that highlight topics of interest to consumers
- "On the Job" activities that highlight topics of interest to workers
- "Focus on Calculators" activities that teach you how to use a calculator to compute the answers to a wide variety of problems

In addition, *Math Skills That Work* contains:

- special activities designed to teach you how and when to estimate instead of finding an exact answer
- unit Skill Reviews that recap the skills taught in each unit
- a comprehensive Post-Test that gives you a chance to test your mastery of many of the skills taught in this book

On a number of pages, a row of Skill Builders comes before the practice exercises. Skill Builders are problems that have been started for you. Look at the steps that have been done, then complete each problem.

To get the most out of your work, do each problem and activity carefully. Check your answers to make sure you are computing accurately. A complete answer key starts on page 186.

UNIT ONE

Numbers Smaller than One

Customer: Excuse me, sir. I'd like to buy a good electric drill, but I don't want to spend too much money. Can you show me what you have?

Salesman: You've come to the right place. We have several models on sale right now, and some have manufacturer's rebates. This WorkRite drill, for example, is regularly priced at $36.00. But with a rebate of $.25 for every dollar spent, you'd save $9.00.

Customer: My brother has the same drill and likes it. What other brands do you have of similar quality?

Salesman: Well, let's see. These drills over here have been marked $\frac{1}{4}$ off the original prices. So this $36.00 drill is now only $27.00. It's a great deal.

Shopping around for sales can save you money.

Customer: I saw the same drill advertised at a department store for 25% off! How am I ever going to figure out what the best deal is?

Salesman: Yeah, I know. Sometimes it seems like you have to be a math genius just to do a few home repairs.

Think About It

- In the passage above, circle the three numbers smaller than one. (**Hint:** one is a decimal [money], one is a fraction, and one is a percent.) Do they have the same or different values?
- Why isn't it easy for this customer to figure out which is the best deal?

How Do Numbers Smaller than One Play a Part in *Your* Life?

Decimals, fractions, and percents are all ways to express numbers smaller than one. You may not have realized it, but you use these numbers all the time in real life. Answer the following questions to see how.

Describe a time when you used a decimal in a conversation with someone. (Remember, money can be expressed in decimal form, and *everybody* talks about money!

____

____

Describe a time when you *wrote* a fraction. (**Hints:** Do you write down recipes? Do you write checks?)

____

____

Where have you seen the percent sign (%) used frequently? Have you ever written a percent sign? When?

____

____

Of the three different ways to express numbers smaller than one, which are you most comfortable using? Why?

____

____

Imagine that you own a store. Which of the three methods (decimal, fraction, percent) would you use to advertise a sale? Why?

____

____

Skills You Will Learn

Number Skills

- reading and writing decimal fractions
- reading and writing mixed decimals
- comparing decimal fractions
- reading and writing proper fractions
- reading and writing mixed numbers
- comparing proper fractions
- reading and writing percents

Life and Workplace Skills

- working with decimal fractions
- using equivalent fractions, for sorting
- writing part as a fraction of a whole

Thinking Skills

- understanding decimals, fractions, and percents
- solving one-step math problems
- solving multistep math problems

Calculator Skills

- calculator basics

Becoming Familiar with Numbers Smaller than One

You, and the people around you, talk about numbers smaller than 1 all the time.

"You'll need a quarter pound of butter for the cake."
"Go about two-tenths of a mile down this road and take a left."
"Seventy percent of the workers attended the meeting."

You can take a whole object such as a pound, a mile, or a group of workers and divide it into smaller parts. Each part of that whole is represented by a number smaller than 1.

In this chapter, you'll learn the meaning and uses of the three ways to express numbers smaller than 1:

- fractions—$\frac{1}{4}$ or one-fourth or one-quarter
- decimals—.2 or two-tenths
- percents—70% or 70 percent or seventy percent

▼ Practice

A. Write the correct number on each blank line.

One Whole Object **Divided into Smaller Parts**

1.

__________ **How many parts?**

____ **out of** ____ **How many left?**

____ **out of** ____ **How many were eaten?**

2.

__________ **How many parts?**

____ **out of** ____ **How many left?**

____ **out of** ____ **How many spent?**

3.

__________ **How many parts?**

____ **out of** ____ **How many shaded?**

____ **out of** ____ **How many unshaded?**

B. For each statement below, circle the whole that is being discussed, and underline the part. The first one is done as an example.

1. "Your calculation is off about twelve-hundredths of an inch."
2. "We're about two-thirds of the way through this job."
3. "I should have gotten a half dollar in change, sir."
4. "Is this sale item fifteen percent off the original price?"
5. "The house is situated on a quarter acre of land."
6. "My son's school is only about eight-tenths of a mile away."
7. "The recipe calls for an eighth of a teaspoon of salt."
8. "I got eighty percent of the math test correct."
9. "Half my time was spent on the telephone!"
10. "Jim had to finance ninety percent of the price of the new car."

C. Listed below are words standing for parts. Be sure to know the meaning and spelling of these words.

For practice, write the correct word on each blank line in the Skill Check column.

	Whole Object	**Shaded Amount**	**Skill Check**	
1.		one-half	1 of 2 parts is called one-	**half**
2.		one-third	1 of 3 parts is called one-	________
3.	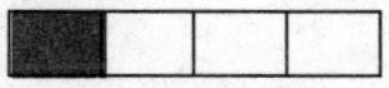	one-fourth	1 of 4 parts is called one-	________
4.	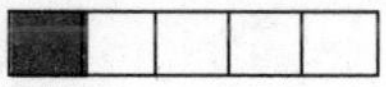	one-fifth	1 of 5 parts is called one-	________
5.	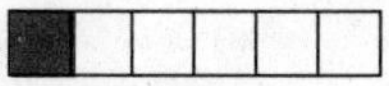	one-sixth	1 of 6 parts is called one-	________
6.	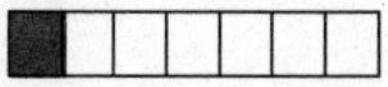	one-seventh	1 of 7 parts is called one-	________
7.	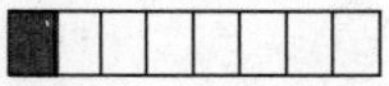	one-eighth	1 of 8 parts is called one-	________
8.	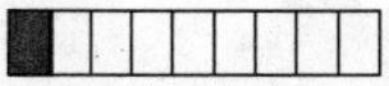	one-ninth	1 of 9 parts is called one-	________
9.	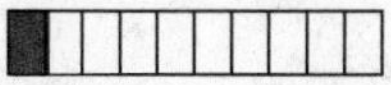	one-tenth	1 of 10 parts is called one-	________

Decimal Fractions

Dollars and Cents

Each of us sees or uses **decimal fractions** every day. This is because our money system is based on them.

- With dollars and cents, we use two decimal places:

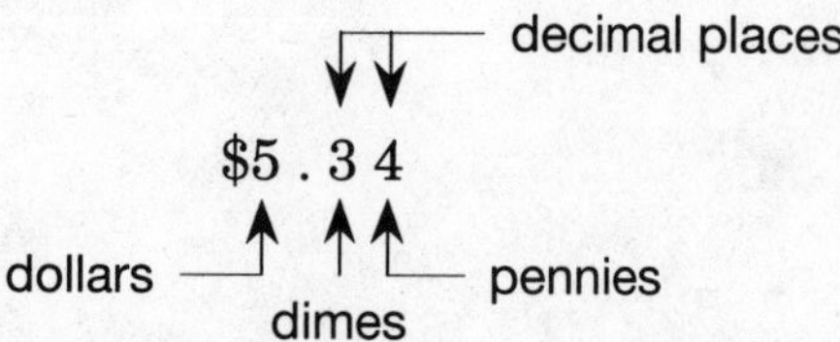

.1 dollar

- One dime ($.10) is one-tenth of a dollar.
- One penny ($.01) is one-hundredth of a dollar.

.01 dollar

The First Three Decimal Places

From dollars and cents you already know the first two decimal place values: **tenths** and **hundredths**.

- The third decimal place value is **thousandths.**

. X X X

tenths, hundredths, thousandths

Examples:

.3	3-tenths
.8	8-tenths
.04	4-hundredths
.09	9-hundredths
.002	2-thousandths
.007	7-thousandths

Look for These "th" Words

Most decimal fractions you'll ever use will have three or fewer digits. So, when you think about decimal fractions, think about these three "th" words: tenth, hundredth, and thousandth.

Value	**Decimal Fraction**	**Meaning**
one-tenth	.1	one part out of 10 parts
one-hundredth	.01	one part out of 100 parts
one-thousandth	.001	one part out of 1,000 parts

The number of digits to the right of the decimal point is called the **number of decimal places**. Here's a memory aid to help you remember decimal place names:

- 10 has one zero, and tenth has one decimal place.
- 100 has two zeros, and hundredth has two decimal places.
- 1,000 has three zeros, and thousandth has three decimal places.

Reading Decimal Fractions

A decimal fraction may have one or more nonzero digits.
To read a decimal fraction:

- Read the number just as you would a whole number.
- Read the place value of the digit at the far right.

Example	Number +	Place Value	Read as
.4	4	tenths	4 tenths
.04	4	hundredths	4 hundredths
.35	35	hundredths	35 hundredths
.035	35	thousandths	35 thousandths
.150	150	thousandths	150 thousandths

▼ Practice

1. Write a decimal fraction to represent the part of each figure that's shaded.

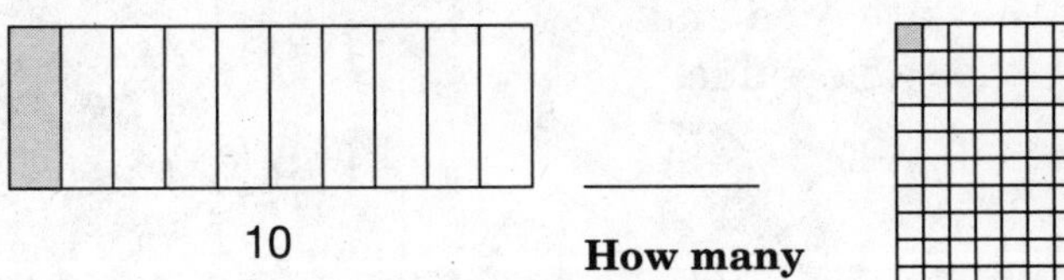

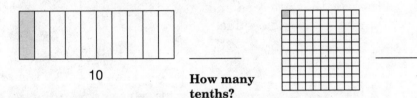

10 ______ **How many tenths?**

100 ______

1,000 ______

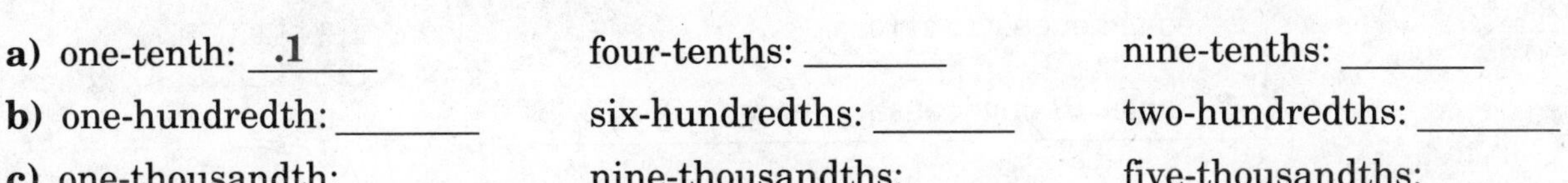

2. Write each amount as a decimal fraction.

a) one-tenth: **.1** four-tenths: ______ nine-tenths: ______

b) one-hundredth: ______ six-hundredths: ______ two-hundredths: ______

c) one-thousandth: ______ nine-thousandths: ______ five-thousandths: ______

3. A co-worker is dictating the following decimal numbers to you. For each statement, circle the correct number.

a) "The length is five-tenths of a centimeter."

.05 5.0 .5

b) "The correct amount of change is nine cents."

$.90 $.09 $.009

c) "Your calculation is eighteen-hundredths of a gram off."

18 .018 .18

d) "One hundred eighty-two thousandths is correct."

1.82 .182 18.2

Writing Zero as a Place Holder

Although 0 has no value, it is used as a **place holder.**

- Placed between the decimal point and a digit, *zero changes the value of a decimal fraction.*

Example 1: .08 differs from .8 because of the 0 in the tenths place. The 0 *holds* the 8 in the hundredths place.

.8

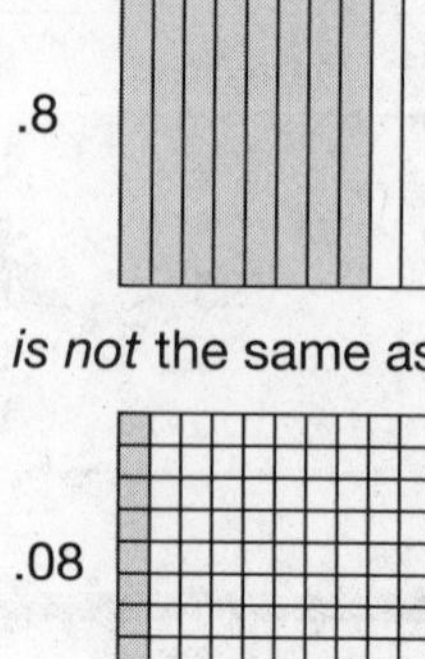

is not the same as

.08

> A zero that comes between the decimal point and the last nonzero digit is called a **necessary zero.** A necessary zero cannot be removed without changing the value of a number.
>
> **Examples of necessary zeros:** .04 .506 .009

- Placed at the far right of a decimal fraction, a zero changes the way a fraction is read, *but does not change its value.*

Example 2: .80 and .8 differ in the way they are read and spoken aloud, yet they have the same value.

Read .80 as "eighty-hundredths."

Read .8 as "eight-tenths."

.8

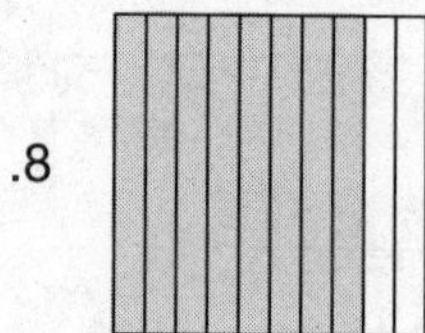

is the same as

.80

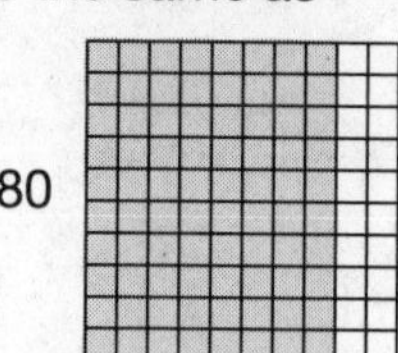

> Because zeros at the far right do not change the value of a decimal fraction, these zeros are called **unnecessary zeros:**
>
> **Examples of unnecessary zeros:** .20 .150 .800

▼ Practice

Underline each necessary zero. Cross out each unnecessary zero (.001, .1~~00~~).

1. .05 .106 .007 .30 .650 .800

2. .109 .048 .070 .050 .004 .097

When you multiply the following numbers on a calculator, the calculator does not display the right-hand zero. For each answer, circle the correct money value.

3. $\$.05 \times 4 =$ [**.2**] $.02 $.020 $.20 $2.00

4. $\$.25 \times 2 =$ [**.5**] $.50 $5.00 $.05 $.050

Writing Decimal Fractions

To write a decimal fraction, first identify the "th" word to decide **place value.**

- The place value gives the position of the right-hand digit of the decimal fraction.
- Write the number, and write 0s as place holders if needed.

Example: Write thirty-six thousandths as a decimal fraction.

The "th" word is thousandths.

Write 36 so that the 6 ends up in the thousandths place—the third place to the right of the decimal.

0 is written as a place holder.

.036

6 ends up in the thousandths place.

Answer: Thirty-six thousandths is written .036.

▼ Practice

1. Bill took an order over the phone. The customer ordered pipe of various wall thicknesses. Write each quoted thickness on the Purchase Order at right.

"Type A, forty-eight thousandths of an inch."

"Type D, two-tenths of an inch."

"Type F, fifteen-thousandths of an inch."

"Type R, one hundred twenty-five thousandths of an inch."

"Type G, five-hundredths of an inch."

"Type M, four-tenths of an inch."

PURCHASE ORDER

ITEM TYPE	WALL THICKNESS
Type A	**.048** inch
Type D	______ inch
Type F	______ inch
Type R	______ inch
Type G	______ inch
Type M	______ inch

2. Reporting on a 100-meter race, the announcer told by how much each runner "just missed the world record." Write these times as decimal fractions on the form at right.

"Johnson, forty-seven thousandths of a second."

"Whiteside, three-tenths of a second."

"Morris, thirty-one hundredths of a second."

"Handly, one hundred nine thousandths of a second."

"George, seven-hundredths of a second."

Runner	Time off Record
Johnson	______ sec.
Whiteside	______ sec.
Morris	______ sec.
Handly	______ sec.
George	______ sec.

Comparing Decimal Fractions

Decimal fractions are easy to compare when they have the same number of decimal places.

.75 is larger than .45 because 75 is larger than 45.

.013 is larger than .009 because 13 is larger than 9.

When decimals do not have the same number of places, add 0s until they do.

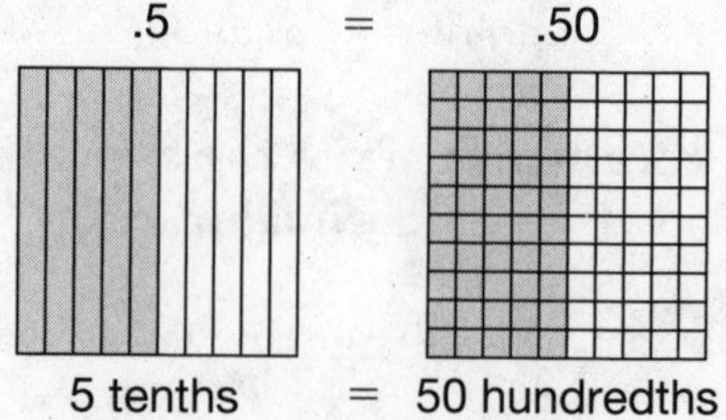

Remember, adding a 0 after the last digit of a decimal does not change its value.

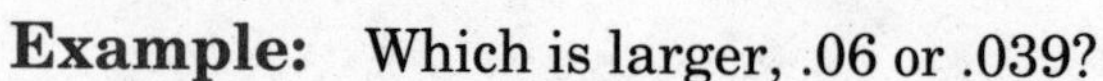

Example: Which is larger, .06 or .039?

Step 1. Give .06 and .039 the same number of places.
Add 0 to .06: .06 = .060

Step 2. Compare .060 and .039.
.060 is larger than .039 because 60 is larger than 39.

Answer: .06 is larger than .039.

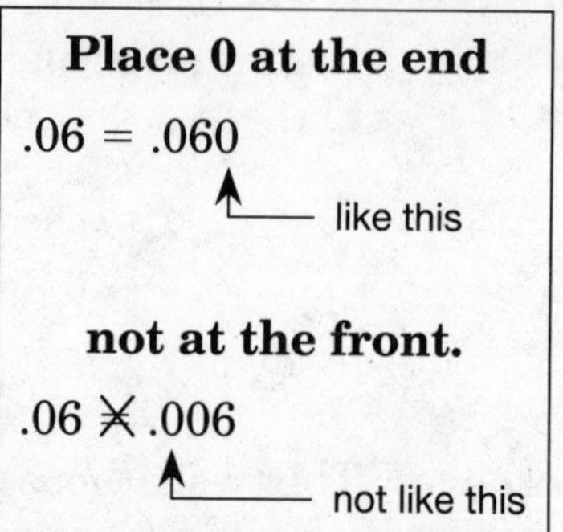

Place 0 at the end
.06 = .060
like this
not at the front.
.06 ≠ .006
not like this

▼ Practice

In each pair below, circle the larger decimal fraction.

1. .9 or .7	**4.** .07 or .13	**7.** .125 or .087
2. .3 or .1	**5.** .50 or .05	**8.** .200 or .175
3. .5 or .8	**6.** .53 or .29	**9.** .450 or .625

10. As a jeweler, you sort gold wire threads by weight. Look at the weight given for each thread, and decide which envelope it belongs in. (First, add zeros so each decimal has three decimal places.)

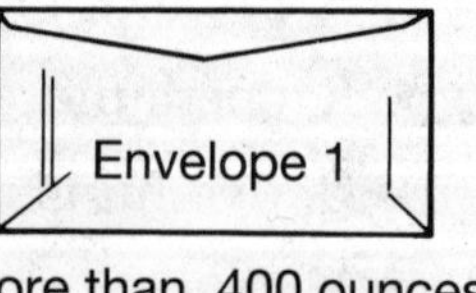

more than .400 ounces

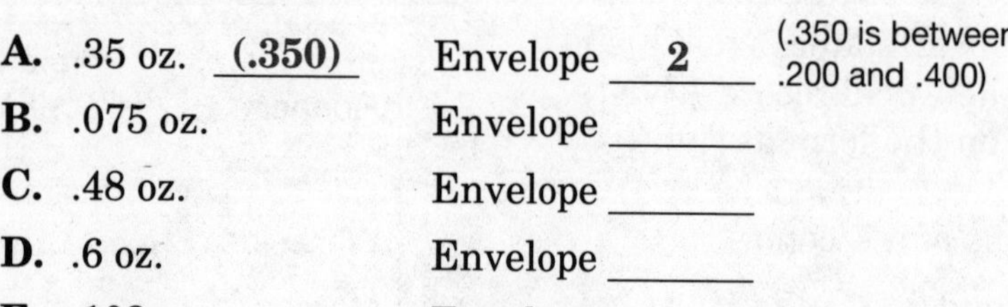

A. .35 oz. (.350) Envelope 2 (.350 is between .200 and .400)
B. .075 oz. Envelope ______
C. .48 oz. Envelope ______
D. .6 oz. Envelope ______
E. .102 oz. Envelope ______
F. .204 oz. Envelope ______

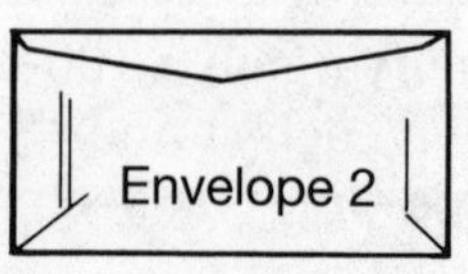

between .200 and .400 ounces

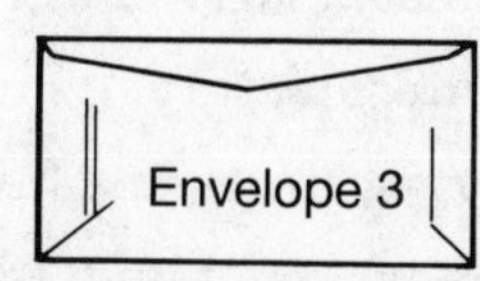

less than .200 ounces

Mixed Decimals

A **mixed decimal** is a whole number plus a decimal fraction.

13.05 is a mixed decimal

whole number — decimal point — decimal fraction

- A decimal point separates the whole number from the decimal fraction.
- The most common use of mixed decimals is with money. The amount $8.59 is a mixed decimal.
- When you read a mixed decimal, read the decimal point as the word *and.*

  $8.59 is read, "Eight dollars *and* fifty-nine cents."

  8.59 is read, "Eight *and* fifty-nine hundredths."

Comparing Mixed Decimals

- To compare mixed decimals, compare the whole numbers first. Then compare the decimal fractions if necessary.

  $5.62 is larger than $3.99 because 5 is larger than 3.
- 7.4 and 7.06 have the same whole number, so compare the decimal fractions. 7.4 is larger than 7.06 because .4 (.40) is larger than .06.

▼ MATH TIP

Studied together, mixed decimals and decimal fractions are commonly just called "decimals."

▼ Practice

A. Write the following mixed decimals as numbers.

1. three and two-tenths ________ four and eighty-four hundredths ________

2. fifteen and six-tenths ________ eleven dollars and seventy-five cents ________

3. six and eight-thousandths ________ twenty-six dollars and five cents ________

B. The Community Athletic Association asked you to help organize the track and field events. For each race result below, circle the names of the two fastest runners.

Remember: The shorter the time, the faster the runner.

RACE #1	RACE #2	RACE #3	RACE #4
Brent: 50.15 sec.	Patrick: 53.09 sec.	Harriet: 59.01 sec.	Roxanne: 61.29 sec.
Avril: 51.51 sec.	Joseph: 53.90 sec.	Meg: 59.90 sec.	Randy: 60.81 sec.
Gary: 50.32 sec.	Ryan: 52.08 sec.	Veralee: 60.70 sec.	Belinda: 59.08 sec.
Dan: 51.08 sec.	Joshua: 53.17 sec.	Linda: 60.07 sec.	Elaine: 60.98 sec.

Proper Fractions

A proper fraction also stands for part of a whole. A proper fraction is written as one number above a second number.

- The top number is called the **numerator.** The numerator tells the number of parts you're describing.
- The bottom number is called the **denominator.** The denominator tells the number of equal parts the whole is divided into.

How much of the circle is shaded?

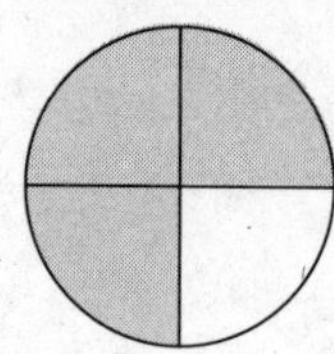

$\frac{3}{4}$ ← numerator / denominator

3 parts are shaded. The circle is divided into 4 equal parts.

What fraction of a dollar is shown below?

$\frac{40}{100}$ ← numerator / denominator

40 cents are shown. A dollar contains 100 cents.

▼ Practice

On the line next to each figure, write a fraction to show how much of that figure is shaded.

$\frac{X}{X}$ ← shaded parts / total equal parts

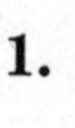

1. 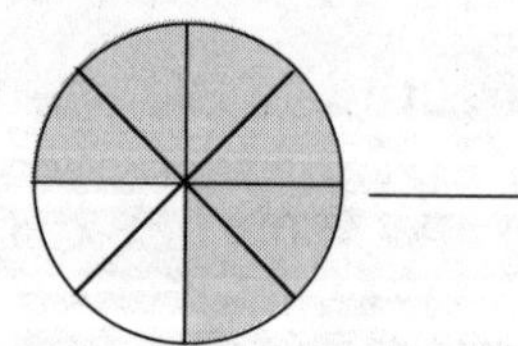 ____

3. 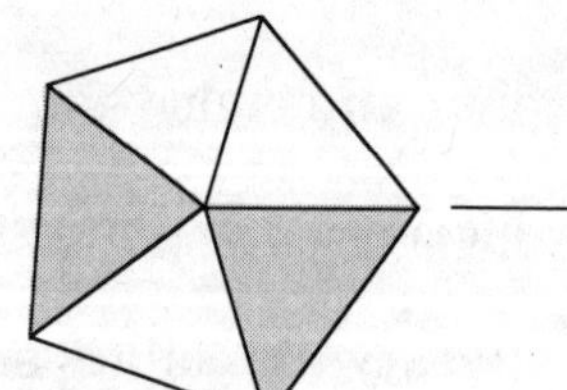 ____

5. 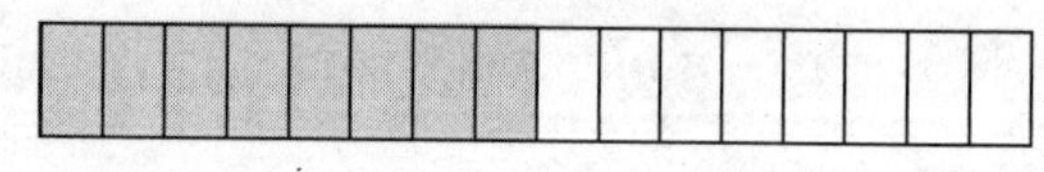 ____

2. 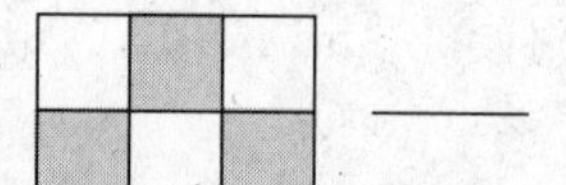 ____

4. 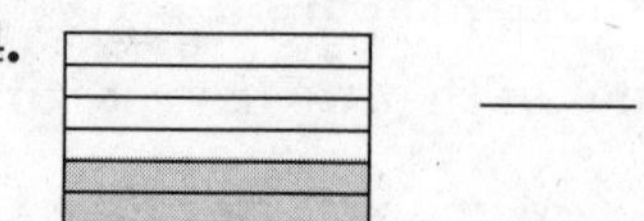 ____

6. Shade $\frac{2}{3}$ of this circle:

7. Shade $\frac{7}{8}$ of the distance between 0 and 1:

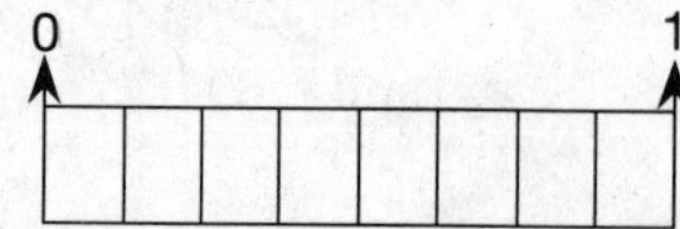

8. What fraction of a dollar is shown at right? (Remember: There are 100 cents in a dollar.)

Writing Equivalent Fractions

The cups at right contain equal amounts of syrup.

- The cup on the left is divided into 4 equal measuring units.
- The cup on the right is divided into 8 equal measuring units.

$\frac{3}{4}$ and $\frac{6}{8}$ represent the same amount, and are called **equivalent fractions.**

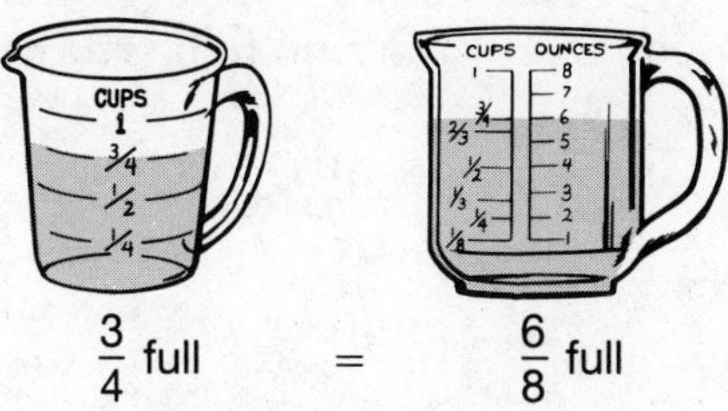

$\frac{3}{4}$ full = $\frac{6}{8}$ full

▼ Practice

Write equivalent fractions for each pair of figures as indicated.

1. Fraction of each rectangle that's shaded

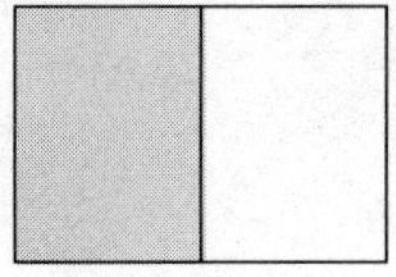

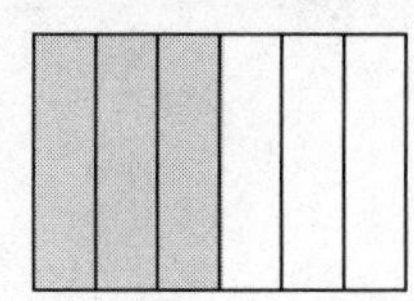

$\frac{1}{2} = \frac{\quad}{6}$

2. Fraction of each pizza eaten

$\frac{\quad}{\quad} = \frac{\quad}{8}$

3. Fraction of each cup filled with water

$\frac{\quad}{\quad} = \frac{\quad}{\quad}$

4. Fraction of each circle that's shaded

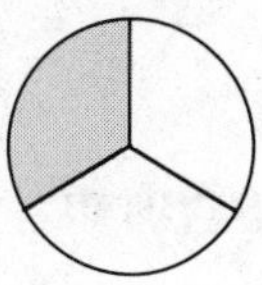

$\frac{\quad}{\quad} = \frac{\quad}{\quad}$

5. Fraction of each pizza remaining

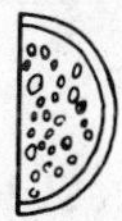

$\frac{\quad}{\quad} = \frac{\quad}{\quad}$

6. Fraction of an inch that each bar measures

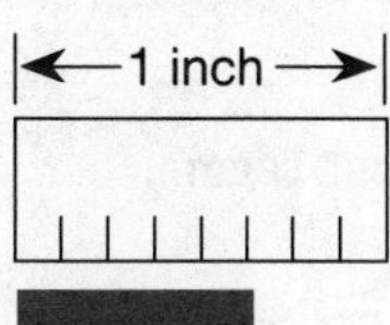

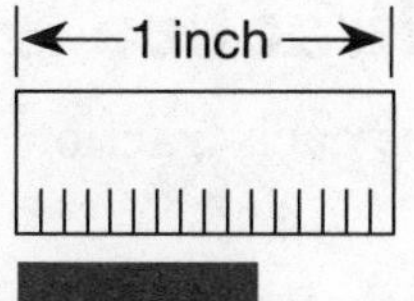

$\frac{\quad}{\quad} = \frac{\quad}{\quad}$

Simplifying Fractions

To **simplify (reduce)** a fraction is to rewrite it as an equivalent fraction with smaller numbers.

When a fraction is in its simplest form—smallest numbers possible—it is said to be **reduced to lowest terms.**

Examples: **a)** $\frac{2}{4} = \frac{1}{2}$

b) $\frac{8}{12} = \frac{2}{3}$

reduced to lowest terms

Equivalent Fractions

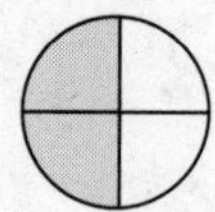
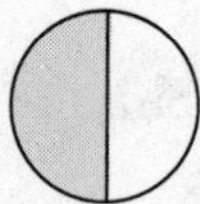

$\frac{2}{4}$ reduces to $\frac{1}{2}$.

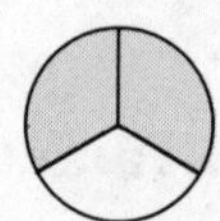

$\frac{8}{12}$ reduces to $\frac{2}{3}$.

> To reduce a fraction to lowest terms, divide both numerator and denominator by the largest whole number that divides evenly into each.

Example 1: Reduce $\frac{6}{9}$ to lowest terms.

Divide both numerator (6) and denominator (9) by 3. $\frac{6 \div 3}{9 \div 3} = \frac{2}{3}$

Answer: $\frac{2}{3}$

> Sometimes you don't know the largest number you need to divide by. When this happens, you may need to divide twice or more. In Example 2 below, you could have saved a step by dividing by 4.

Example 2: Reduce $\frac{20}{32}$ to lowest terms.

Divide both 20 and 32 by 2.
Divide again by 2.

$\frac{20 \div 2}{32 \div 2} = \frac{10}{16} \quad \frac{10 \div 2}{16 \div 2} = \frac{5}{8}$

Answer: $\frac{5}{8}$

▼ Practice

Reduce each fraction to lowest terms.

1. $\frac{4}{12} =$ $\frac{6}{8} =$ $\frac{4}{6} =$ $\frac{3}{9} =$ $\frac{12}{16} =$

2. $\frac{9}{15} =$ $\frac{14}{16} =$ $\frac{8}{32} =$ $\frac{10}{24} =$ $\frac{28}{64} =$

ON THE JOB

Using Equivalent Fractions for Sorting

Part of Ned's job at Value Hardware involves keeping supply bins organized. Ned must make sure that each bin holds the correct wood screws. The label on each bin gives the length of the screw size reduced to lowest terms.

Ned has 7 sizes of wood screws to place in the supply bins. Unfortunately, the manufacturing company gave the sizes only in 32nds of an inch.

By reducing each size to lowest terms, Ned determines where to place each size of wood screw.

Example: Ned first reduces Size A to lowest terms.

$$\frac{16}{32} = \frac{16 \div 2}{32 \div 2} = \frac{8}{16} \qquad \frac{8 \div 8}{16 \div 8} = \frac{1}{2} \text{ inch}$$

Then, Ned matches his answer with the labeled bins.

Answer: Size A goes in Bin #4 as shown below. (Ned didn't see it, but he could have saved a step by first dividing by 16—$\frac{16 \div 16}{32 \div 16} = \frac{1}{2}$.)

▼ Practice

Write the size of the wood screw (A, B, and so on) on the line to the left of the correct bin. Size A has been done for you.

Wood Screws		Supply Bins
Size A: $\frac{16}{32}$ inch ($\frac{16}{32} = \frac{1}{2}$)	**1.** ______	BIN #1: $\frac{1}{8}$ inch
Size B: $\frac{12}{32}$ inch	**2.** ______	BIN #2: $\frac{1}{4}$ inch
Size C: $\frac{4}{32}$ inch	**3.** ______	BIN #3: $\frac{3}{8}$ inch
Size D: $\frac{28}{32}$ inch	**4.** **A**	BIN #4: $\frac{1}{2}$ inch
Size E: $\frac{24}{32}$ inch	**5.** ______	BIN #5: $\frac{5}{8}$ inch
Size F: $\frac{8}{32}$ inch	**6.** ______	BIN #6: $\frac{3}{4}$ inch
Size G: $\frac{20}{32}$ inch	**7.** ______	BIN #7: $\frac{7}{8}$ inch

Writing a Part as a Fraction of a Whole

Suppose you work in an arts and crafts shop where gold sequin twine sells for $1.80 per foot. A customer comes in and would like to buy 8 inches of the twine. How can you figure out the cost?

You need to find out what fraction of a foot 8 inches equals.

Place the part → 8
over the whole → 12   (1 foot = 12 inches)

Reduce the fraction: $\frac{8}{12} = \frac{8 \div 4}{12 \div 4} = \frac{2}{3}$

- Eight inches is equal to $\frac{2}{3}$ of a foot. The twine would cost $\frac{2}{3}$ of $1.80.

▼ Practice

A. Another customer buys the following items. As your first step in determining cost, write each length as a fraction of a foot or yard as indicated.

1 yard = 36 inches	1 foot = 12 inches

1. 9 inches of red felt = $\frac{9}{12}$ = ______________ foot

2. 6 inches of gold lamé = ______________ foot

3. 12 inches of silver braid = ______________ yard

4. 24 inches of vinyl backing = ______________ yard

5. 30 inches of corduroy = ______________ yard

6. 9 inches of striped ribbon = ______________ yard

7. 10 inches of sequin twine = ______________ foot

B. At the end of each week, you're supposed to write overtime minutes as a fraction of an hour. Do this for the overtime periods below. Be sure to reduce your answers to lowest terms.

1 hour = 60 minutes

Monday	15 minutes = __________	hour
Tuesday	20 minutes = __________	hour
Wednesday	45 minutes = __________	hour
Thursday	50 minutes = __________	hour
Friday	30 minutes = __________	hour

Raising Fractions to Higher Terms

You'll see in the next lesson that you may sometimes want to raise a fraction to **higher terms.** Most often, you'll know the denominator of the fraction you want to write. When a fraction is raised to higher terms, the new fraction is **equivalent** (equal in value) to the original fraction.

Equivalent Fractions

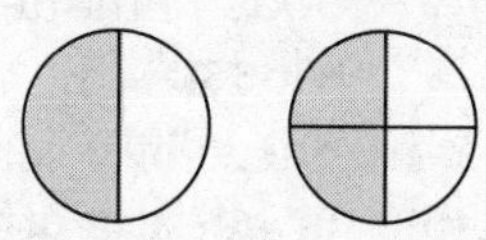

$$\frac{1}{2} = \frac{1 \times 2}{2 \times 2} = \frac{2}{4}$$

> To raise a fraction to higher terms, multiply both numerator and denominator by the same number.

Example 1: Write $\frac{3}{8}$ as a fraction that has 16 as a denominator.

Step 1. Look at the denominators.
Ask, "What do I multiply 8 by to get 16?"

Answer: 2

To Solve

$$\frac{3}{8} = \frac{?}{16}$$

Step 2. Multiply the numerator (3) by 2: $3 \times 2 = 6$
The new numerator is 6.

Think

$$\frac{3 \times 2}{8 \times 2} = \frac{6}{16}$$

Answer: $\frac{3}{8} = \frac{6}{16}$

Example 2: $\frac{3}{4} = \frac{?}{12}$

Step 1. Ask, "What do I multiply 4 by to get 12?"
Answer: 3

Step 2. Multiply the numerator by 3:

Answer: $\frac{3 \times 3}{4 \times 3} = \frac{9}{12}$

Example 3: $\frac{4}{5} = \frac{?}{25}$

Step 1. Ask, "What do I multiply 5 by to get 25?"
Answer: 5

Step 2. Multiply the numerator by 5:

Answer: $\frac{4 \times 5}{5 \times 5} = \frac{20}{25}$

▼ Practice

Raise each fraction to higher terms.

1. $\frac{1}{2} = \frac{}{8}$ (× 4 numerator, × 4 denominator) $\quad \frac{1}{3} = \frac{}{6} \quad \frac{1}{4} = \frac{}{8} \quad \frac{2}{3} = \frac{}{9} \quad \frac{3}{4} = \frac{}{12}$

2. $\frac{2}{5} = \frac{}{10} \quad \frac{3}{4} = \frac{}{8} \quad \frac{1}{3} = \frac{}{12} \quad \frac{5}{7} = \frac{}{14} \quad \frac{1}{2} = \frac{}{10}$

3. $\frac{1}{3} = \frac{}{15} \quad \frac{2}{5} = \frac{}{30} \quad \frac{5}{14} = \frac{}{28} \quad \frac{11}{12} = \frac{}{24} \quad \frac{4}{7} = \frac{}{42}$

Comparing Proper Fractions

"I'd like the widest roll of tape you have. It doesn't matter what color it is, I just want the widest!"

If you're in charge of a company's stockroom, you're responsible for getting other employees the supplies they ask for. But because of the way tape is boxed, it's difficult to tell which is the widest. You read the following widths on the box labels.

$\frac{11}{16}$ inch	$\frac{3}{8}$ inch	$\frac{9}{16}$ inch	$\frac{1}{2}$ inch	$\frac{5}{8}$ inch

"Nothing is easy," you think to yourself. "Now, which tape is the widest?"

Your first step is to make these **like fractions**—fractions with the same denominator. Like fractions are easy to compare: $\frac{11}{16}$ is larger than $\frac{9}{16}$ because 11 is larger than 9.

To compare **unlike fractions** (fractions with different denominators):

1. Find a common denominator. In the example above, rewrite $\frac{3}{8}$, $\frac{1}{2}$, and $\frac{5}{8}$ as like fractions with a denominator of 16.

$\frac{3 \times 2}{8 \times 2} = \frac{6}{16}$; $\frac{1 \times 8}{2 \times 8} = \frac{8}{16}$; $\frac{5 \times 2}{8 \times 2} = \frac{10}{16}$

2. Compare the numerators of the like fractions:

Numerators: 11, 9, 6, 8, and 10

From smallest to largest, the fractions are:

$\frac{3}{8}$ $(\frac{6}{16})$ $\frac{1}{2}$ $(\frac{8}{16})$ $\frac{9}{16}$ $\frac{5}{8}$ $(\frac{10}{16})$ $\frac{11}{16}$

Answer: The widest tape measures $\frac{11}{16}$ inch.

▼ **MATH TIP**

Learning to write like fractions is a very important skill. You'll need to write like fractions as your first step in adding or subtracting fractions that have unlike denominators. You'll learn these skills on page 86.

▼ Practice

A. Circle the larger fraction in each pair. Use the larger denominator in each pair as the common denominator.

1. $\frac{2}{3}$ or $\frac{7}{12}$ $\frac{3}{10}$ or $\frac{2}{5}$ $\frac{7}{8}$ or $\frac{13}{16}$ $\frac{4}{9}$ or $\frac{1}{3}$

Hints: $\frac{2}{3} = \frac{?}{12}$ $\frac{2}{5} = \frac{?}{10}$ $\frac{7}{8} = \frac{?}{16}$ $\frac{1}{3} = \frac{?}{9}$

2. $\frac{3}{4}$ or $\frac{10}{12}$ $\frac{6}{7}$ or $\frac{11}{14}$ $\frac{1}{4}$ or $\frac{3}{8}$ $\frac{5}{8}$ or $\frac{1}{2}$

B. At the hardware store where you work, you need to label the drawers that contain screws. Each set of screws is placed from shortest to longest in the drawers as pictured. As your first step, give fractions a common denominator.

1. sheet metal screws

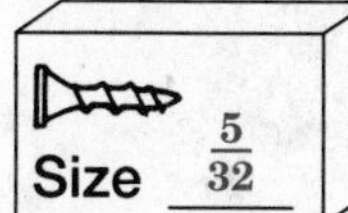
Size $\frac{5}{32}$

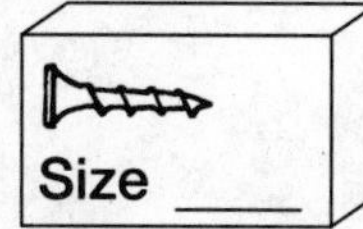
Size ____

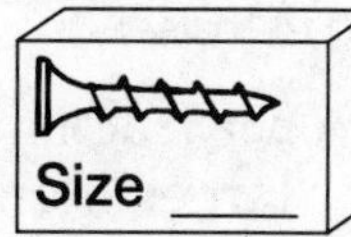
Size ____

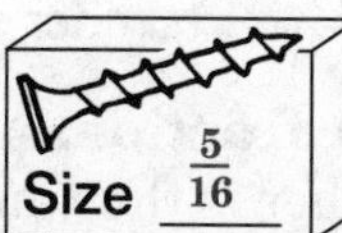
Size $\frac{5}{16}$

Write the following sizes on the drawers:

$\frac{3}{16}$ inch $\frac{1}{4}$ inch $\frac{5}{32}$ inch $\frac{5}{16}$ inch

$(\frac{3}{16} = \frac{6}{32})$ $(\frac{1}{4} = \frac{8}{32})$ $(\frac{5}{32})$ $(\frac{5}{16} = \frac{10}{32})$

Hint: Compare the numerators after changing the measurements to like fractions.

2. machine screws

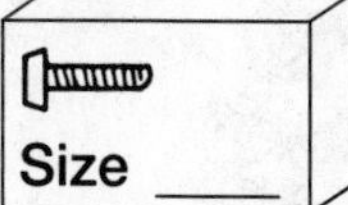
Size ____

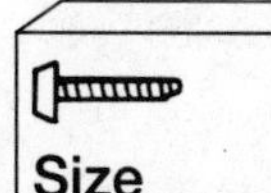
Size ____

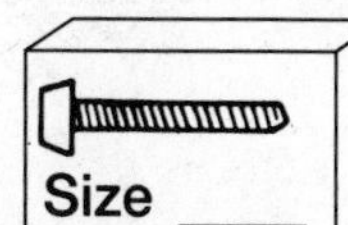
Size ____

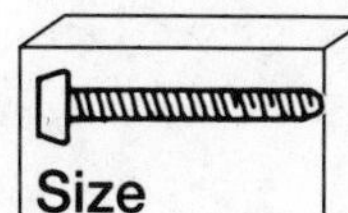
Size ____

Write the following sizes on the drawers:

$\frac{1}{2}$ inch $\frac{3}{8}$ inch $\frac{7}{16}$ inch $\frac{10}{32}$ inch

3. wood screws

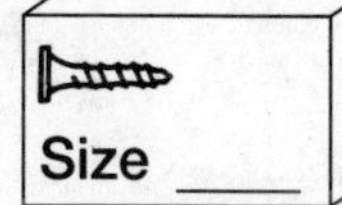
Size ____

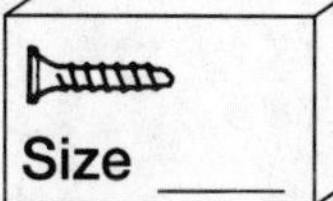
Size ____

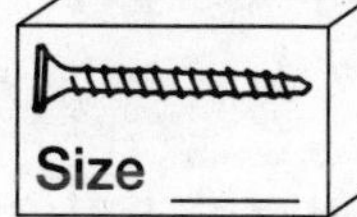
Size ____

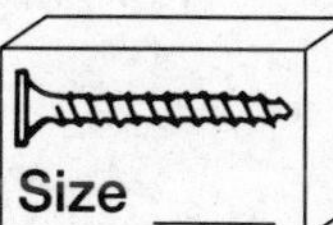
Size ____

Write the following sizes on the drawers:

$\frac{3}{4}$ inch $\frac{5}{8}$ inch $\frac{1}{2}$ inch $\frac{9}{16}$ inch

4. Sheetrock screws

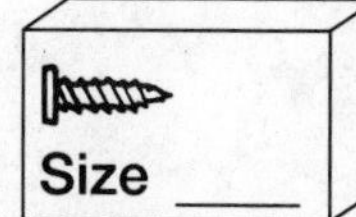
Size ____

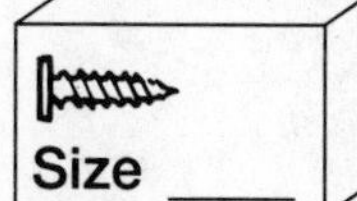
Size ____

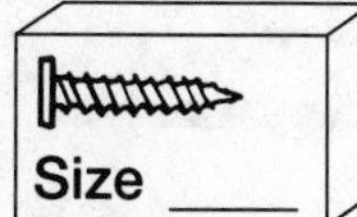
Size ____

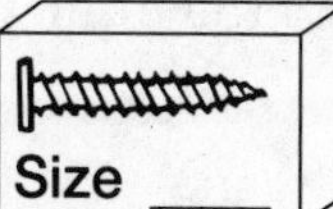
Size ____

Write the following sizes on the drawers:

$\frac{29}{32}$ inch $\frac{7}{8}$ inch $\frac{15}{16}$ inch $\frac{3}{4}$ inch

Mixed Numbers and Improper Fractions

Suppose you manage a pizza parlor. A co-worker, Harry, cuts whole pizzas into 8 slices. He then sells the individual slices. Friday night there were 27 slices left unsold at 8:00.

After 8:00 P.M., you sell whole pizzas made up of leftover slices. For one of these "leftover whole pizzas," you charge less than you charge for a regular pizza.

CLOSING TIME SPECIAL
Whole Pizzas from Leftovers!
Only $7.50

"How many pizzas are left over?" Harry asks you.

There are two ways to answer Harry.

Example 1: $\frac{27}{8}$ ← 27 slices left (numerator); number of slices per pizza (denominator)

$\frac{27}{8}$ is an **improper fraction.** An improper fraction is one in which the top number is the same as or larger than the bottom number.

Other examples of improper fractions:

$\frac{3}{3}$ $\frac{9}{8}$ $\frac{100}{100}$ $\frac{13}{5}$

Chances are that Harry would rather your answer be a **mixed number,** which is often easier to understand.

Example 2:

Step 1. Divide 8 into 27:

$$\begin{array}{r} 3 \text{ r } 3 \\ 8\overline{)27} \\ \underline{24} \\ 3 \end{array}$$

Step 2. Write the remainder (r 3) over the divisor (8) to form a proper fraction: $\frac{3}{8}$

Step 3. Put the whole number and fraction together: $3\frac{3}{8}$

You can tell Harry that there are $\mathbf{3\frac{3}{8}}$ **pizzas left over.**

$3\frac{3}{8}$ is a **mixed number.** A mixed number is a whole number plus a fraction.

To change an improper fraction to a mixed number, divide the denominator into the numerator.

▼ **MATH TIP**

When a number of equal-size parts adds to more than 1, you'll most often write the answer as a mixed number.

▼ Practice

A. To figure out how much money you made by selling "leftover whole pizzas," you ask Harry to determine how many of these pizzas he made each night this week. Eight slices equals one pizza.

	Slices Left Over	Improper Fraction		Mixed Number
Monday	35	$\frac{35}{8}$	=	$4\frac{3}{8}$
Tuesday	20	______	=	______
Wednesday	32	______	=	______
Thursday	16	______	=	______
Friday	27	______	=	______
Saturday	19	______	=	______
Sunday	8	______	=	______

B. Now imagine that you work in a fabric store. On the remnant table, there are numerous leftover pieces of cloth, some one-fourth yard long, some one-third yard, some one-eighth yard, and some one-half yard. Your supervisor asks you to total the yards of each length of fabric.

Fabric Length	Number of Pieces	Improper Fraction		Mixed Number
1. $\frac{1}{4}$ yard	13	$\frac{13}{4}$	=	$3\frac{1}{4}$
2. $\frac{1}{3}$ yard	20	______	=	______
3. $\frac{1}{2}$ yard	9	______	=	______
4. $\frac{1}{8}$ yard	21	______	=	______

Percent

Percent is the third way to write part of a whole.

Percent means *parts out of 100.*

Percent always refers to a whole that is divided into 100 equal parts.

is 1% of

Do you know why?

You write percent as the number of hundredths followed by the percent sign (%).

1 percent is written as 1%.
1% means 1 part out of 100.

Here are some examples:

Each square is divided into 100 smaller squares.

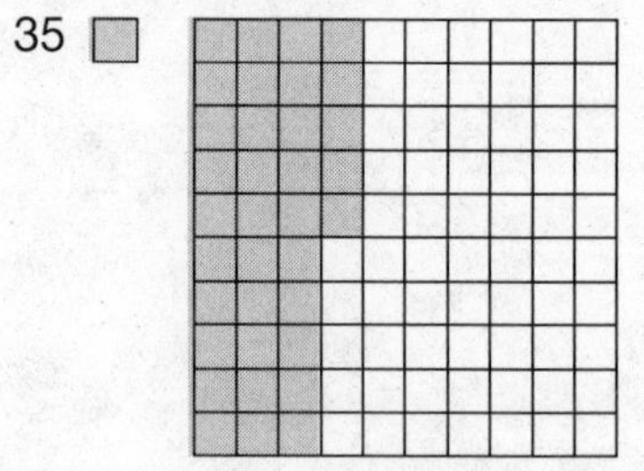

35% of the large square is shaded.

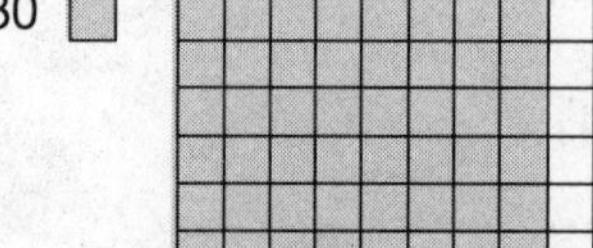

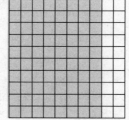

80% of the large square is shaded.

75% of a dollar is shown.

What Is 100%?

100% represents a whole amount. | 100% = 1 |

At right, 30% of the large square is shaded; 70% is unshaded.

30% + 70% = 100%

shaded + unshaded = whole square

100%

30%

70%

How about Percents Larger than 100%?

Any percent larger than 100% represents a number larger than 1.

200% stands for 2 whole objects.
300% stands for 3 whole objects, and so on.

You will seldom see percents larger than 100%, but you need to understand them.

▼ MATH TIP

If sales increased from \$100 to \$210, that would be a 110% increase.

▼ Practice

Write what percent of each square below is shaded, what percent is unshaded, and what the total of the two percents equals.

1. 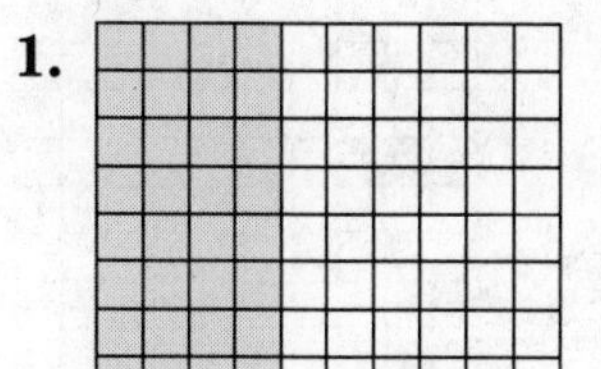

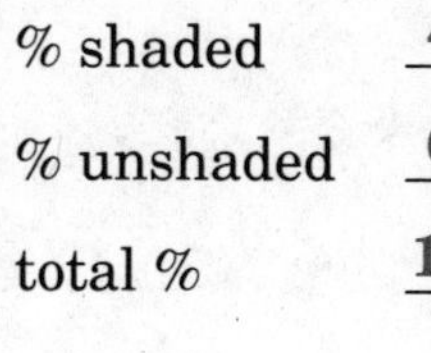

% shaded 40%

% unshaded 60%

total % 100%

3. 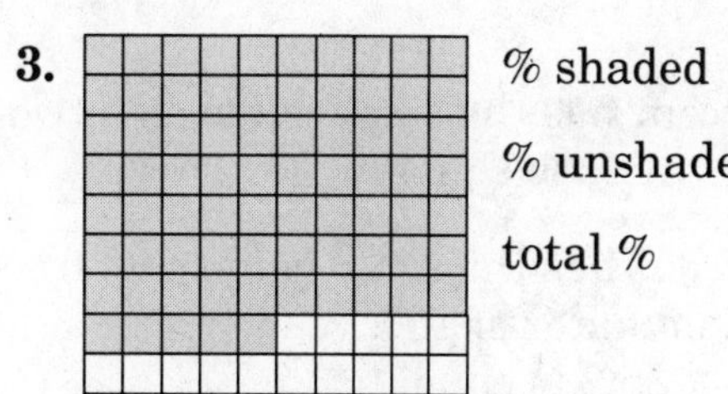

% shaded ____

% unshaded ____

total % ____

2. 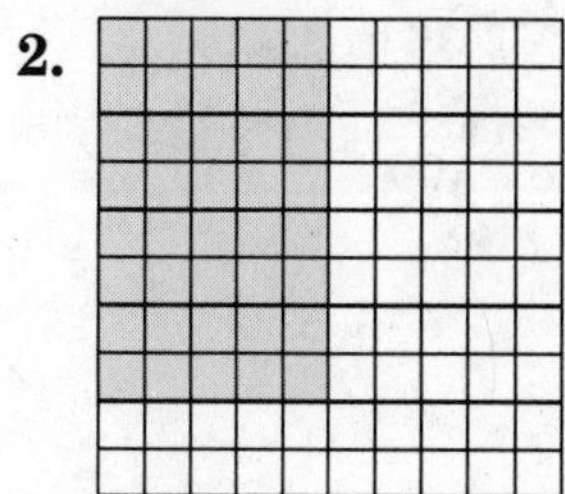

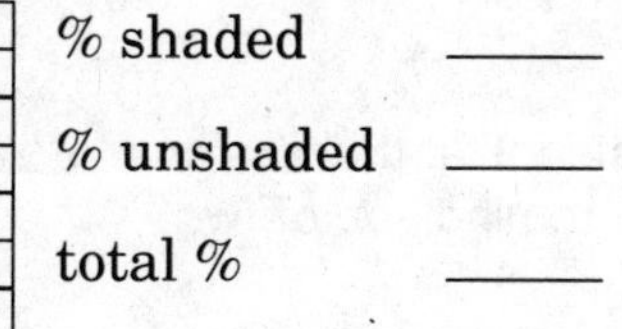

% shaded ____

% unshaded ____

total % ____

4. 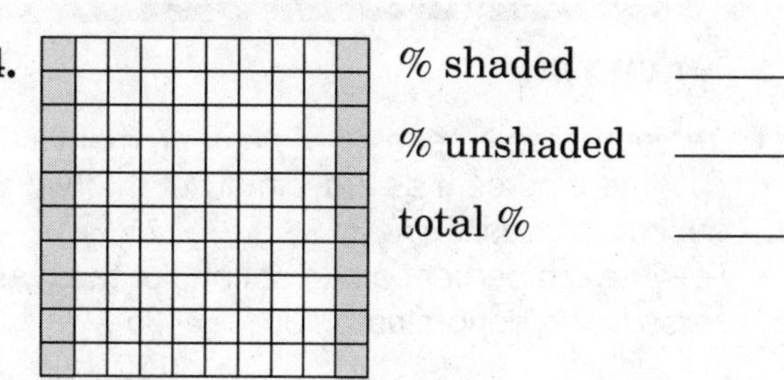

% shaded ____

% unshaded ____

total % ____

If 1 circle represents a whole, write a percent larger than 100% to represent each group of circles below.

5. 100% × 3 = ________%

6. ________%

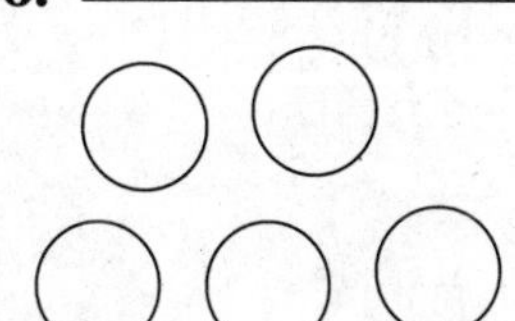

7. ________%

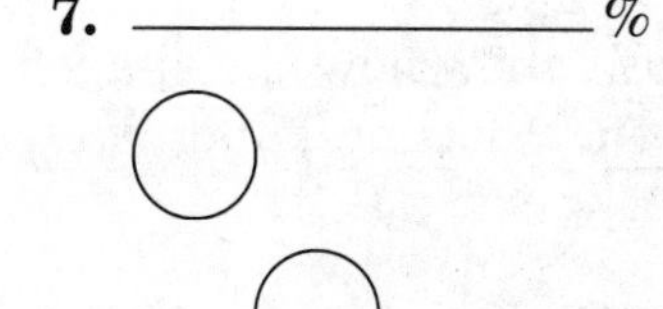

---

8. Gary, Jesse, and Amy agreed to split their profit from their garage sale as shown at right.

Gary: 30 percent
Jesse: 25 percent
Amy: 45 percent

How much money did each person receive out of $100 profit?

Gary: ______ Jesse: ______ Amy: ______

What percent of each square below is unshaded?

9. 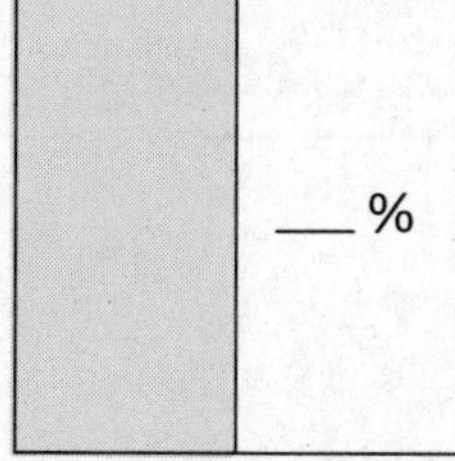

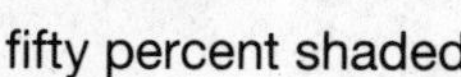

fifty percent shaded

10. 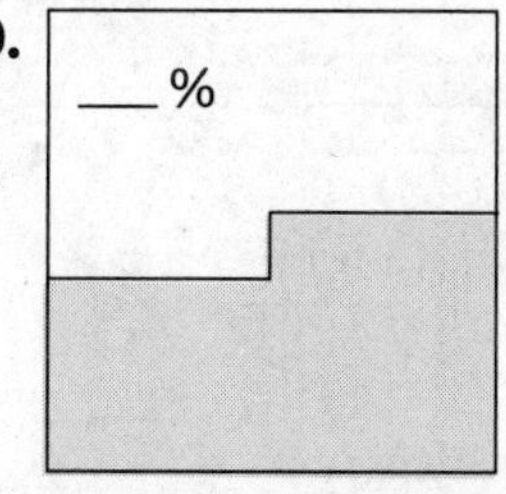

forty-five percent shaded

11. 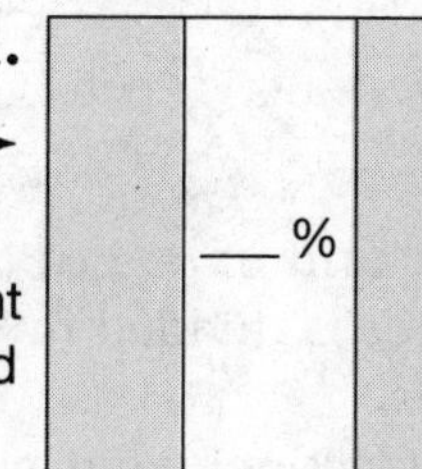

Writing Percent as a Decimal or a Fraction

Any percent can easily be written as an equivalent decimal or fraction.

- Percent has the same value as a two-place decimal.
  35% is equal to .35.
- Percent has the same value as a fraction that has a denominator of 100.
  35% is equal to $\frac{35}{100}$.

100 Equal Parts

35

35% is shaded.
.35 is shaded.
$\frac{35}{100}$ is shaded.

▼ MATH TIP

To remember the meaning of percent, many students just look at the % sign.

- To write a percent as a decimal, let the two zeros in % remind you of two decimal places: 35% = .35
- To write the percent as a fraction, let the two zeros in % remind you of two zeros in the denominator: 35% = $\frac{35}{100}$

▼ Practice

In each figure below, show how the shaded part can be written as a fraction, a decimal, and a percent. The first one is done for you.

1. 

$\frac{21}{100}$

.21

21%

3. 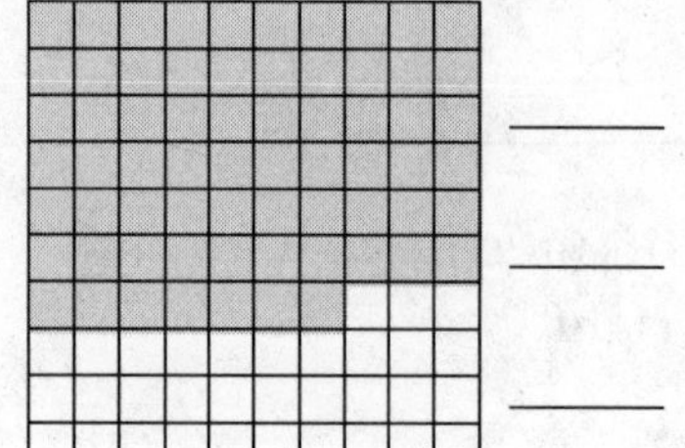

______
______
______

5. 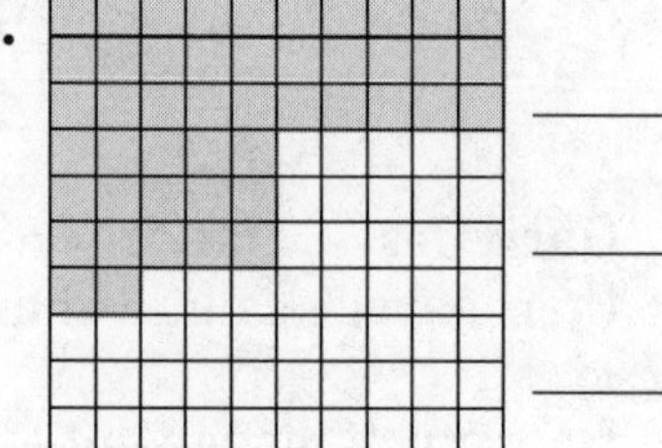

______
______
______

2. 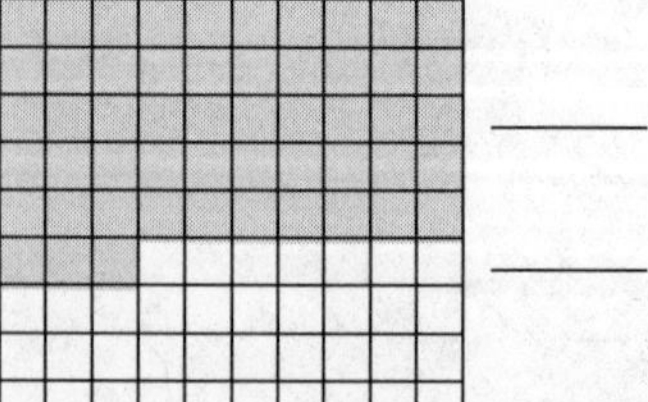

______
______
______

4. 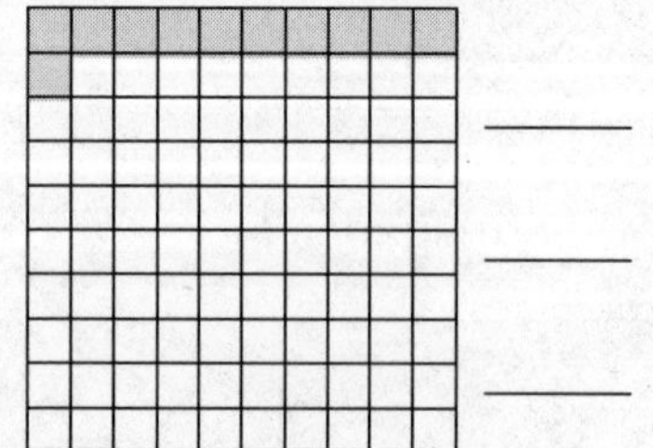

______
______
______

6. 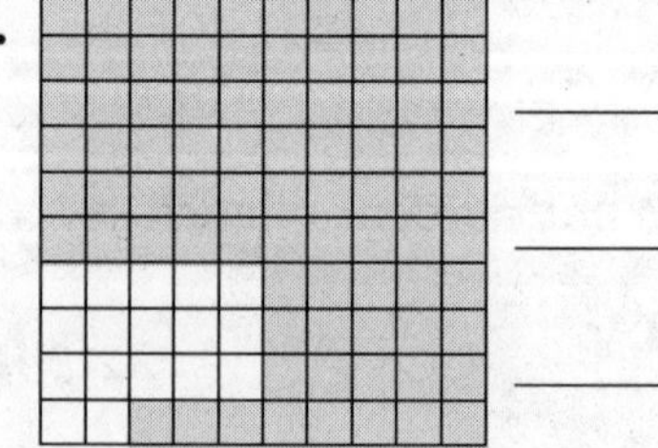

______
______
______

7. A meter is a metric unit of length that is a little longer than a yard. A meter is divided into 100 smaller units called **centimeters.**

a) Expressed as a fraction, what part of a meter is a length of 91 centimeters (about 1 yard)? ______

b) Expressed as a percent, what part of a meter is a length of 30 centimeters (about 1 foot)? ______

8. A **kilometer** equals 1,000 meters. What part of a kilometer is 350 meters? Express your answer three ways:

a) as a decimal: __________

Hint: 350 meters is 350 thousandths of a kilometer.

b) as a fraction reduced to hundredths: __________

Hint: $\frac{350}{1,000} = \frac{?}{100}$

c) as a percent: __________

Hint: See answer *b.*

9. Suppose you keep attendance records at Little Bear Preschool. There were 100 students enrolled for the week shown below. Fill in the correct percents for each day as indicated.

Day	Total Enrollment	Total Present	Percent Present	Percent Absent*
Monday	100	89	89%	11%
Tuesday	100	93	______	______
Wednesday	100	96	______	______
Thursday	100	86	______	______
Friday	100	79	______	______

*Percent Absent = 100% − Percent Present

10. Suppose you work at Fleming Truck Rental. Your boss asks you to complete the report below. The boss wants to express the number of trucks that needed repairs each month as a percent, a decimal, and a fraction. Fill out this report.

		TRUCKS NEEDING REPAIRS			
Month	Total Number of Trucks	Number	Percent	Decimal	Fraction
January	100	17	17%	.17	$\frac{17}{100}$
February	100	23	______	______	______
March	100	26	______	______	______
April	100	21	______	______	______
May	100	16	______	______	______

Thinking about Decimals, Fractions, and Percents

Since decimals, fractions, and percents are so similar, you may wonder why we use all three. Wouldn't one do just fine?

The answer is yes! But, like so many other things, math has a history. As math developed, each method of writing part of a whole became popular for certain uses:

- Decimals became the basis of our money system and of the metric measuring system.

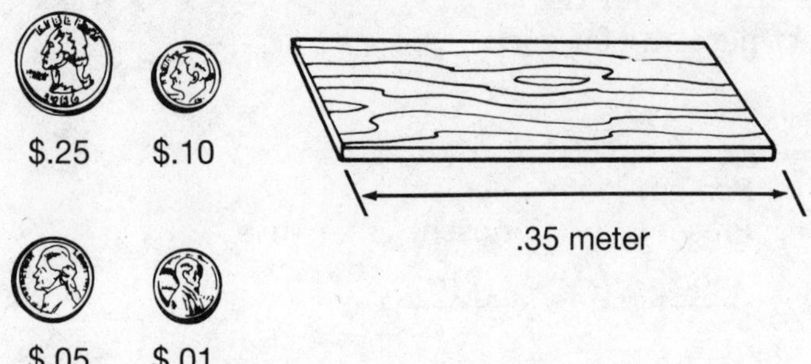

- Fractions became the basis of the English measuring system.

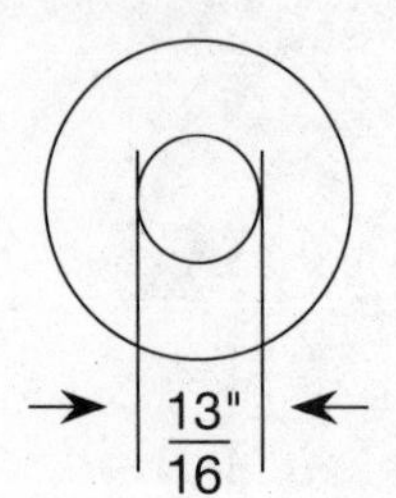

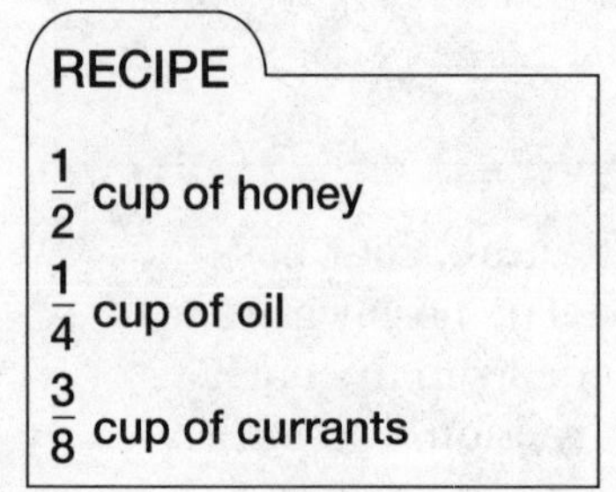

RECIPE
1/2 cup of honey
1/4 cup of oil
3/8 cup of currants

- Percents came to be used with such things as store sales, taxes, finance charges, and rates of increase and decrease.

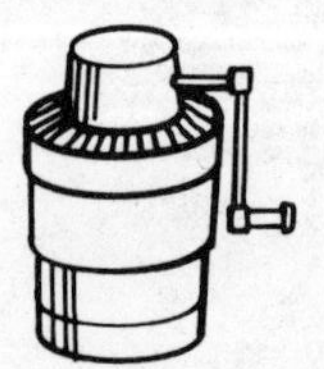

Save 19%

Ice-Cream Freezer

FIRST BANK
$ SAVINGS RATE $
NOW 5%

New Home Loans
30-Year Fixed Rate 12%
Home Savings and Loan

Why All Three?

5%

.05

$\frac{5}{100}$

▼ MATH TIP

In the metric system, a meter is divided into 100 equal parts called centimeters. A length such as 35 centimeters is often written as the decimal fraction .35 meter.

As you've seen, a number smaller than 1 can be written in any one of three equivalent ways. Look how decimal fractions, proper fractions, and percents can be used to write cents as part of a dollar.

Examples:

Cents	Written as a Decimal Fraction	Written as a Proper Fraction	Written as a Percent
1¢	\$.01	$\frac{1}{100}$ of a dollar	1% of a dollar
34¢	\$.34	$\frac{34}{100}$ of a dollar	34% of a dollar
80¢	\$.80	$\frac{80}{100}$ of a dollar	80% of a dollar

▼ Practice

Complete the following chart to show the three equally correct ways of writing cents as part of a dollar.

Cents	Written as a Decimal Fraction	Written as a Proper Fraction	Written as a Percent
1. 4¢		$\frac{4}{100}$	
2. 9¢			9%
3. 16¢	\$.16		
4. 46¢			
5. 70¢			
6. 99¢			

On the line above each of the following pictures, write *decimal fraction*, *proper fraction*, or *percent* to identify which is being used.

7. ____________

NEW-CAR LOANS
NOW ONLY 11%

9. ____________

$\frac{15}{16}$ in.

11. ____________

STOCK MARKET PRICES ON THE RISE

Stock	Changes
IBM	$+\frac{1}{2}$
MDU	$+\frac{5}{8}$
TRW	$+\frac{3}{4}$

8. ____________

\$.50

10. ____________

Normal Human Body Temperature 98.6° F

94 96 98 100 102 104 106

12. ____________

Save 33%
All ski clothes on sale

Thinking about Math Problems

In your everyday life, in your job, in school, and on tests, you'll have to solve many types of math problems. Whether you must add up expenses in order to establish a household budget or divide decimals on a certification exam, math problems are a challenge.

There is no "one correct way" to solve every math problem.

- Some problems you'll be able to solve "in your head." Other problems will require a step-by-step plan to solve.
- You'll be able to use a calculator to solve some problems.
- For other problems, you may be more comfortable with a pencil and some paper.

One-Step Problems

Many math problems require only one operation (addition, subtraction, multiplication, or division) to solve them.

Example 1: On a test, you are required to solve the following word problem:

A client pays $235 per month in rent. What does she pay in a year?

You know that there are 12 months in a year. Therefore, you should multiply:

$$\begin{array}{r} \$235 \\ \times \quad 12 \\ \hline \$2{,}820 \end{array}$$

▼ MATH TIP

An answer like $28.20 or $28,200 would be a clue that you made an error.

Your math common sense will often tell you when an answer "just doesn't seem right."

Multistep Problems

Other math problems require two or more operations to solve them. Think of these problems as two or more one-step problems. Look at the example on the next page.

Example 2: You are buying a $7.89 cassette tape, and you know that the tax is $.39. You give the clerk a $20 bill. You want to be sure you get the right amount of change.

Think of Example 2 as two one-step problems:

Problem #1: How much are you spending in all?
Add the two amounts:

$$\begin{array}{r} \$7.89 \\ + \quad .39 \\ \hline \$8.28 \end{array}$$

Problem #2: How much change should you get?
Subtract:

$$\begin{array}{r} \$20.00 \\ - \quad 8.28 \\ \hline \$11.72 \end{array}$$

▼ **MATH TIP**

Of course, you can always just estimate to make sure you've received *approximately* the right amount of change:

$7.89 is about $8.00
.39 is about .40
Total is about $8.40

Estimated Change:

$20.00 − $8.40 = $11.60

▼ Practice

Solve each multistep problem below.

1. Before writing two checks last week, you had a checking account balance of $256.85. If the two checks were for $25.50 and $12.89, what is the new balance in your account?

Think:
Problem 1: What did the two checks total?
Problem 2: What is the new balance?

2. Christy's two daughters visited the dentist. Amy's bill was $47.65; Jenny's bill was $76.50. If Christy's insurance pays a total of $50.00, how much will she have to pay?

Think:
Problem 1: What was the total dental bill?
Problem 2: How much was left after the insurance paid?

3. At the Super Sunday Sale, a friend bought 3 vases priced at $7.85 each and 2 ceramic figures priced at $14.99 each. What total amount did your friend spend?

4. You baked 72 cookies for the picnic. You put 30 in a bowl for adults. The remaining cookies were divided evenly among 14 children. How many cookies did each child get?

5. One hundred students signed up to take swimming lessons. At the first meeting, 47 girls and 39 boys showed up.
a) What percent of the total class showed up?
b) What percent of the total class did not show up?

Estimating: Your Most Important Math Tool

Sometimes when you work with numbers it is very important for you to find an exact amount.

Examples: giving change to a customer
measuring a shelf to fit your bookcase
adding the correct amount of salt to a dessert recipe

In other cases, however, you may want to estimate.

To **estimate** is to find an approximate answer.

Here are some situations in which estimation is appropriate:

Example 1: Your boss asks you to figure out about how many hours you spend on the computer each week. Instead of adding up the exact number of hours each day, you estimate:

$$\begin{array}{r l} 3 & \text{hours each day (approximately)} \\ \underline{\times\ 5} & \text{days per week} \\ 15 & \end{array}$$

Answer: You spend about 15 hours each week on the computer.

Example 2: You have been busy shopping at the drugstore when you suddenly remember that you have only $10 in your wallet. Do you have enough money to pay for the items in your cart? Instead of adding up the exact prices, you estimate:

		Estimate
toothpaste	$1.89	about $2
razor blades	2.79	about $3
soap	.89	about $1
magazine	1.39	about $1
		about $7

Answer: Your estimate tells you that you *do* have enough money.

▼ **MATH TIP**

Words and phrases such as *about, approximately, around,* and *on average* are clues that an estimate is all that is expected of you.

Example 3: You are given four possible answers to a problem on a multiple-choice math test. Instead of doing the computation exactly, you can estimate, then choose the answer closest to your estimate.

What is $5.95 × 12?

a) $7.14
b) $71.40
c) $175.90
d) $714.00

Estimate: $5.95 is about $6.
$6 × 12 = $72

Answer: Choice b) $71.40 is closest to $72.

▼ **MATH TIP**

Estimating on multiple-choice tests works best when the answer choices given are not too close together in value. For example, if your estimate is $72, it would be difficult to choose between $72.40 and $71.95.

When answer choices are close in value, finding an exact answer is your best strategy.

When you are working with very large numbers, such as the cost of food for a year or the number of people living in New York City, you should usually estimate.

▼ Practice

Look at the following situations, and decide whether an exact answer is needed or an estimate will be enough. Circle the correct choice.

1. You are trying to decide how much sand you'll need to fill a large sandbox.

estimate exact answer

2. Some factory machinery is not cutting exactly the right size hole. Your foreman asks you to figure out how many tenths of a centimeter the drill is off.

estimate exact answer

3. On a test, you are asked to multiply two numbers. Your answer choices are 1.3, 13, 130, and 1,300.

estimate exact answer

4. A customer is purchasing several items, and she wants to write a check. She asks you what the total cost comes to.

estimate exact answer

5. You have to put in about twenty hours of overtime at work. You want to figure out how much extra money will be in your paycheck this week.

estimate exact answer

FOCUS ON CALCULATORS

Calculator Basics

In this book, you'll learn to use a calculator to solve problems involving decimals, fractions, and percents. You'll find that your calculator is an essential math tool.

The Calculator Keyboard*

The calculator below is similar to many of the inexpensive calculators on the market today.

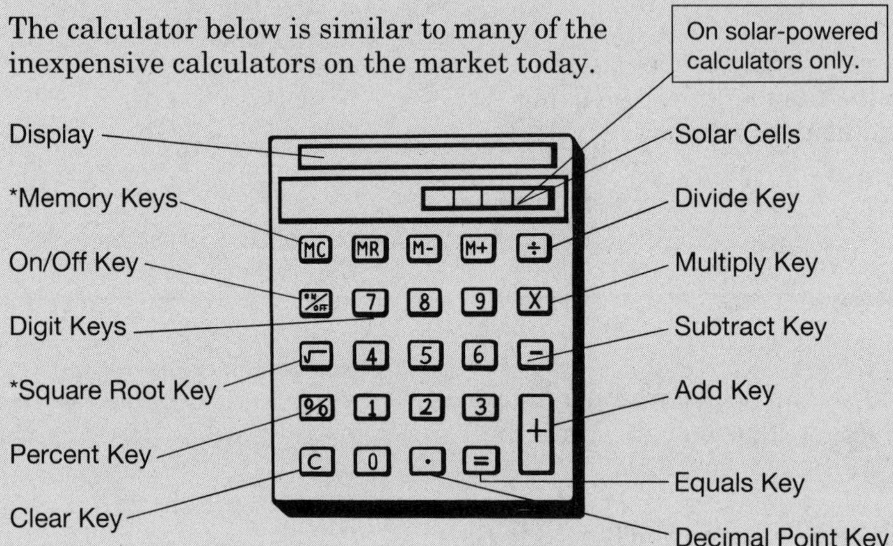

Locate the following keys (or similar keys) on your calculator.

- The **on/off key:** (ON/OFF). You press (ON/OFF) once to turn a calculator on, and press it again to turn it off. Some calculators have separate (ON) and (OFF) keys.

- The **digit keys:** (0), (1), (2), (3), (4), (5), (6), (7), (8), (9). Entering a number on a calculator is similar to dialing on a touchtone telephone. You simply press one digit at a time.

- The **clear key:** (C). Pressing (C) erases the display. You press (C) each time you begin a new problem or when you've made a keying error.

Different calculators use different clear key symbols. Other commonly used symbols are shown below.

(ON/C)	On/Clear	(CE/C)	Clear-Entry/Clear
(CE)	Clear Entry	(AC)	All Clear

*A complete discussion of the square root key and the memory keys can be found in Contemporary's *Calculator Power* text.

Displayed Numbers

Look carefully at these two examples.

Example 1: Enter 3,850 on your calculator.

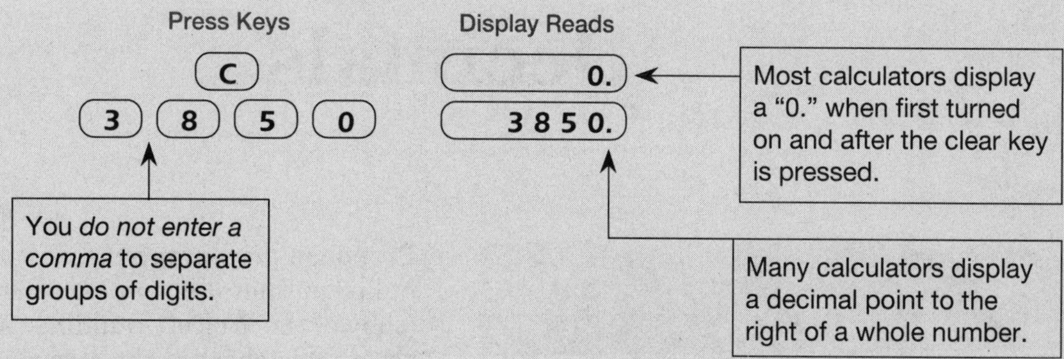
Press Keys
Display Reads
C
3 8 5 0
0.
3850.
Most calculators display a "0." when first turned on and after the clear key is pressed.
You do not enter a comma to separate groups of digits.
Many calculators display a decimal point to the right of a whole number.

Example 2: Enter $6.83 on your calculator.

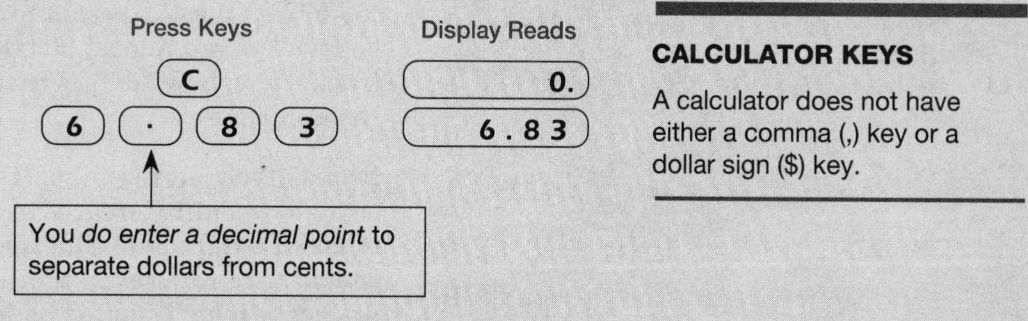
Press Keys
Display Reads
C
6 . 8 3
0.
6.83
You do enter a decimal point to separate dollars from cents.

CALCULATOR KEYS

A calculator does not have either a comma (,) key or a dollar sign ($) key.

▼ Practice

Use your calculator to solve the following problems.

1. With your calculator on, press the whole number keys.

1 2 3 4 5 6 7 8 9

a) How many digits appear on the display? ________

b) What is the largest number your calculator can display? ________

2. What key do you press to clear the display? ________

3. Enter the following on your calculator. Then show how the calculator displays each number or amount.

Enter	Display Reads
a) $.47	
b) $2.35	
c) 187	
d) 2,683	

UNIT TWO

Decimals

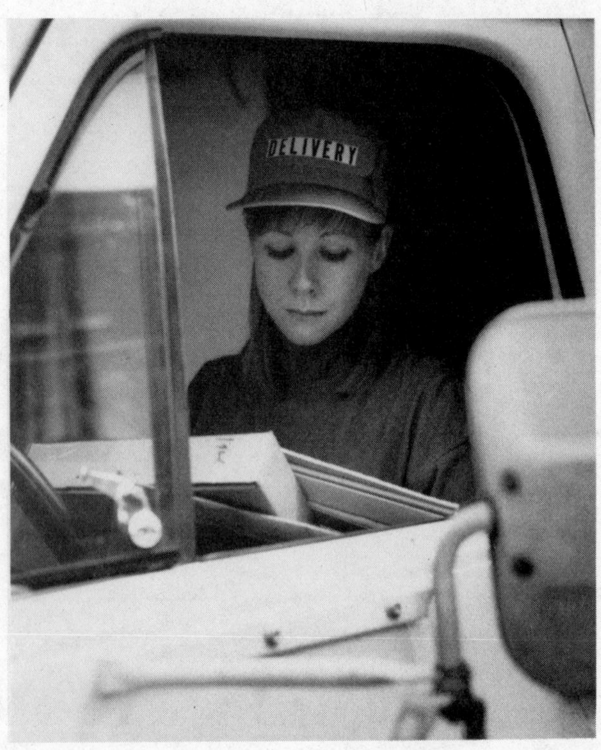

Mileage is recorded using decimals.

Brenda, a driver for a messenger service, pulled out her delivery log as she left the lobby of the Wolcott Building. As always, she double-checked the recorded times for the deliveries at the last stop. Then she got in her truck and wrote down the mileage. "89,897.9 miles," she said to herself. "I can't believe I've put almost 90,000 miles on this truck. Now, how do I get to this next stop, Driscoll House?"

Brenda took out her map. "Let's see, if I go straight about two-tenths of a mile, I need to make a right onto Elm Avenue. Then I should take Elm seven-tenths of a mile to Anchor Street. Then take a left, and Driscoll should be about a tenth of a mile down on the left."

"Perfect," she said to herself. "That's about a mile's drive from here. Before I head back, I'll need to figure out my total mileage for these five deliveries. That won't take long."

Brenda Rafferty			Employee #29080
Destination	**Package/Letter**	**Time of Completed Delivery**	**Mileage**
Dawes' Drugs	pkg	7:09 A.M.	89,864.7
Mason Building	pkg	7:21 A.M.	89,866.9
City Hall	letter	7:29 A.M.	89,875.7
Wolcott Building	letter	8:03 A.M.	89,897.9
Driscoll House	pkg		

Think About It

- Can you see how decimals are a part of a delivery person's job?
- How did Brenda figure out that she was about a mile from Driscoll House?
- How will she figure out how many miles she has driven for the last five deliveries?

How Do Decimals Play a Part in *Your* Life?

Answer the following questions to see how you already use decimals. Don't forget, you can always refer to examples using money—our most common use of the decimal.

Describe a time when you added or subtracted two decimals. Was there anything particularly difficult about this?

____

____

____

Have you ever multiplied one decimal by another? If not, have you multiplied a decimal by a whole number? Think about when you are shopping and want to buy more than one of an item. How do you determine the cost?

____

____

____

Have you ever had to "round" a decimal to a whole number? Why? How did you do this?

____

____

Skills You Will Learn

Number Skills
- adding decimals
- subtracting decimals
- multiplying decimals
- dividing decimals

Life and Workplace Skills
- reading a clinical thermometer
- computing total earnings
- working with averages
- improving quality control
- figuring gas mileage
- computing distance, rate, and time

Thinking Skills
- estimating with decimals
- rounding decimals
- solving one-step math problems
- solving multistep math problems

Calculator Skills
- adding and subtracting decimals
- multiplying and dividing decimals
- using memory keys
- changing fractions to decimals

Estimating: Building Confidence with Decimals

In this chapter, you'll learn the skills to solve decimal problems like these:

Example 1: As a carpenter's apprentice, you nail a 6.5-centimeter piece of molding alongside a 12.3-centimeter mantel. You need to know the approximate total width of the mantel with molding.

Example 2: On a test, you are asked to subtract 3.62 from 5.4. Your answer choices are 17.8, 1.78, and 0.178.

Before you learn how to do computations like these, take some time to learn how to **estimate** with decimals. Estimation is useful when you don't really need an exact number. And if you are confused about where to put the decimal point in an answer, estimating can help.

Rounding Mixed Decimals

- To round a mixed decimal to a whole number, look at the digit in the *tenths* place:
  - If the digit is 5 or more, round up.
  - If the digit is less than 5, discard all decimal digits.

Example 1: 12.3-cm mantel + 6.5-cm molding =
12.3 rounds down to 12 (less than 5)   6.5 rounds up to 7 (5 or more)

12 + 7 = 19

Answer: The total width of the mantel and molding is *about* 19 centimeters.

Example 2: 5.4 − 3.62 =
5.4 rounds to 5 (less than 5)   3.62 rounds to 4 (5 or more)

5 − 4 = 1

Answer: The correct answer choice is 1.78. (See the answer choices listed at the top of the page.)

▼ MATH TIP

When rounding to a whole number, just ignore any digit to the right of the tenths place.

▼ Practice

Round each mixed number to the nearest whole number or dollar.

1. a) 4.8 miles **b)** 2.54 meters **c)** 3.62 ounces

2. a) $7.95 **b)** 21.6 miles per gallon **c)** $12.38

3. a) 3.52 tons **b)** 11.74 pounds **c)** 11.75 inches

4. a) $6.50 **b)** $2.44 **c)** $24.61

Imagine you are taking a test. You've been asked to estimate an answer for each problem below. *You are not to find exact answers*. To find an estimated answer, round each number to a whole number or dollar as your first step.

5.

Problem	Estimate	Problem	Estimate	Problem	Estimate
$5.88 + 3.14		6.7 + 2.26		14.78 − 3.9	

6.

Problem	Estimate	Problem	Estimate	Problem	Estimate
12.23 − 7.875		$5.83 × 3.5		9.375 × 4.25	

7.

Problem	Estimate	Problem	Estimate
$27.80 ÷ 4.2 =		3.14)36.24	

As an administrative assistant at a day-care center, you purchase food. After weighing the following items, you want to **estimate** their costs to see if you are within your $75.00 budget.

Complete the chart that has been started for you.

	Item	Number of Pounds		Price per Pound	Estimate
8.	cheese	5.03	×	$2.79	**5 × $3 = $15**
9.	bologna	8.91	×	$3.09	______
10.	grapes	3.56	×	$1.29	______
11.	apples	10.49	×	$ .89	______
12.	bananas	2.79	×	$1.19	______
13.	hot dogs	6.43	×	$1.89	______
				14. TOTAL:	______

15. Are you within the $75 budget? ______

Imagine that, as part of a job application, you are taking a pre-employment math test. You decide to use your estimating skills to solve the following decimal problems.

Round the numbers given in each problem, then solve using the rounded numbers. *Using your estimate as a clue*, circle the letter of the correct answer.

One-Step Problems

16. James placed two tiles side by side. One measures 8.375 inches wide, and the other 6.75 inches wide. What total width is spanned by the two tiles? (**Hint:** 8 + 7 = 15)

a) .15125 in.
b) 1.5125 in.
c) 15.125 in.
d) 25.125 in.

17. As a typist, Myrta earns $7.28 per hour. How much did Myrta earn last week if she worked 34.75 hours?

a) $252.98
b) $2,529.80
c) $298.45
d) $328.40

18. Blake bought a beef roast on sale for $6.28. If the roast weighs 3.17 pounds, how much did Blake pay per pound?

a) $.89
b) $1.06
c) $1.57
d) $1.98

Multistep Problems

19. Kate bought an 11.3-pound turkey and paid $.93 per pound. How much should Kate write a check for if she wants to get back $10 in change?

a) $14.89
b) $20.51
c) $28.74
d) $34.35

20. Last week, Mark worked 40 hours at his regular pay rate of $6.19 per hour. He also worked 9.75 hours of overtime at a rate of $9.29 per hour. What total salary did Mark earn last week?

a) $304.80
b) $309.50
c) $338.18
d) $375.29

Rounding Decimal Fractions to the Lead Digit

In a machine shop, you've been asked to estimate the amount of stainless steel that must be cut off a shaft so that it can fit through a hole. The diameter of the shaft is .305 inches. The hole measures .087 inches. How do you do this estimate?

Estimating with decimal fractions is a little tricky. The first step is learning to round to the lead digit.*

The **lead digit** is the first nonzero digit to the right of the decimal point.

To round to the lead digit, look at the digit just to the right of the lead digit.

- If the digit to the right is 5 or more, round up. Add 1 to the lead digit. Discard all other digits.

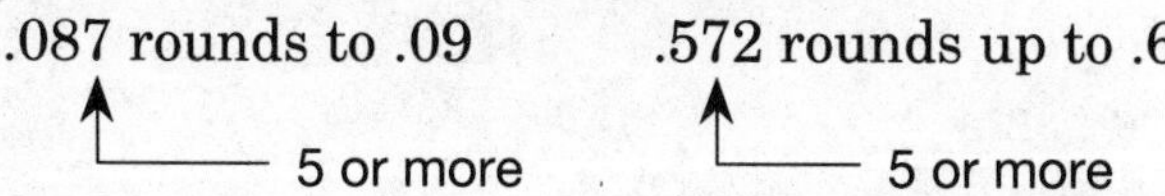

- If the digit to the right is less than 5, round down. Leave the lead digit alone. Discard all other digits.

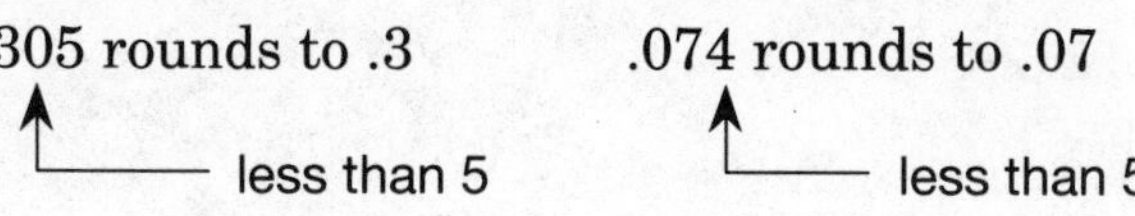

▼ MATH TIP

When you round to the lead digit, *you round to the place value of the lead digit.*

The examples are rounded as follows:

Fraction	Rounded to
.087 ≈ .09	hundredths
.572 ≈ .6	tenths
.305 ≈ .3	tenths
.074 ≈ .07	hundredths

≈ means "approximately equal to"

▼ Practice

Round each decimal fraction to its lead digit.

1. .24 ↖ less than 5 ≈ **.2**   .48   .37   .864   .107   .250

2. .069 ↖ 5 or more ≈ **.07**   .024   .096   .038   .041   .067

3. .0058 ↖ 5 or more ≈ **.006**   .0082   .0069   .0034   .0074   .0088

*We'll use this skill several times in the following pages.

Rounding Numbers to a Chosen Place Value

Smaller Place Values

Once in a while, you may see a decimal fraction with more than 3 decimal places. Because of this, you'll want to be familiar with place values smaller than one-thousandth (.001).

.1 one-tenth
.01 one-hundredth
.001 one-thousandth
.0001 one ten-thousandth
.00001 one hundred-thousandth
.000001 one-millionth

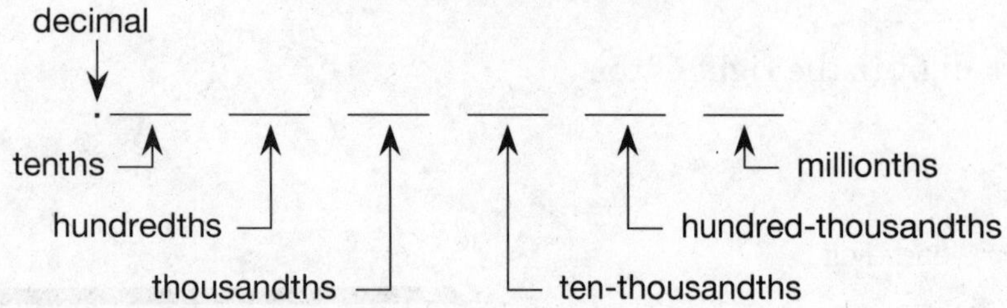

Rounding Numbers

Sometimes, when a number has several decimal digits, you may need to *round to a chosen place value.*

Example: You've measured two stacks of boards on a construction site, and you've written down the lengths. Your foreman asks you to label the length of each stack to the *nearest hundredth* meter.

Stack #1: 1.635 meters Stack #2: 2.584 meters

In this example, the measurements are given in *thousandths* of a meter. To write these lengths as *hundredths* of a meter, you have to round the numbers.

> To *round* a number, look at the digit just to the right of the chosen place value.
> - If the digit is 5 or more, round up.
> - If the digit is less than 5, round down.

$1.635 \approx$ 1.64 meters (5 or more) $2.584 \approx$ 2.58 meters (less than 5)

Your foreman could also have asked you to give the same measurements to the *nearest tenth* meter.

$1.635 \approx$ 1.6 meters (less than 5) $2.584 \approx$ 2.6 meters (5 or more)

Before you round, be sure you know what place you're asked to round to.

▼ MATH TIP

The symbol ≈ means "is approximately equal to."

▼ Practice

Round each decimal fraction in row 1 to the tenths place.

1. .68 ↖ 5 or more   .25   .73   .265   .483   .915

≈ **.7**

Round each decimal fraction in row 2 to the hundredths place.

2. .463 ↖ less than 5   .583   .823   .7526   .5075   .2691

≈ **.46**

3. At the grocery store where you work, you put prices on all labels in the meat and poultry case. Each label already shows the weight of the meat and the price per pound.

You use a calculator to multiply *pounds* × *dollars per pound*, and you come up with the numbers in the chart below. Round each calculator answer to the hundredths place (nearest cent).

	Weight (lb.)		Price ($ per lb.)	Calculator Answer	Selling Price
Chicken					
whole	5.03	×	$.89	4.4767	a) $4.48
breasts	3.89	×	$3.40	13.226	b) ______
pieces	1.36	×	$1.16	1.5776	c) ______
livers	2.77	×	$1.19	3.2963	d) ______
thighs	4.62	×	$2.49	11.5038	e) ______
legs	3.50	×	$2.19	7.665	f) ______
Beef					
ground	3.09	×	$2.19	6.7671	g) ______
flank steak	2.79	×	$5.99	16.7121	h) ______
sirloin	1.74	×	$2.39	4.1586	i) ______
liver	1.45	×	$1.09	1.5805	j) ______
T-bone	2.63	×	$4.18	10.9934	k) ______

Note: A calculator does not display a dollar sign ($).

4. Round each drill bit size below to the nearest thousandth of an inch.

	Bit Size	**Nearest Thousandth Inch**
a)	$\frac{1}{16}$" (.0625")	______
b)	$\frac{5}{64}$" (.078125")	______
c)	$\frac{11}{32}$" (.34375")	______

FOCUS ON CALCULATORS

Decimal Numbers

Adding Decimal Numbers

To add two or more decimal numbers . . .

- Enter each number, and press (+) after each.
- Press (=) only after entering the final number.

▼ **MATH TIP**

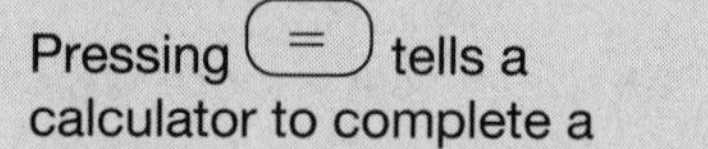

Pressing (=) tells a calculator to complete a calculation and to display the answer.

Example 1: If you place these three spacers end-to-end, what total distance will be covered?

To solve, add the three lengths as shown at right.

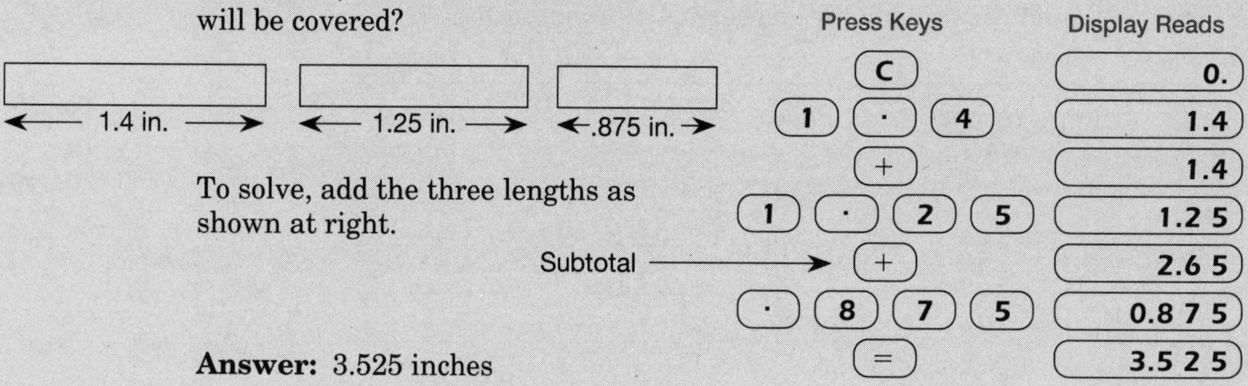

Answer: 3.525 inches

Subtracting Decimal Numbers

To subtract one or more decimal numbers . . .

- Enter the largest number, then press (−) .
- Enter the number(s) to be subtracted, and press (−) after each.
- Press (=) only after entering the final number.

▼ **MATH TIP**

If you accidentally subtract a larger number from a smaller number, your calculator will display a minus sign next to the answer.

Example 2: At work, you cut 0.235 inch off a 1.364-inch shaft. You then cut another 0.06 inch off. What is the width of the completed shaft?

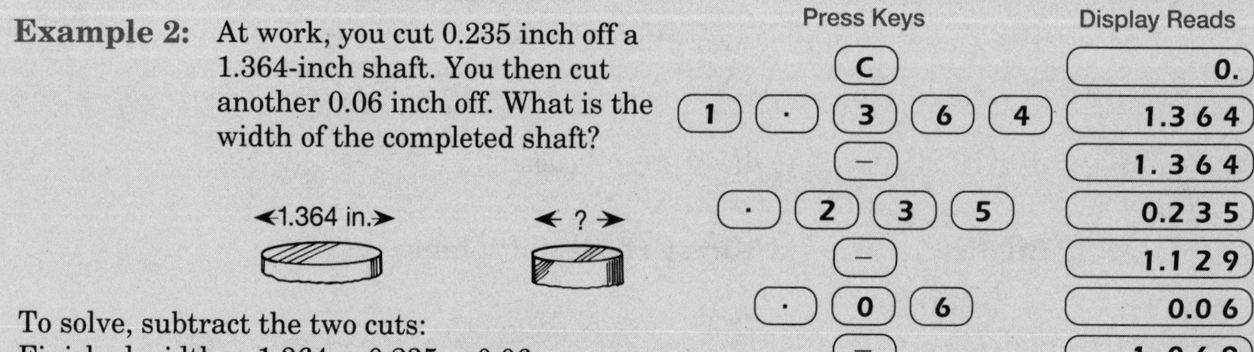

To solve, subtract the two cuts:
Finished width = 1.364 − 0.235 − 0.06

Answer: 1.069 inches

▼ Practice

Use your calculator to solve the following problems.

1. Add or subtract as indicated.

2.4	3.73	9.05	2.7	4.5	$9.00
+ 1.9	+ 2.065	4.5	− 1.6	− 2.875	− 3.58
		+ 3.875			

2. $12.45 + $8 + $3.67 =

3. 2.5 in. + 3.125 in. + 1.875 in. =

4. 7.01 in. − 3.875 in. − 2.75 in. =

5. Suppose you kept a record of the hours you worked last week (shown at right).

a) How many hours did you work last week?

b) How many more hours did you work on Thursday than on Friday?

c) If your normal work week is 38.5 hours, how many overtime hours did you work?

Monday:	7.25 hours
Tuesday:	8.5 hours
Wednesday:	8 hours
Thursday:	9.25 hours
Friday:	7.75 hours
Saturday:	3.5 hours
Total:	

6. Imagine you are using a computer-controlled lathe to cut bolts to specified lengths. The lathe is not cutting correctly, and your boss wants to know why. Listed below are the results of three test cuts.

Bolt #	Specified Length	Actual Length Cut by Lathe	Difference
1	2.35 in.	2.344 in.	________
2	4.5 in.	4.494 in.	________
3	5.875 in.	5.869 in.	________

a) For each bolt, subtract to find the difference between Specified Length and Actual Length.

b) What can you conclude about the cutting error being made?

Multiplying Decimal Numbers

To multiply two or more decimal numbers . . .

- Enter each number, and press × after each.
- Press = only after entering the final number.

Example 3: On Saturday, a co-worker worked 4.5 hours of overtime. His overtime pay rate is 1.5 times his regular rate of \$7.60 per hour. How much did he earn on Saturday?

Overtime rate = \$7.60 × 1.5

To solve, multiply the overtime rate by 4.5.

Total earnings = \$7.60 × 1.5 × 4.5

Press Keys	Display Reads
C	0.
7 · 6 0	7.6 0
×	7.6 0
1 · 5	1.5
×	1 1.4
4 · 5	4.5
=	5 1.3

Answer: \$51.30

Dividing Decimal Numbers

To divide one decimal number by another . . .

- Enter the **dividend,** then press ÷.
- Enter the **divisor,** and press =.

Example 4: If you paid \$6.35 for 1.3 pounds of salmon, how much were you charged per pound?

To solve, divide \$6.35 by 1.3.

\$6.35 ÷ 1.3

dividend ↑ ↑ divisor

Round the displayed answer to the nearest cent.

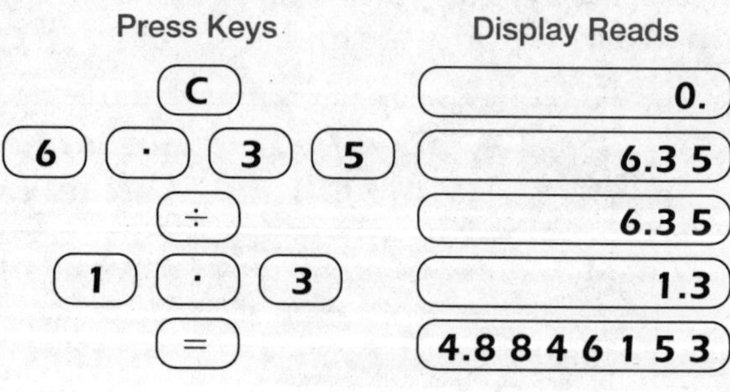

Answer: \$4.88 per pound

▼ **MATH TIP**

A calculator carries out division until there is no remainder—or until the display is full. For this reason, the displayed answer may contain more decimal places than the dividend. See Example 4.

▼ Practice

Using your calculator, multiply or divide as indicated. Round money answers to the nearest cent.

1.

$$\begin{array}{r} \$6.05 \\ \times\ \ 4.5 \\ \hline \end{array} \qquad \begin{array}{r} 7.9 \\ \times\ \ 8 \\ \hline \end{array} \qquad \begin{array}{r} 8.03 \\ \times\ \ 4.2 \\ \hline \end{array} \qquad 3\overline{)\$39.84} \qquad .05\overline{)16}$$

2. $8.40 × 1.5 × 5 = $32.92 ÷ 4 = 32.4 ÷ 1.6 =

3. Compute the daily receipts for the sale of each item below.

Item	Pounds Sold		Price per Pound		Daily Receipts (Nearest Cent)
turkey	27.8	×	$3.88	=	________
ham	23.4	×	$4.79	=	________
roast beef	38.3	×	$3.29	=	________

4. Compute the hourly rate each employee was paid for the amount each earned below.

Employee	Amount Earned		Hours Worked		Hourly Pay Rate
Jesse	$264.10	÷	38	=	________
Ella	$202.23	÷	27	=	________
Debbie	$335.40	÷	39	=	________

5. A decimal fraction may be terminating or repeating.

A **terminating decimal fraction** has a limited number of decimal digits.

Example: 7 ÷ 4 = 1.75

A **repeating decimal fraction** has a never ending, repeating pattern of one or more digits.

Example: 4 ÷ 3 = 1.3333333 . . .

Using your calculator, divide. Indicate with a check (✔) the type of decimal fraction you obtain.

a) $4\overline{)5}$ ____ terminating
____ repeating

b) $3\overline{)13}$ ____ terminating
____ repeating

c) 17 ÷ 11 ____ terminating
____ repeating

d) 35 ÷ 16 ____ terminating
____ repeating

Adding Decimals

Suppose you work at a gas station where the price of gas is \$1.389 per gallon. Your boss tells you that she is raising the price \$.012, and she wants you to display the new price on the sign in front of the station. What do you do?

To add decimals:

- line up the decimal points and add the columns;
- place a decimal point in the answer directly below the decimal points in the problem.

$$\begin{array}{r} \$1.389 \\ .012 \\ \hline 1.401 \end{array}$$

Line up decimal points

The new gas price will be \$1.401 per gallon.

- To add decimals that do not have the same number of decimal places, use 0s as place holders. Extra 0s keep columns in line.
- A whole number is "understood" to have a decimal point to the right of the ones digit.

Example: You have 3 cups. One contains 7 grams of weights, the second 3.125 grams, and the third 1.5 grams. Do you have the right weight to balance a scale set at 11.5 grams?

Step 1. Write a decimal point to the right of the 7, and line up the three decimal points. Use 0s as place holders.

Step 2. From right to left, add the columns.

$$\begin{array}{r} 7.000 \\ 3.125 \\ +\ 1.500 \\ \hline 11.625 \end{array}$$

place-holding 0s

place-holding 0s

Answer: No, you don't have the right weight—11.625 is more than 11.5 (11.500).

▼ MATH TIP

Write place-holding 0s at the right end of decimal fractions. In this way, you don't change their values.

2.5 = 2.50

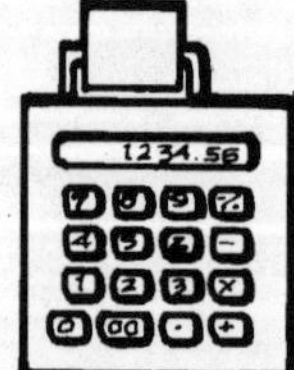

Calculator Solution of Example

Press Keys: C 7 + 3 . 1 2 5 + 1 . 5 =

Answer: 11.625

▼ Practice

Add. Use zeros as place holders where necessary.

1. $.6 + .3$ $.75 + .54$ $\$.95 + .25$ $\$5.80 + 3.40$ $15.9 + 6.5$ $4.375 + 2.250$

2. $.65 + .2$ $.7 + .15$ $2.75 + 1.5$ $.437 + .2$ $\$12.85 + 1.55$ $14.8 + 3.625$

3. .34 + .12   .64 + .5   2.15 + .375 $4 + $3.28

.34
+ .12
.46

4. 7 + 3.65 + 1.2 $4.20 + $3 + $.85   6.81 + 4 + 3.9

Round each answer in row 5 to the hundredths place.

5. 2.675 + 1.846   1.025 + .95   .8125 + .125   2.1 + .9375

2.675
+ 1.846
4.521
≈ 4.52

6. At right is a record of your gas purchases. Add to determine the amount of gas you purchased during June and the amount you spent for gas.

	Gallons	Cost
6/1	12.9	$19.22
6/10	14.3	$20.45
6/19	13.8	$20.15
6/27	9.4	$14.29

7. At the end of each week, a store clerk adds the daily totals of each type of meat sold. His daily totals are shown below:

	Turkey	Roast Beef	Ham
Monday	14.75 lb.	20.82 lb.	15.64 lb.
Tuesday	9.9 lb.	10.37 lb.	8 lb.
Wednesday	12 lb.	11.5 lb.	7.5 lb.
Thursday	3.45 lb.	6 lb.	9.1 lb.
Friday	8.2 lb.	9.74 lb.	6.19 lb.

a) Rounding to whole numbers, estimate each total for the week:

Turkey: _____ lb. Roast Beef: _____ lb. Ham:_____ lb.

b) Add each column to determine each exact total for the week:

Turkey: _____ lb. Roast Beef: _____ lb. Ham:_____ lb.

Subtracting Decimals

You're working as a lab assistant in an industrial plant.

> "I've got a 2.750-liter jug of solvent here, and I'm about to use 1.250 liters of it," says a co-worker. "Will we have enough left for the other experiment?"

You know that the second experiment requires 1.5 liters of solvent. Will there be enough left over for that experiment? To find out, you'll need to subtract decimals.

▼ **MATH TIP**

Liter is a metric unit that's slightly larger than one quart.

Example 1:

Step 1. Write 1.250 below 2.750, and line up the decimal points. Subtract as you do with whole numbers.

$$\begin{array}{r} 2.750 \\ -\ 1.250 \\ \hline 1.500 \end{array}$$

↑ Line up decimal points.

Step 2. Place a decimal point in the answer directly below the decimal points in the problem.

Answer: There are 1.5 (1.500) liters left. Yes, there will be enough solvent to do the second experiment.

▼ **MATH TIP**

Remember that 1.500 has the same value as 1.5.

- To subtract numbers that do not have the same number of decimal places, use 0s as place holders—just as you do when adding decimals.

Example 2: If you pour 4.375 liters of solvent from an 8-liter jug, how many liters will be left?

Lining up the decimal points	Using 0s as place holders
$\begin{array}{r} 8. \\ -\ 4.375 \\ \hline \end{array}$	$\begin{array}{r} {}^{7\ 9\ 9\ 10} \\ \not{8}.\not{0}\not{0}\not{0} \\ -\ 4.375 \\ \hline 3.625 \end{array}$

Answer: 3.625 liters

▼ **MATH TIP**

Estimating can help you check that you lined up your decimals and put in 0s correctly.

Estimate

$$\begin{array}{r} 8 \\ -\ 4 \\ \hline 4 \end{array}$$

$4 \approx 3.625$ (actual answer)

Calculator Solution of Example 2

Press Keys: (C) (8) (−) (4) (·) (3) (7) (5) (=)

Answer: (3.625)

▼ Practice

1.

.8	.97	$2.58	13.9	$7.00	3.375
− .4	− .25	− .39	− 5.6	− 5.28	− 1.625

2.

.89	.972	1.45	.467	5.7	6
− .5	− .7	− 1.3	− .29	− 2.75	− 2.375

3. .95 − .8   1.45 − .3   .504 − .3 $5 − $2.75

.95
− .80
.15

4. $7 − $5.37   8 − 4.275   12.4 − 7.85 $20 − $9.39 − $2.89

Round each answer in row 5 to the tenths place.

5. .85 − .46   1.3 − .82   .275 − .062   3.54 − 1.9

.85
− .46
.39
≈ .4

6. At the weekend track meet, the top five finishers completed the 440-yard run in the times shown at right. The field record is 49.65 seconds.

a) How much slower did each runner run than the field record? Write your answers on the lines in the table.

b) What is the difference between the fastest and slowest times?
_______ seconds

Name	Time (sec.)	Amount Over Field Record
Barton	51.6	_______
Clancy	52	_______
Ewa	50.875	_______
Hanson	50.49	_______
McDougal	53.1	_______

7. Your co-worker at the machine shop must cut stock metal rod down to specified finished sizes. Fill in the table below to show how much he must cut. Write both an estimate and an exact answer.

Stock Size	Finished Size	Estimate of Difference	Exact Difference
a) .25 inch	.175 inch	_______ inch	_______ inch
b) .375 inch	.29 inch	_______ inch	_______ inch
c) 2.6 inches	1.175 inches	_______ inches	_______ inches
d) 3.25 inches	1.148 inches	_______ inches	_______ inches

IN YOUR LIFE

Reading a Thermometer

During many illnesses, the temperature of the human body rises. Because of this, the first thing a doctor often wants to know about a patient is his or her temperature.

Temperature is measured in units called **degrees**. The symbol for degrees is °. Instruments used to measure temperature are called **thermometers**.

A **clinical thermometer** is used to measure body temperature. The two types of clinical thermometers are the **Fahrenheit** and the **Celsius** thermometers.

- On the Fahrenheit thermometer, normal human body temperature is 98.6°. Notice that each small mark on this thermometer is .2° F away from the mark next to it.

Fahrenheit
normal human body temperature → 98.6° F

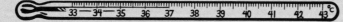

94 96 98 100 102 104 °F

- On the Celsius thermometer, normal human body temperature is 37° C. On this thermometer, each mark is .1° C away from the next mark.

Celsius
normal human body temperature → 37° C

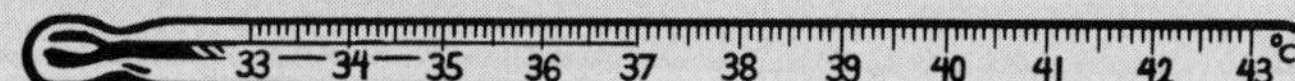

▼ MATH TIP

Both thermometers show normal body temperature.

To read the temperature, read the point on the scale directly above the right-hand end of the horizontal line passing through the center of each thermometer.

▼ Practice

A. Become familiar with both types of thermometers by answering the following questions.

1. What is the temperature range shown on the Fahrenheit thermometer? ______ ° F to ______ ° F

2. What is the temperature range shown on the Celsius thermometer? ______ ° C to ______ ° C

3. What is normal human body temperature? ______ ° F or ______ ° C

B. Problems 4–6 refer to the Fahrenheit thermometer below.

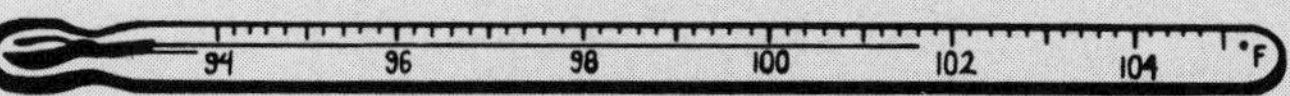

4. Put an ↓ above the thermometer scale to show the reading for normal human body temperature.

5. At 8 o'clock Saturday evening, a child complains of feeling sick. His temperature is shown on the thermometer above.

a) What is the child's temperature at 8 o'clock? _______

b) By 9 o'clock, his temperature has risen another 1.6° F. What is his temperature at 9 o'clock? _______

6. You treat the fever with medicine and put a cool towel on the child's forehead. By 9:30, his temperature drops to 99.3° F.

a) How much has his temperature dropped between 9:00 and 9:30? _______

b) How much is his temperature still above normal at 9:30? _______

C. Problems 7–9 refer to the Celsius thermometer below.

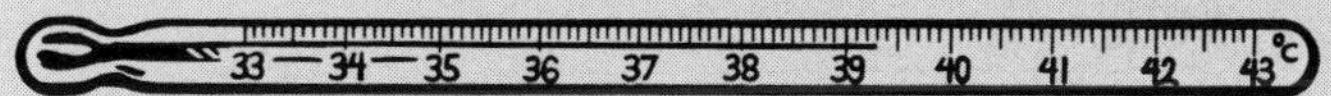

7. Put an ↓ above the thermometer scale to show the reading for normal human body temperature.

8. When you had the flu, you took your own temperature, as shown above.

a) What was your temperature? _______

b) How much was your temperature above normal? _______

9. When you called your doctor's office, the nurse advised you to take two non-aspirin tablets, to put a cool towel on your forehead, and to lie down—all of which you did. Twenty minutes later, your temperature had dropped to 37.9° C.

a) How much did your temperature drop during those 20 minutes? _______

b) How much was your temperature still above normal? _______

▼ MATH TIP

The Fahrenheit thermometer is part of the English measuring system. You may be most familiar with this type of thermometer.

The Celsius thermometer is part of the metric system of measurement. Both types of thermometers are in common use in the United States.

Fact to Remember:
98.6° F = 37° C

HEALTH FACTS

Low-Fever Range:
99° F–101° F
or
37.2° C–38.3° C

High-Fever Range:
102° F–104° F
or
38.8° C–40° C

Note: A temperature above 104° F or 40° C can be serious and may require medical attention.

Multiplying Decimals

Occasionally on the job or on math tests, you may be asked to multiply a decimal by a decimal. In most cases, you would use a calculator to multiply. However, in case a calculator is not available, you'll want to know how to multiply with paper and pencil.

Example: Multiply 2.85 × .7

Step 1. Multiply the numbers.

Step 2. Count the number of decimal places in each number being multiplied.

		Estimate
2.85	2 places	3
× .7	+ 1 place	× .7
1995	3 places	2.1

Step 3. Add these two numbers (2 + 1 = 3) to see how many decimal places belong in the answer.

Place a decimal point in the answer.

1.995
321

Start at the right.
Count to the left.

Answer: 1.995

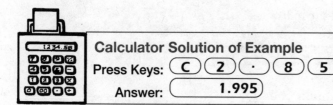

Calculator Solution of Example

Press Keys: C 2 · 8 5 × · 7 =

Answer: 1.995

▼ Practice

Find each product below. First complete each row of Skill Builders by placing a decimal point in each answer.

REMINDER

The number of decimal places in a number is the number of digits to the right of the decimal point. A whole number has no decimal places.

Multiplying Decimals by Whole Numbers

Skill Builders

1.	1.35	2 places	47	0 places	125	0 places	390	0 places
	× 4	0 places	× .05	2 places	× .9	1 place	× .005	3 places
	540	2 places	235	2 places	1125	1 place	1950	3 places

2. 5.7 × 3   .82 × 6   42 × 1.4   2.8 × 5   23 × .08

3. \$.38 × 5   123 × .05   \$2.75 × 7   .055 × 4   \$6.13 × 9

Round each answer in row 4 to the tenths place.

4. 24 × .06 = 1.44   215 × .004   78 × .35   5.75 × 3   .015 × 6

= 1.44 ≈ 1.4

Multiplying Decimals by Decimals

Skill Builders

5.

.9 8 × .7 = 6 8 6	2 places, 1 place	4.7 × .8 = 3 7 6	1 place, 1 place
2.3 5 × .7 6: 1 4 1 0, 1 6 4 5, 1 7 8 6 0	2 places, 2 places	.6 4 5 × .5 8: 5 1 6 0, 3 2 2 5, 3 7 4 1 0	3 places, 2 places

6. .59 × .7   .43 × .5   3.8 × .9   5.46 × .05   3.25 × 1.4

Round each answer in row 7 to the hundredths place.

7. 3.4 × .005 = .0170   \$5.73 × 1.5   .85 × 2.4   6.75 × .008   \$4.84 × 2.5

= .017 ≈ .02

Compute an estimate for each problem in row 8. Do not find an exact solution.

8. 1.9 × .87 **Estimate**   \$5.25 × 2.1 **Estimate**   .906 × 4.2 **Estimate**   .412 × .89 **Estimate**

Place-Holding Zeros

Example: Multiply .13 × .05

```
      .13     2 places
    × .05     2 places
  . _ _ 65    4 places     = .0065
     ↑  ↑
Add two  Although there are only
zeros    two numbers, there must
         be four decimal places.
```

▼ MATH TIP

In some problems, it is necessary to write one or more zeros as place holders before you can write the decimal point in the answer.

In the example at left, two zeros must be placed in the answer to the left of the 6 before the decimal point is written.

Compute each product below. First complete the Skill Builders by placing a decimal point in each answer after adding needed zeros.

Skill Builders

9.

.3	1 place	.05	2 places	.16	2 places	7	0 places
× .3	1 place	× .9	1 place	× .03	2 places	× .005	3 places
9	2 places	45	3 places	48	4 places	35	3 places

10. .4 × .2   .6 × .5   .7 × .6   .14 × .2   .9 × .03

11. .08 × .9   .05 × .3   .006 × .04   9 × .005   7.5 × .02

12. You work as a billing clerk for the Electric Power Company. To compute amount owed, you multiply electric power usage times cost per kWh (kilowatt-hour). The cost per kWh is given to the nearest thousandth cent. After multiplying, you round each bill to the nearest cent.

Compute the amount owed by each customer below.

Name	Electric Power Usage (kWh)		Cost per kWh		Amount Owed (Rounded to Nearest Cent)
Franklin	700	×	\$.06372	≈	______
Garland	650	×	\$.06372	≈	______
NAD Co.	8,000	×	\$.08456	≈	______
ALU Inc.	7,400	×	\$.08456	≈	______

Imagine that you are taking a math exam. Write an estimate for each problem below. *Then, using only your estimate as a clue,* choose the correct answer. To estimate:

- Round each money amount to the nearest dollar.
- Round each mixed decimal to the nearest whole number.
- Round each decimal fraction to its lead digit.

	Estimate	**Choose one based on your estimate**
13. Paying $4.98 per pound, how much should Stella pay for a fillet of salmon that weighs .79 pound?		**a)** $3.14 **b)** $3.52 **c)** $3.93 **d)** $4.26
14. A medium-sized shipping box is packed with 72 cans of corn. If each can weighs 14 ounces (.875 pound), how many pounds does the box weigh?		**a)** 59 **b)** 63 **c)** 67 **d)** 71
15. In the metric system, weight is measured in grams, a unit much smaller than one ounce. In fact, 1 ounce equals 28.35 grams. Knowing this, determine the weight in grams of a 6-ounce can of tuna.		**a)** 170.1 **b)** 198.4 **c)** 215.7 **d)** 236.8
16. How much change would you expect to receive if you bought 5.9 pounds of nails on sale for $.96 per pound and you paid with a twenty-dollar bill?		**a)** $10.82 **b)** $11.04 **c)** $12.76 **d)** $14.34
17. Bert used his calculator to find the product of .382 times .071. What answer should appear on the calculator display?		**a)** 0.0027122 **b)** 0.027122 **c)** 0.27122 **d)** 2.7122
18. In the metric system, road distance is measured in kilometers (one kilometer is about .62 mile). Giving your answer in miles, how much shorter is 10 kilometers than 10 miles?		**a)** 2.4 **b)** 2.8 **c)** 3.2 **d)** 3.8

10 miles

10 kilometers

? miles ? miles

Multiplying by 10, 100, or 1,000

Decimal multiplication gives you three shortcuts to use when multiplying by 10, 100, or 1,000.

- To multiply a decimal by 10, move the decimal point *one place* to the right.

$3.52 \times 10 = 3.52 = 35.2$ (decimal point moved 1 place)

$.08 \times 10 = .08 = .8$ (decimal point moved 1 place) — You can drop this 0 after you move the decimal point.

- To multiply a decimal by 100, move the decimal point *two places* to the right.

$7.3 \times 100 = 7.3\_ = 730$ (decimal point moved 2 places) — Add a 0.

$.4 \times 100 = .4\_ = 40$ (decimal point moved 2 places) — Add a 0.

Note: You add 0s so you can move the decimal point the correct number of places. *The added 0s become part of the answer.*

- To multiply a decimal by 1,000, move the decimal point *three places* to the right.

$12.5 \times 1{,}000 = 12.5\_\_ = 12{,}500$ (decimal point moved 3 places) — Add two 0s.

▼ MATH TIP

To remember these rules, notice that you always move the decimal point the same number of places as there are 0s in the multiplying number.

▼ Practice

1. Using the shortcuts, compute each product below.

$.35 \times 10 =$ $.04 \times 100 =$ $2.09 \times 1{,}000 =$

2. Multiply to compute the weight of the contents of each packed shipping box below.

	Contents	Weight of Each	Total Weight
Box A	100 clocks	.415 pound	______
Box B	10 dictionaries	3.2 pounds	______
Box C	1,000 erasers	.03 pound	______
Box D	100 rulers	.11 pound	______
Box E	1,000 pencils	.02 pound	______
Box F	10 tape dispensers	2.7 pounds	______

ON THE JOB

Computing Total Earnings

Imagine that you work as a payroll clerk for Alsea Manufacturing. At the end of each week, you fill out a form that shows the total weekly earnings of company employees. Your partially filled out form for this week is shown below.

Here's how you computed Amberg's weekly earnings:

Total hours worked = 43.75
= 40 regular hours + 3.75 overtime hours

Overtime Rate (A)

$$\begin{array}{r} \$6.80 \\ \times\ 1.5 \\ \hline 3\ 400 \\ 6\ 80 \\ \hline 10\ 200 \end{array}$$

(base) (time and a half)

= $10.20

Regular Earnings (B)

$$\begin{array}{r} \$6.80 \\ \times\ 40 \\ \hline \$272.00 \end{array}$$

(hours)

Overtime Earnings (C)

$$\begin{array}{r} \$10.20 \\ \times\ \ 3.75 \\ \hline 5100 \\ 7\ 140 \\ 30\ 60 \\ \hline 38\ 2500 \end{array}$$

(from A) (overtime hours)

= $38.25

Total Earnings (D)

$$\begin{array}{r} \$272.00 \\ +\ 38.25 \\ \hline \$310.25 \end{array}$$

Last Name	Total Hours	Base Rate (1st 40 Hours)	Overtime Rate (1.5 × Base) (A)	Regular Earnings (B)	Overtime Earnings (C)	Total Earnings (D)
Amberg	43.75	$6.80	**$10.20**	**$272.00**	**$38.25**	**$310.25**
Heiden	41.5	$6.40	______	______	______	______
Loude	44.25	$7.20	______	______	______	______
Varley	42.5	$10.00	______	______	______	______
Waxman	43	$7.60	______	______	______	______

▼ Practice

Use the form above to answer the questions.

1. Complete the form above for each of the other four employees.

2. How many more hours did Loude work this week than Amberg?__________

3. Determine the average number of hours worked this week by company employees. (Add the Total Hours column, then divide the sum by 5.)__________

Dividing a Decimal by a Whole Number

Suppose that you and three friends have just finished eating in a restaurant. The bill comes to \$7.84, and you agree to split it evenly four ways. How do you divide?

To divide a decimal by a whole number, place a decimal point in the answer directly above its position in the problem. Then divide.

Example: Divide 7.84 by 4.

Step 1. Set up the problem for division. Place a decimal point where it goes in the answer.

Step 2. Divide as you would with whole numbers.

Step 1.

$$4\overline{)\$7.84}$$

Decimal points are lined up.

Step 2.

$$\begin{array}{r} \$1.96 \\ 4\overline{)\$7.84} \\ -4 \\ \hline 3\,8 \\ -3\,6 \\ \hline 24 \\ -24 \\ \hline \end{array}$$

Answer: 1.96

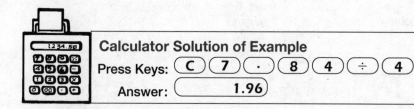

Calculator Solution of Example

Press Keys: C 7 . 8 4 ÷ 4 =

Answer: 1.96

Estimate

$$\begin{array}{r} 2 \\ 4\overline{)8} \end{array}$$

(Your answer should be close to \$2.00.)

▼ Practice

Divide. First complete each row of Skill Builders.

Skill Builders

1. $3\overline{)6.96}$ $6\overline{).744}$ $4\overline{)33.2}$ $8\overline{)6.608}$ $2\overline{).584}$

2. $4\overline{)8.48}$ $5\overline{)45.5}$ $2\overline{).68}$ $3\overline{)30.6}$ $5\overline{).675}$

3. $4\overline{)\$31.44}$ $20\overline{)132.0}$ $6\overline{)\$.84}$ $8\overline{)\$9.44}$ $14\overline{)2.884}$

Estimate an answer for each problem in row 4. Do not try to find exact answers.

4. $5\overline{)40.05}$ $3\overline{).86}$ $7\overline{)\$252.14}$ $4\overline{).824}$ $9\overline{)9.179}$

Using Zeros When You Can't Divide

As shown at right, a zero is used to hold a place when you can't divide.

Since you can't divide 6 into 2, put a 0 above the 2. Now divide 6 into 21. Place a 3 above the 1 and continue.

Example:

$6\overline{).216}$ → $6\overline{).216}$ = .036

```
  .036
6).216
 - 18
   36
 - 36
```

Skill Builders

5. $4\overline{).248}$ (.0) $7\overline{).497}$ (.0) $6\overline{).384}$ (.0) $8\overline{).424}$ (.0) $12\overline{)1.08}$ (.0)

6. $8\overline{).648}$ $3\overline{).096}$ $7\overline{).0084}$ $15\overline{)1.05}$ $25\overline{)2.075}$

7. $9\overline{).297}$ $6\overline{).0774}$ $13\overline{)1.105}$ $27\overline{).0567}$ $4\overline{).0504}$

Zeros can also be added at the end of a number. At right, a 0 is added to 2.4 to give 2.40. Now we can divide by 60.

Example:

$60\overline{)2.4}$ ⟶ $60\overline{)2.40}$

```
     .04
60)2.40
  -2 40
```

Skill Builders

8. $4\overline{).2}$ ⟶ $4\overline{).20}$ $20\overline{).16}$ ⟶ $20\overline{).160}$ $24\overline{).012}$ ⟶ $24\overline{).0120}$

9. $6\overline{).3}$ $8\overline{).4}$ $32\overline{)1.6}$ $40\overline{)2.4}$ $60\overline{)1.2}$

ON THE JOB

Working with Averages

Lin Chang works as an assistant at the Emerald Crop Research Institute. Part of her job is to record the growth of seed samples and to compute average monthly growth rates. Some samples are grown for only two months, while others are grown for as many as four months.

To compute an average monthly growth rate, Lin adds the growth amounts for the months indicated, then she divides the sum by the number of months over which the growth took place. Lin's partially completed table is shown below.

Here's how Lin computed the average monthly growth rate of the Sample #3 seeds.

a) Add the 3 growth amounts shown:

June	.103
July	.134
August	+ .147
	.384

b) Divide by 3:

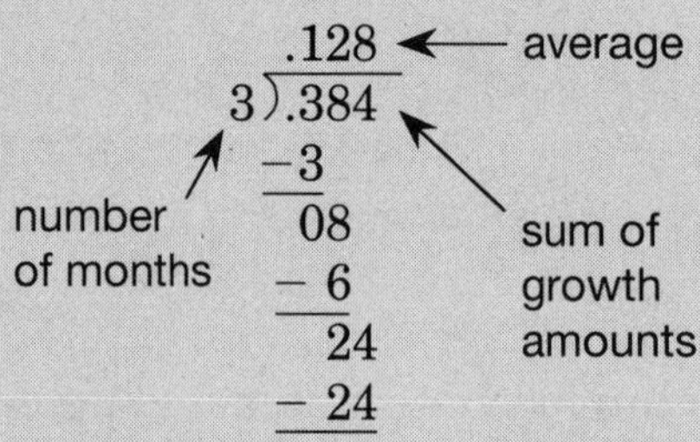

REMINDER

An average is usually not equal to any of the numbers in the group you add.

However, the average is often close to the middle value of the group.

▼ Practice

Compute the average monthly growth rate for each sample listed below. Round each average to the nearest thousandth meter.*

PLANT GROWTH DATA
(growth given in fractions of a meter*)

Sample #	June	July	August	September	Average Monthly Growth Rate
1	.063	.071			m
2	.086	.098			m
3	.103	.134	.147		**.128 m**
4	.089	.105	.118		m
5	.195	.206	.217	.216	m
6	.221	.234	.246	.265	m

*A meter is a metric unit of length. One meter is just over 39 inches long.

Dividing a Larger Whole Number into a Smaller Whole Number

Adding zeros also makes it possible to:

- divide a larger whole number into a smaller whole number;
- change a proper fraction into an equivalent decimal fraction.

As shown in Example 2 at right, adding several zeros while dividing can often eliminate any remainder.

Example 1: Change $\frac{4}{5}$ to a decimal fraction.

$$5\overline{)4} \longrightarrow \begin{array}{r} .8 \\ 5\overline{)4.0} \\ \underline{-\,4\,0} \end{array}$$

Example 2: Divide $8\overline{)5}$

$$\begin{array}{r} .625 \\ 8\overline{)5.000} \\ \underline{-\,4\,8} \\ 20 \\ \underline{-\,16} \\ 40 \\ \underline{-\,40} \end{array}$$

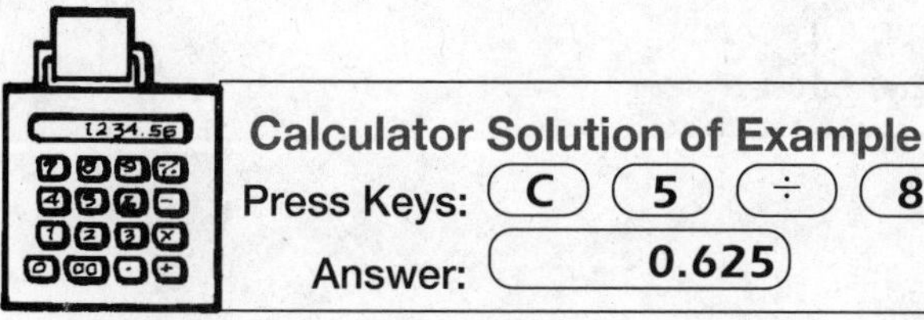

Calculator Solution of Example 2

Press Keys: (C) (5) (÷) (8) (=)

Answer: (0.625)

▼ Practice

Divide. First complete the row of partially worked Skill Builders. In each problem, add enough 0s so that each answer ends without a remainder.

Skill Builders

1. $2\overline{)1} \longrightarrow 2\overline{)1.0}$ $\qquad 8\overline{)6} \longrightarrow 8\overline{)6.00}$ $\qquad 8\overline{)3} \longrightarrow 8\overline{)3.000}$

2. $4\overline{)1}$ $\qquad 8\overline{)2}$ $\qquad 5\overline{)2}$ $\qquad 4\overline{)3}$ $\qquad 8\overline{)7}$

Divide to change each proper fraction into an equivalent decimal fraction. Before dividing, reduce proper fractions to lowest terms.

3. $\frac{2}{4} =$ $\qquad \frac{4}{5} =$ $\qquad \frac{6}{8} =$ $\qquad \frac{8}{10} =$ $\qquad \frac{5}{16} =$

4. $\frac{3}{4} =$ $\qquad \frac{12}{20} =$ $\qquad \frac{5}{8} =$ $\qquad \frac{3}{16} =$ $\qquad \frac{15}{60} =$

ON THE JOB

Improving Quality Control

Manufacturing companies try to make each of their products perfectly. Unfortunately, this goal is impossible to achieve. Machines break down, and employees are sometimes overworked. **Quality control** is the effort a company makes to reduce the number of its defective products.

To measure quality control, Blue Dolphin Toys keeps a record of the number of defective toys its employees produce each work shift. Management tries to arrange working conditions to keep this number as low as possible.

During February, Blue Dolphin ran a test. It put teams of employees on different-length shifts for a few days each week. The object was to determine the number of defects per hour each shift would average. The results of the study are shown below.

To compute defects per hour, divide the number of defective products (column a) by length of shift (column b). For the 4-hour shift, divide 2 by 4:

```
                    .5   <— defects per hour
length of shift —> 4)2.0  <— number of defective products
                   - 2 0
```

▼ Practice

1. Compute the defects per hour for each shift listed. Round any long decimal fraction to the thousandths place.

		Number of Defective Products (a)		Length of Shift (hours) (b)		Defects per Hour (a ÷ b)
Part-Time Employees	Shift A	2	÷	4	=	.5
	Shift B	3	÷	5	=	______
	Shift C	4	÷	6	=	______
Full-Time Employees	Shift D	5	÷	8	=	______
	Shift E	7	÷	10	=	______
	Shift F	10	÷	12	=	______

2. For each type of employee, which shift is *most* efficient (has the lowest number of defects per hour)? Part-time: ______ Full-time: ______

3. a) Overall, which shift is *least* efficient? __________

b) Why do you think this is the least efficient of the shifts in the study?

IN YOUR LIFE

Working with Drill Bits

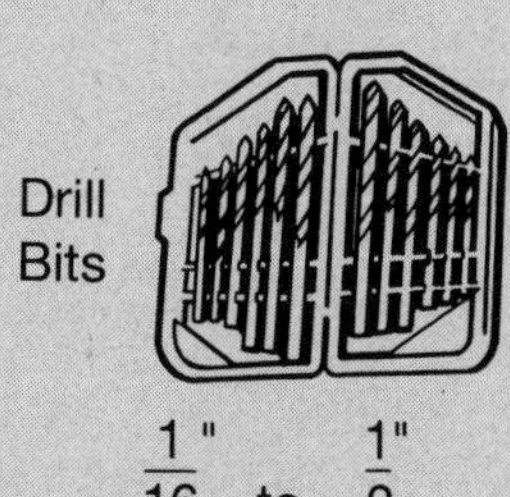

The most common power shop tool used in homes is the electric drill. Drill bits (the pointed, threaded tool that the drill spins) come in a variety of sizes. Most common are those whose diameters (width) are from $\frac{1}{16}$ inch to $\frac{1}{2}$ inch.

Drill bits are usually purchased in sets where each "next larger" bit is $\frac{1}{64}$ inch wider than the next smaller bit. Each bit size is given as a reduced fraction.

Sample Bits

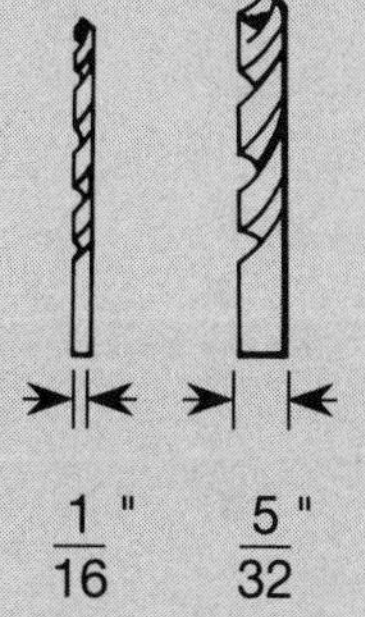

Here are some typical bit sizes—given in fractions of an inch. (Below, for comparison, are equivalent sizes given in 64ths of an inch.)

Bits	$\frac{1}{16}$"	$\frac{5}{64}$"	$\frac{3}{32}$"	$\frac{7}{64}$"	$\frac{1}{8}$"	$\frac{9}{64}$"	$\frac{5}{32}$"
64ths	$\frac{4}{64}$"	$\frac{5}{64}$"	$\frac{6}{64}$"	$\frac{7}{64}$"	$\frac{8}{64}$"	$\frac{9}{64}$"	$\frac{10}{64}$"

▼ MATH TIP

The symbol " is used to stand for *inch.*

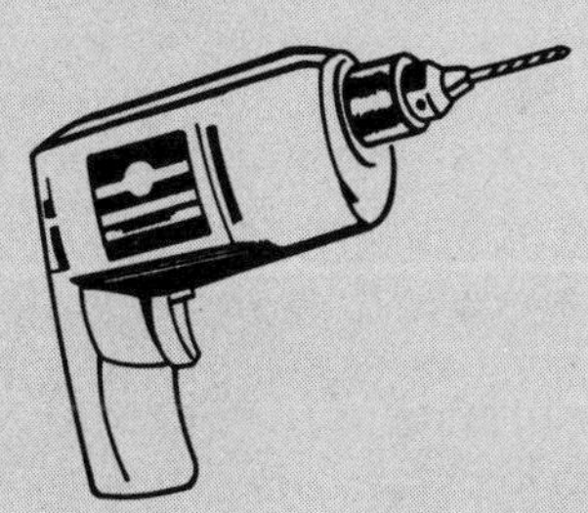

▼ Practice

In the following problems, change each fraction to a decimal as you learned on page 59.

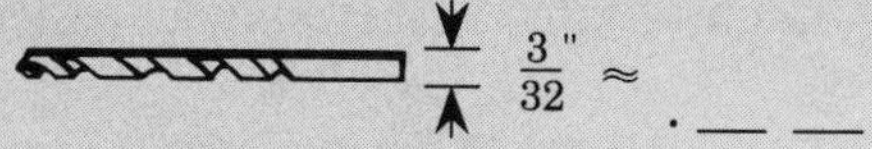

1. To the nearest hundredth of an inch, what is the diameter of a $\frac{3}{32}$" drill bit?

2. Erin needs to drill a hole that will allow a 0.18-inch-diameter wire to pass through. She wants the wire to fit as tightly as possible. Which of the three bits shown at right should she use?

Bit #	Diameter
#1	$\frac{5}{32}$"
#2	$\frac{11}{64}$"
#3	$\frac{3}{16}$"

3. Circle each of the following bits that could be used to drill a drainage hole that is supposed to be "no wider than 0.35 inch."

$\frac{1}{4}$" $\frac{5}{16}$" $\frac{21}{64}$" $\frac{11}{32}$" $\frac{23}{64}$" $\frac{3}{8}$" $\frac{1}{2}$"

ON THE JOB

Working with a Digital Scale

A **digital scale** shows weight as a mixed decimal number of pounds (see box at right). On most digital scales, the weight is rounded to the nearest hundredth pound. Many markets, delis, and other shops use a digital scale to weigh a customer's purchase.

Scale	
Total Price	$14.35
5.81 lb.	$ 2.47
Weight	$ per lb.

Vinnie works at Sal's Deli. One disadvantage of Sal's new digital scale is that customers *never* order by the hundredths of a pound! They order by fractions of a pound.

To give customers what they want, Vinnie had to learn:

- how to change fractions to equivalent decimals; and
- how to give customers "about how much" they order.

Mrs. Lantz ordered "two and one-half pounds of ham." Vinnie knows that "two and one-half" is the same as 2.5. He also knows that any amount between 2.4 and 2.6 pounds is "close enough."

To help with all orders, Vinnie made a chart (shown on page 63), which he taped beside the scale. He listed the fractions that customers most commonly use when buying meat.

To complete this chart, Vinnie follows these rules:

- Divide to change a proper fraction to an equivalent decimal. (You can use your calculator for this.)

Example 1: To change $\frac{1}{4}$ to a decimal, divide 4 into 1:

$\frac{1}{4} = .25$

$$\begin{array}{r} .25 \\ 4\overline{)1.00} \\ -\ 8 \\ \hline 20 \\ -\ 20 \\ \hline \end{array}$$

- Add .10 to the equivalent decimal to find the high end of the acceptable range; subtract .10 to find the low end.

NOTE

Vinnie's way of computing an "acceptable range" by adding and subtracting .10 is his own idea. This range may not be acceptable to every customer!

Example 2: *Step 1.* Add .10 to .25 to find the high end of the range.

$$\begin{array}{r} .25 \\ +\ .10 \\ \hline \textbf{high end: }\ .35 \end{array}$$

Step 2. Subtract .10 from .25 to find the low end.

$$\begin{array}{r} .25 \\ -\ .10 \\ \hline \textbf{low end: }\ .15 \end{array}$$

Vinnie's Chart

Fraction in Words	Proper Fraction		Decimal Equivalent	Acceptable Range
one-fourth (one-quarter)	$\frac{1}{4}$		.25	.15–.35
one-third	______	≈	______	______
one-half	______		______	______
two-thirds	______	≈	______	______
three-fourths (three-quarters)	______		______	______

▼ Practice

1. Complete the table above for Vinnie. (Round one-third and two-thirds to the hundredths.)

2. Frank Lawson came into Sal's Deli and ordered "four pounds of white chicken meat." Using Vinnie's rule, what would be the acceptable range of weight that Vinnie would consider "close enough" to fill Mr. Lawson's order?

   from ______ to ______ pounds

3. Vinnie often takes orders over the phone. He then prepares packages, which are delivered to the customers.

   Match each package below with the order received over the phone. Write the letter of the package on the line to the left of each order.

Package		Order
A. 3.16 lb.	______	"two and three-fourths pounds of beef"
B. 2.67 lb.	______	"two and one-half pounds of beef"
C. 3.58 lb.	______	"two and one-third pounds of beef"
D. 2.24 lb.	______	"three pounds of beef"
E. 2.58 lb.	______	"three and two-thirds pounds of beef"
F. 3.09 lb.	______	"three and one-quarter pounds of beef"

▼ MATH TIP

When written as decimals, the fractions $\frac{1}{3}$ and $\frac{2}{3}$ form repeating decimals.

- Remember, a repeating decimal has a nonending, repeating pattern of decimal digits.

When changing $\frac{1}{3}$ and $\frac{2}{3}$ to decimal fractions, round each to the hundredths place.

Dividing by a Decimal

To divide a decimal by a decimal, follow these steps:

- Change the divisor to a whole number by moving its decimal point to the far right.
- Move the decimal point in the dividend an equal number of places to the right.

▼ MATH TIP

Dividing a decimal by a decimal is a skill you won't use very often.

However, you may need to use this skill on a job or on a math test sometime!

Example: Divide 3.76 by .04

Step 1. Set up the problem for division, then move the decimal points.

- Move the decimal point in the divisor (.04) two places to the right.
- Move the decimal point in the dividend (3.76) two places to the right also.

$.04\overline{)3.76}$

$$\begin{array}{r} 94. \\ 04.\overline{)376.} \\ -36 \\ \hline 16 \\ -16 \\ \hline 0 \end{array}$$

Step 2. Divide 4 into 376.

Answer: 94

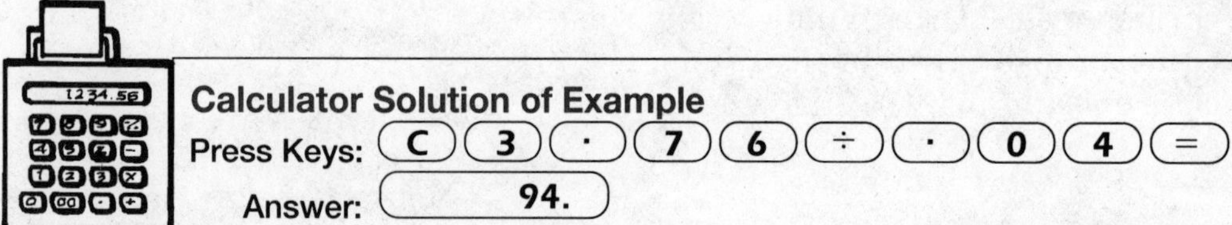

1234.56
Calculator Solution of Example
Press Keys: C 3 · 7 6 ÷ · 0 4 =
Answer: 94.

▼ Practice

Solve each division problem. First complete the Skill Builders. Remember to place a decimal point in each answer.

Skill Builders

1. $\begin{array}{r} 52 \\ .03\overline{)1.56} \end{array}$ $\begin{array}{r} 46 \\ .06\overline{).276} \\ -24 \\ \hline 36 \\ -36 \\ \hline \end{array}$ $\begin{array}{r} 12 \\ 1.8\overline{)21.6} \\ -18 \\ \hline 36 \\ -36 \\ \hline \end{array}$ $.14\overline{).728}$ $4.2\overline{)9.66}$

2. $.04\overline{)2.8}$ $.12\overline{).36}$ $2.6\overline{).806}$ $.002\overline{)6.508}$ $.07\overline{)42.21}$

3. $2.3\overline{).529}$ $.006\overline{)91.44}$ $1.2\overline{)27.84}$ $5.6\overline{)29.12}$ $.08\overline{).52}$

Adding Zeros Before Moving the Decimal Point

Before you can move the decimal point in the dividend, it may be necessary to add one or more zeros as place holders.

In the example at right, two zeros must be added to the dividend.

Example: $.003\overline{)2.7}$

$$\begin{array}{r} 900. \\ .003\overline{)2.700.} \end{array}$$

Answer: 900

Skill Builders

4. $.04\overline{).8} \rightarrow .04\overline{).80.}$ $.005\overline{)2.5} \rightarrow .005\overline{)2.500.}$ $.0025\overline{).5} \rightarrow .0025\overline{).5000.}$

5. $.04\overline{)1.2}$ $.016\overline{).208}$ $.004\overline{)9.36}$ $.024\overline{)26.4}$ $.012\overline{).144}$

Dividing Whole Numbers by Decimals

To divide a whole number by a decimal:

- Add a decimal point to the whole number.
- Move the decimal points, adding zeros as needed to the dividend.
- Divide.

Example: $.05\overline{)4}$

$$\begin{array}{r} 80. \\ .05\overline{)4.00} \end{array}$$

Answer: 80

Skill Builders

6. $.05\overline{)10} \rightarrow .05\overline{)10.00.}$ $.08\overline{)168} \rightarrow .08\overline{)16800.}$ $2.5\overline{)50} \rightarrow 2.5\overline{)500.}$

7. $.04\overline{)12}$ $.07\overline{)21}$ $3.5\overline{)735}$ $1.6\overline{)320}$ $2.3\overline{)483}$

IN YOUR LIFE

Figuring Gas Mileage

Gas mileage tells the number of miles a car can drive on one gallon of gas. When a car engine is tuned up, it gets higher gas mileage than when it needs to be tuned.

Brett Lance keeps a record of his car's gas mileage. He does this by recording the reading on the odometer (mileage indicator) each time he buys gas. He also records the number of gallons that he buys to refill the tank.

- By subtracting the previous odometer reading from the present reading, Brett determines the number of miles driven.
- The amount of gas used is equal to the number of gallons it now takes to refill the tank.

Example: Here's how Brett figured his gas mileage for the week of October 3:

Present odometer reading	68,972.8
Previous odometer reading	− 68,734.9
Miles driven	237.9

$$\text{Gas Mileage} = \frac{\text{Miles Driven}}{\text{Gallons Used}}$$

$$= \frac{237.9}{9.4}$$

$=$ **25.3 miles per gallon**
(rounded to nearest tenth mile per gallon)

```
        2 5.3 0
9.4 ) 2 3 7.9 0 0
    - 1 8 8
        4 9 9
      - 4 7 0
          2 9 0
        - 2 8 2
              8 0
```

▼ Practice

1. Determine the gas mileage of Brett's car during each of the weeks shown on the table below:

Date	Odometer Reading	Gallons	Gas Mileage (nearest tenth)
9/26	68,734.9	8.65	24.9
10/3	68,972.8	9.4	25.3
10/10	69,272.8	11.95	______
10/17	69,492.2	12.9	______
10/24	69,674.0	10	______

2. Brett's mechanic discovered that a spark plug was broken in the engine of Brett's car. During which week did this plug most likely break? What is the clue? ______________

Dividing by 10, 100, or 1,000

You can use three shortcuts when dividing decimals by 10, 100, or 1,000.

- To divide a decimal by 10, move the decimal point *one place* to the left.

Add a 0.

7.5 ÷ 10 = 7.5 (1) = .75   .8 ÷ 10 = ._.8 (1) = .08

Note: You add 0s so you can move the decimal point the correct number of places. *The added 0s become part of the answer.*

- To divide a decimal by 100, move the decimal point *two places* to the left.

Add a 0.   Add two 0s.

3.4 ÷ 100 = ._3.4 (2 1) = .034   .5 ÷ 100 = .__.5 (2 1) = .005

- To divide a decimal by 1,000, move the decimal point *three places* to the left.

Add a 0.   Add two 0s.

31.5 ÷ 1,000 = ._31.5 (3 2 1) = .0315   6 ÷ 1,000 = .__6. (3 2 1) = .006

▼ MATH TIP

To remember these rules, notice that you always move the decimal point the same number of places as there are 0s in the dividing number.

▼ Practice

1. Using the shortcuts, compute each quotient below.

   8.2 ÷ 10 =   .85 ÷ 100 =   45.6 ÷ 1,000 =

2. Rick's Clothing Store orders clothes and other items in large quantities from manufacturers. On the invoice below, divide to find the price that Rick pays for each item.

Item	Total Paid		Number Purchased		Price of Each
jackets	$250.80	÷	10	=	______
dress shirts	$1,289.00	÷	100	=	______
pairs of socks	$2,450.00	÷	1,000	=	______
raincoats	$375.90	÷	10	=	______
watches	$2,478.00	÷	100	=	______

REMINDER

Write each price as dollars and cents by rounding each quotient to the hundredths place.

Putting It All Together

Computing Distance, Rate, and Time

While traveling, Jody's daughter Sarah always asks three questions:

- How far is it?
- How fast are we going?
- How long will it take?

If you have children, these questions may sound familiar!

To answer these questions, Jody uses the following information.

Distance, rate (speed), and time are related by the **distance formula:** distance equals rate times time.

Distance (D)	=	Rate (R)	×	Time (T)
(miles)		(miles per hour)		(hours)

Written in short form as $D = RT$, this formula is used to find the distance when the rate and the time are known.

Example 1: How far can a car travel in 3 hours and 30 minutes if the car averages 40 miles per hour?

Step 1. Identify R and T.

$R = 40$ miles per hour

$T = 3.5$ hours (since 30 min. $= \frac{30}{60}$ hr. $= .5$ hr.)

Step 2. Substitute these values into the distance formula and multiply.

$D = 40 \times 3.5 = 140$ miles

REMINDER

To change a proper fraction to a decimal, divide the denominator into the numerator.

The distance formula can also be written as a **rate formula** (speed) or as a **time formula**.

Rate Formula: $R = D \div T$

Example 2: If a car travels 250 miles in 6 hours and 15 minutes, at what average speed is the car moving?

Step 1. Identify D and T.

$D = 250$ miles

$T = 6.25$ hours (since 15 min. $= \frac{15}{60}$ hr. $= .25$ hr.)

Step 2. Substitute these values into the rate formula and divide.

$R = 250 \div 6.25 = 40$ miles per hour

Time Formula: $T = D \div R$

Example 3: How long will it take to drive 180 miles in a car averaging 50 miles per hour?

Step 1. Identify D and R.

$D = 180$ miles $R = 50$ miles per hour

Step 2. Substitute these values into the time formula and divide.

$T = 180 \div 50 = 3.6$ hours $= 3$ hours 36 minutes
(since .6 hr. $= .6 \times 60$ min.)

▼ Practice

In this exercise, you will practice several decimal skills you have learned in this unit.

During a vacation in July, Jody and Sarah were driving to Chicago, a distance of 341 miles from their home. As usual, Sarah had plenty of questions.

1. "If we drive the speed limit of 55 miles per hour, how long will it take to go from home to Chicago?" (Express your answer in hours and minutes.)

2. After they had driven for 2 hours, Sarah noticed a sign that said, "Chicago, 234 miles." At that point, Sarah asked:

a) "How many miles have we driven so far?"

b) "What average speed have we been driving?"

3. Due to road construction, Jody could average only 45 miles per hour during the next 3 hours and 30 minutes, at which time they stopped for lunch. During lunch, Sarah asked:

a) "How far have we driven since we saw the sign?"

b) "How far are we from Chicago now?"

c) "If we average 45 miles per hour for the rest of the trip, can we make it to Chicago in the next hour and a half?"

4. "If an airplane could average 500 miles per hour between our home and Chicago, how many minutes would the flight take?"
(Express your answer to the nearest minute.)

UNIT THREE

Fractions

Leandra works as a teacher's assistant in a community day-care center. As you might expect, the job requires the ability to work closely with young children in a creative and caring environment. Leandra also must be energetic and flexible in meeting the head teacher's needs. She must read and write well. What you may not realize, however, is that Leandra also must have excellent math skills. Let's see why.

Fractions make it easy to share equally.

Head Teacher: Leandra, here is the play dough recipe. Please get everything ready so that when the children arrive, they can help you mix it right away.

Leandra: The last time we made it, there wasn't really enough for everyone. Do you mind if I double the recipe?

Head Teacher: Not at all. But remember to separate the finished product into six equal batches so that the afternoon sessions get plenty, too.

Leandra: No problem. Now I'll just rewrite the recipe, multiplying everything by two. Let's see . . . $1\frac{1}{2}$ cups flour times two equals 3 cups. $1\frac{1}{3}$ cups salt times two equals $2\frac{2}{3}$ cups, and $2\frac{3}{4}$ teaspoons cream of tartar times two equals $5\frac{1}{2}$ teaspoons.

Head Teacher: I see that we have only $\frac{1}{2}$ cup of salt in the storage room. How much more should I buy?

Leandra: We'll need a total of $2\frac{2}{3}$ cups. $2\frac{2}{3}$ minus $\frac{1}{2}$ is close to $2\frac{1}{2}$ cups by my estimate. So I'd buy at least two boxes.

Think About It

- Why was it important for Leandra to have a good understanding of fractions?
- Can you think of any other situations in which a day-care worker would have to use fractions?

How Do Fractions Play a Part in *Your* Life?

Do you use fractions at home or at work? Answer the questions that follow.

Fractions are common in speech. For example, we seldom say, "I spent 50% of my vacation sleeping." Instead we would say, "I spent half my vacation sleeping." Write down a situation in which you used a fraction in conversation.

____

____

____

Do you ever have to figure out the number of hours you've spent working? Do you use fractions to show parts of an hour?

____

____

Have you ever used a recipe that made more or less than the number of servings you needed? How did you change the recipe? Was it easy for you or challenging? Why?

____

____

People often use fractions in measurements. Can you think of some examples?

____

____

Skills You Will Learn

Number Skills

- adding fractions and mixed numbers
- subtracting fractions and mixed numbers
- multiplying fractions and mixed numbers
- dividing fractions and mixed numbers

Life and Workplace Skills

- calculating dimensions
- finding the sum of partial quantities
- working with weight limits
- recording changes in growth
- using measurement in home projects
- increasing a recipe
- buying fabric

Thinking Skills

- estimating with fractions
- estimating with mixed numbers
- solving problems with fractions and decimals

Calculator Skills

- converting fractions to decimals
- solving fraction problems

Estimating: Building Confidence with Fractions

In this unit, you'll learn to solve math problems like these:

Example 1: You know that a pallet on the factory floor can hold $30\frac{1}{4}$ boxes, if each contains $20\frac{1}{2}$ pounds of books. You want to find out the total weight so that you know how much weight can be put on the pallet before it collapses.

Example 2: A problem on a math exam asks what $8\frac{4}{5}$ minus $5\frac{1}{2}$ equals. The answer choices given are $2\frac{1}{10}$, $3\frac{3}{10}$, and $4\frac{7}{10}$.

People often say that computations with fractions are the most troublesome topics in math. Why is this? Here's a typical response:

> "I just don't have a *feeling* about how answers should turn out."

Estimation can help if you have trouble working with fractions. Let's see how.

- To estimate with mixed numbers, round each mixed number to the nearest whole number.
  - *Round up* if the fraction is equal to or larger than $\frac{1}{2}$.
  - *Round down* if the fraction is less than $\frac{1}{2}$.

Example 1: $30\frac{1}{4}$ boxes $\times$ $20\frac{1}{2}$ pounds per box is about how many pounds?

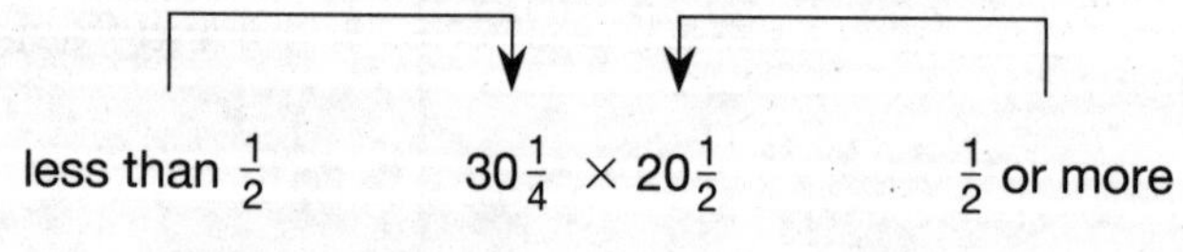

Estimate: $30 \times 21 = 630$ pounds

Answer: The pallet can hold about 630 pounds before collapsing.

▼ **MATH TIP**

If a fraction is $\frac{1}{2}$ or more, round up.

If a fraction is less than $\frac{1}{2}$, round down.

Examples: $3\frac{5}{8}$ rounds to 4
$3\frac{3}{8}$ rounds to 3

Example 2: $8\frac{4}{5} - 5\frac{1}{2} = ?$

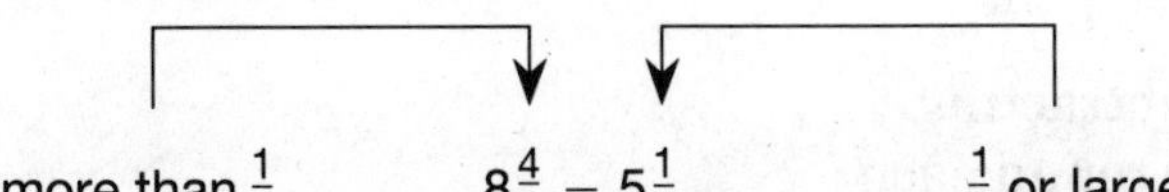

more than $\frac{1}{2}$ $8\frac{4}{5} - 5\frac{1}{2}$ $\frac{1}{2}$ or larger

Estimate: 9 − 6 = 3

Answer: The approximate answer is 3. This is closest to the answer choice of $3\frac{3}{10}$.

▼ MATH TIP

A fraction is larger than $\frac{1}{2}$ when two times the numerator is larger than the denominator.

$\frac{2}{3}$ is more than $\frac{1}{2}$ because

2 (× 2) = 4
3 ← is larger than

A fraction is less than $\frac{1}{2}$ when two times the numerator is less than the denominator.

$\frac{3}{10}$ is less than $\frac{1}{2}$ because

3 (× 2) = 6
10 ← is smaller than

▼ Practice

Round each mixed number to the nearest whole number.

1. $5\frac{1}{3}$ acres $3\frac{3}{5}$ pieces $4\frac{7}{16}$ pints

2. $6\frac{5}{8}$ pounds $2\frac{2}{6}$ feet $7\frac{2}{3}$ crates

Estimate an answer to each problem below. *Do not find exact answers.*

3. You add $4\frac{2}{3}$ cups of water to $1\frac{1}{4}$ cup of oil. *Approximately* how much liquid do you have altogether?

____

4. A customer has a chain that measures $9\frac{11}{12}$ yards long, and you cut a $7\frac{2}{3}$-yard piece from it. *About* how long is the chain now? ________________

5. You've filled $8\frac{1}{4}$ cases with $3\frac{1}{2}$ pounds of canned goods in each. How much is the total weight, *approximately*?

____

6. A manager at the shop where you work plans to divide a $36\frac{1}{3}$-inch piece of plastic into strips that measure $5\frac{3}{4}$ inches wide. She asks you to estimate *about* how many strips she'll get. ________________

Estimating to Add Proper Fractions

Estimating is especially useful when adding or subtracting proper fractions. The first step in estimating is to round each proper fraction.

To round a proper fraction, replace it by one of the three following values: 0, $\frac{1}{2}$, or 1.

- Round a proper fraction to 0 if its denominator is much larger than its numerator.

  Fractions that round to 0: $\frac{1}{5}, \frac{1}{6}, \frac{1}{8}, \frac{1}{10}, \frac{3}{16}$

- Round a proper fraction to $\frac{1}{2}$ if its denominator is equal to about twice its numerator.

  Fractions that round to $\frac{1}{2}$: $\frac{1}{3}, \frac{3}{5}, \frac{4}{7}, \frac{5}{9}, \frac{7}{12}$

- Round a proper fraction to 1 if its numerator and denominator are about the same size.

  Fractions that round to 1: $\frac{3}{4}, \frac{4}{5}, \frac{5}{6}, \frac{9}{10}, \frac{11}{12}$

When estimating a sum of proper fractions, group two $\frac{1}{2}$s to make a whole (1). Then add the 1s, $\frac{1}{2}$s, and 0s.

Example 1:

$$\begin{array}{rl} \frac{3}{8} & \rightarrow \frac{1}{2} \\ \frac{4}{9} & \rightarrow \frac{1}{2} \\ + \frac{6}{7} & \rightarrow 1 \end{array} \quad \left.\frac{1}{2}, \frac{1}{2}\right\} \rightarrow 1$$

Estimate: 2

Example 2:

$$\begin{array}{rl} \frac{4}{7} & \rightarrow \frac{1}{2} \\ \frac{3}{6} & \rightarrow \frac{1}{2} \\ \frac{1}{8} & \rightarrow 0 \\ + \frac{3}{5} & \rightarrow \frac{1}{2} \end{array} \quad \left.\frac{1}{2}, \frac{1}{2}\right\} \rightarrow 1$$

Estimate: $1\frac{1}{2}$

Example 3:

$$\begin{array}{rl} \frac{11}{12} & \rightarrow 1 \\ \frac{7}{8} & \rightarrow 1 \\ \frac{9}{10} & \rightarrow 1 \\ + \frac{3}{7} & \rightarrow \frac{1}{2} \end{array}$$

Estimate: $3\frac{1}{2}$

▼ Practice

Find an estimated answer for each problem. *Do not find an exact answer.*

7. $\begin{array}{r} \frac{11}{16} \\ \frac{3}{4} \\ + \frac{1}{2} \\ \hline \end{array}$ $\begin{array}{r} \frac{2}{4} \\ \frac{7}{8} \\ + \frac{9}{10} \\ \hline \end{array}$ $\begin{array}{r} \frac{7}{8} \\ \frac{1}{5} \\ + \frac{3}{5} \\ \hline \end{array}$ $\begin{array}{r} \frac{1}{6} \\ \frac{8}{9} \\ + \frac{3}{7} \\ \hline \end{array}$ $\begin{array}{r} \frac{15}{16} \\ \frac{6}{10} \\ + \frac{3}{8} \\ \hline \end{array}$

Imagine that you are taking a math test. The problems below appear on the test. Write an estimate for each problem. Then, *using only your estimate as a clue,* choose the correct answer. You may need to round the answer choices as in problem 8.

To estimate:

- Round each mixed number to the nearest whole number.
- Round each proper fraction to 0, $\frac{1}{2}$, or 1.
- Round each money amount to the nearest dollar.

One-Step Problems

Estimate, then choose one

8. Laurie bought the following material to make her own clothes:
$2\frac{1}{4}$ yards for a dress
$2\frac{7}{8}$ yards for a wraparound skirt
$1\frac{2}{3}$ yards for a blouse
How many total yards of material did Laurie purchase?

a) $4\frac{15}{24}$ (≈ 5)
b) $5\frac{11}{12}$ (≈ 6)
c) $6\frac{19}{24}$ (≈ 7)
d) $7\frac{23}{24}$ (≈ 8)

9. When salmon went on sale, Rhonda bought an uncut fish that weighed $6\frac{1}{8}$ pounds. How much should she be charged?

Whole-Salmon Sale

$2.89/lb.

a) $15.50
b) $17.70
c) $19.80
d) $21.30

10. Lenny wants to move the pile of gravel shown at right. The maximum load his pickup can carry is $1\frac{7}{8}$ tons. How many trips will Lenny need to make?

$16\frac{1}{4}$ tons

a) 3
b) 6
c) 9
d) 12

Multistep Problems

11. Lei mixed the ingredients shown at right in a bowl that can hold $6\frac{7}{8}$ cups. How many more cups can the bowl hold before being full?

Recipe
(in cups)

milk	$2\frac{1}{2}$
sugar	$1\frac{2}{3}$
cream	$1\frac{1}{4}$

a) $1\frac{11}{24}$
b) $2\frac{1}{24}$
c) $2\frac{13}{24}$
d) $2\frac{23}{24}$

12. Stacey practices piano each day after school. How much longer did she practice last week than this week?

This Week		Last Week
Monday:	$\frac{3}{4}$ hour	$3\frac{1}{2}$ hours
Tuesday:	$\frac{2}{3}$ hour	
Wednesday:	$\frac{1}{8}$ hour	
Thursday:	$\frac{1}{6}$ hour	
Friday:	$\frac{3}{6}$ hour	

a) $\frac{1}{2}$ hour
b) $1\frac{7}{24}$ hours
c) $1\frac{19}{24}$ hours
d) $1\frac{23}{24}$ hours

FOCUS ON CALCULATORS

Mixed Numbers

A co-worker at the vegetable stand where you work yells,

> "Mrs. Maynard is buying $4\frac{3}{4}$ pounds of grapes at $1.19 a pound, and the computerized scale is down again! Grab the calculator and figure out what she owes, please."

As you learned in the last chapter, fractions are a little tricky on the calculator. But you think quickly and figure out the following:

Example 1: Change $4\frac{3}{4}$ to a mixed decimal.

Step 1. First, divide to change $\frac{3}{4}$ to a decimal fraction.

$4\frac{3}{4} = 4.75$

Press Keys	Display Shows
C	0.
3	3.
÷	3.
4	4.
=	0.75

Step 2. Multiply pounds by price per pound.

$4.75 \times \$1.19 =$

Display Shows: 5.6525

Step 3. Round off to the nearest hundredth to get the correct price.

$5.6525 \approx 5.65$

Answer: $5.65

To use your calculator with fractions:

- change fractions to decimals;
- then do the math indicated.

Example 2: $4\frac{9}{16} \times 5$

Step 1. Change $\frac{9}{16}$ to a decimal. 9 ÷ 16 = → .5625

Step 2. Add the decimal to the whole number. 4 + .5625 = → 4.5625

Step 3. Multiply. 4 · 5 6 2 5 × 5 = → 22.8125

Answer: 22.8 (rounded to the nearest tenth)

▼ Practice

Using your calculator, solve each problem below. In problems 1–4, circle your answer from the choices given.
Hint: Change each answer choice to a mixed decimal.

1. $5\frac{3}{8} + 2\frac{5}{6}$

a) $8\frac{5}{24}$
b) $8\frac{17}{24}$
c) $8\frac{11}{24}$

2. $8\frac{5}{6} - 3\frac{4}{5}$

a) $4\frac{10}{11}$
b) $5\frac{1}{30}$
c) $5\frac{1}{15}$

3. $9\frac{7}{8} \times 7 =$

a) $68\frac{7}{8}$
b) $69\frac{1}{8}$
c) $70\frac{3}{8}$

4. $7\frac{5}{16} \div 3 =$

a) $2\frac{5}{16}$
b) $2\frac{3}{8}$
c) $2\frac{7}{16}$

▼ MATH TIP

Can you use estimation to solve problems 1–4? Probably not!

When answer choices are very close in value, as they are here, estimation may not be of much help.

However, these problems will help you build a lot of confidence in your calculator!

5. When tomatoes are on sale for $.89 per pound, how much would $6\frac{3}{8}$ pounds of tomatoes cost, to the nearest penny?
Hint: Change $6\frac{3}{8}$ to a mixed decimal, then multiply.

6. Lydia paid $6.43 for $8\frac{3}{4}$ pounds of oranges. To the nearest penny, how much is Lydia paying per pound?
Hint: Change $8\frac{3}{4}$ to a mixed decimal, then divide.

7. Each member of the Valley Dieter's Club has set a weight-loss goal as shown below. Divide to determine the number of weeks each member will take to reach his or her goal. Round each answer to the nearest whole number of weeks.

Name	Total Weight-Loss Goal (a)	Weight Loss per Week (b)	Number of Weeks (a ÷ b)
Abbott	35	$1\frac{1}{2}$	________
Foote	42	$1\frac{1}{4}$	________
Hughes	29	$1\frac{3}{4}$	________
Riker	56	$\frac{7}{8}$	________

Adding Like Fractions

As a member of a road-building crew, you've been asked to determine the total distance the crew completed on Monday, Tuesday, and Wednesday. The daily distances are Monday, $\frac{3}{8}$ mile; Tuesday, $\frac{1}{8}$ mile; and Wednesday, $\frac{2}{8}$ mile.

You quickly see that you must add fractions to get the answer.

- To add **like fractions** (fractions with the same denominator):
  - add the numerators and place the sum over the denominator;
  - reduce the answer to lowest terms.

Example: Add $\frac{3}{8}$, $\frac{1}{8}$, and $\frac{2}{8}$.

Step 1. Add the numerators, and place the answer over 8. $\frac{3}{8} + \frac{1}{8} + \frac{2}{8} = \frac{6}{8}$

Step 2. Reduce. $\frac{6}{8} = \frac{6 \div 2}{8 \div 2} = \frac{3}{4}$

Answer: $\frac{3}{4}$ mile

▼ Practice

Add. Reduce each answer to lowest terms. The first one in each row has been done for you.

Fractions That Add to Less than 1

1. $\frac{1}{3} + \frac{1}{3} = \frac{2}{3}$ $\quad$ $\frac{5}{8} + \frac{2}{8}$ $\quad$ $\frac{2}{4} + \frac{1}{4}$ $\quad$ $\frac{3}{5} + \frac{1}{5}$ $\quad$ $\frac{7}{12} + \frac{4}{12}$

2. $\frac{3}{8} + \frac{1}{8} = \frac{4}{8}$ $\quad$ $\frac{2}{9} + \frac{1}{9} =$ $\quad$ $\frac{3}{8} + \frac{3}{8} =$ $\quad$ $\frac{1}{4} + \frac{1}{4} =$ $\quad$ $\frac{4}{12} + \frac{4}{12} =$

   Reduce: $\frac{4 \div 4}{8 \div 4} = \frac{1}{2}$

3. $\frac{3}{8} + \frac{2}{8} + \frac{1}{8} = \frac{6}{8}$ $\quad$ $\frac{4}{9} + \frac{1}{9} + \frac{1}{9}$ $\quad$ $\frac{3}{10} + \frac{2}{10} + \frac{1}{10}$ $\quad$ $\frac{2}{6} + \frac{1}{6} + \frac{1}{6}$ $\quad$ $\frac{5}{12} + \frac{3}{12} + \frac{1}{12}$

   Reduce: $\frac{6 \div 2}{8 \div 2} = \frac{3}{4}$

Fractions That Add to a Whole Number

- When adding fractions gives an answer that has the same numerator and denominator, write the answer as 1.

4. $\frac{5}{6} + \frac{1}{6} = \frac{6}{6} = 1$ $\qquad \frac{4}{8} + \frac{4}{8}$ $\qquad \frac{3}{4} + \frac{1}{4}$ $\qquad \frac{2}{3} + \frac{1}{3}$ $\qquad \frac{9}{16} + \frac{7}{16}$

- Fractions may also add to whole numbers larger than 1.

5. $\frac{3}{4} + \frac{2}{4} + \frac{3}{4} = \frac{8}{4} = 2$ $\qquad \frac{2}{3} + \frac{2}{3} + \frac{2}{3} =$ $\qquad \frac{7}{8} + \frac{6}{8} + \frac{5}{8} + \frac{6}{8} =$

Fractions That Add to More than 1

- When adding fractions results in an improper fraction, change the answer to a mixed number, and reduce the proper fraction if possible.

6. $\frac{3}{4} + \frac{2}{4} = \frac{5}{4} = 1\frac{1}{4}$ $\qquad \frac{6}{8} + \frac{5}{8}$ $\qquad \frac{5}{6} + \frac{2}{6}$ $\qquad \frac{9}{12} + \frac{8}{12}$ $\qquad \frac{2}{3} + \frac{2}{3}$

7. $\frac{3}{4} + \frac{3}{4} = \frac{6}{4} = 1\frac{2}{4} = 1\frac{1}{2}$ $\qquad \frac{6}{8} + \frac{4}{8}$ $\qquad \frac{4}{6} + \frac{4}{6}$ $\qquad \frac{7}{10} + \frac{5}{10}$ $\qquad \frac{8}{12} + \frac{6}{12}$

Adding Fractions and Mixed Numbers

- Add fractions and mixed numbers separately. If the sum of fractions is an improper fraction, change it to a mixed number. Combine the whole numbers, and reduce the proper fraction if possible.

8. $3\frac{3}{4} + 2\frac{3}{4} = 5\frac{6}{4}$ $= 5 + 1\frac{2}{4}$ $= 6\frac{2}{4} = 6\frac{1}{2}$ $\qquad 4\frac{2}{3} + 1\frac{2}{3}$ $\qquad 1\frac{5}{8} + \frac{7}{8}$ $\qquad 6\frac{9}{16} + 4\frac{11}{16}$ $\qquad 4\frac{1}{2} + 2\frac{1}{2}$

9.

$$5\frac{4}{6} + 2\frac{4}{6} = 7\frac{8}{6} = 7 + 1\frac{2}{6} = 8\frac{2}{6} = 8\frac{1}{3}$$

$$7\frac{8}{9} + 4\frac{7}{9}$$

$$2\frac{6}{8} + \frac{4}{8}$$

$$3\frac{11}{12} + 1\frac{10}{12}$$

$$10\frac{15}{16} + 5\frac{9}{16}$$

10. As a salesclerk in a fabric store, you add up the amount of each type of fabric sold every day. Write your sums on the lines in the table below. The first sum is done as an example.

Type of Fabric	Pieces Sold (Length in Yards)	Total
cotton	$\frac{3}{4}$, $1\frac{3}{4}$, $\frac{2}{4}$, $3\frac{1}{4}$	$6\frac{1}{4}$
flannel	$1\frac{1}{2}$, $2\frac{1}{2}$, 3, $2\frac{1}{2}$	_____
corduroy	$\frac{2}{3}$, $1\frac{2}{3}$, $1\frac{1}{3}$, $\frac{2}{3}$	_____
wool	$2\frac{1}{4}$, $\frac{3}{4}$, $1\frac{2}{4}$, $\frac{3}{4}$	_____
polyester	$\frac{7}{8}$, $1\frac{5}{8}$, $2\frac{4}{8}$, $\frac{6}{8}$	_____

Example: Cotton

$$\frac{3}{4} + 1\frac{3}{4} + \frac{2}{4} + 3\frac{1}{4} = 4\frac{9}{4} = 4 + 2\frac{1}{4} = 6\frac{1}{4}$$

11. As a payroll clerk, you've been asked to find the total amount of overtime worked by each employee listed below. Write the totals on the lines provided.

OVERTIME HOURS EACH DAY

Employee	Mon.	Tues.	Wed.	Thurs.	Fri.	Total
Frankle	$\frac{3}{4}$	$\frac{2}{4}$	$\frac{1}{4}$	$\frac{2}{4}$	0	_____
Hall	$\frac{3}{4}$	$2\frac{2}{4}$	$1\frac{2}{4}$	0	$\frac{1}{4}$	_____
Lewis	$\frac{1}{2}$	$\frac{1}{2}$	$1\frac{1}{2}$	$\frac{1}{2}$	0	_____
Moore	$2\frac{1}{3}$	$1\frac{1}{3}$	$\frac{2}{3}$	0	$\frac{2}{3}$	_____

Subtracting Like Fractions

Imagine that you have recently moved to a new neighborhood. A neighbor has sketched a map showing you where the day-care center is located compared to your workplace, the Shady Rest Nursing Home.

You want to know how far you live from the day-care center. How do you figure this out? You'll need to subtract fractions.

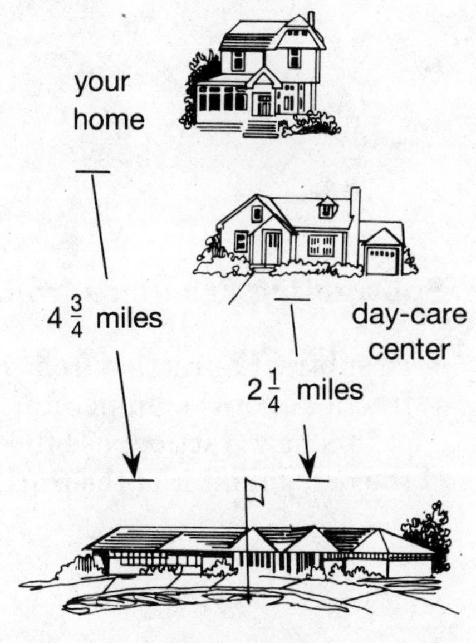

- To subtract **like fractions** (fractions with the same denominator):
  - subtract the numerators, and place the difference over the denominator;
  - reduce the answer to lowest terms.

Example: Subtract $2\frac{1}{4}$ from $4\frac{3}{4}$.

Step 1. Subtract the numerators, and place the answer over 4. $\frac{3}{4} - \frac{1}{4} = \frac{2}{4}$

Step 2. Reduce. $\frac{2 \div 2}{4 \div 2} = \frac{1}{2}$

Step 3. Subtract the whole numbers. $4 - 2 = 2$

Answer: $2\frac{1}{2}$ miles

▼ Practice

Subtract. Reduce each answer to lowest terms. The first one in each row has been done as an example.

Subtracting Two Fractions

1. $\frac{3}{4} - \frac{2}{4} = \frac{1}{4}$ $\qquad \frac{6}{8} - \frac{3}{8}$ $\qquad \frac{4}{5} - \frac{2}{5}$ $\qquad \frac{7}{9} - \frac{5}{9}$ $\qquad \frac{9}{10} - \frac{6}{10}$

2. $\frac{6}{8} - \frac{4}{8} = \frac{2}{8} = \frac{1}{4}$ $\qquad \frac{8}{9} - \frac{2}{9}$ $\qquad \frac{11}{12} - \frac{3}{12}$ $\qquad \frac{13}{16} - \frac{9}{16}$ $\qquad \frac{3}{4} - \frac{1}{4}$

Subtracting Fractions from Mixed Numbers

- To subtract a fraction from a mixed number, first subtract the fractions. Then bring down the whole number.

3. $5\frac{7}{8} - \frac{3}{8} = 5\frac{4}{8} = 5\frac{1}{2}$ $\qquad 6\frac{3}{4} - \frac{1}{4}$ $\qquad 4\frac{5}{6} - \frac{1}{6}$ $\qquad 2\frac{9}{10} - \frac{3}{10}$ $\qquad 7\frac{11}{12} - \frac{4}{12}$

Subtracting Mixed Numbers

- To subtract mixed numbers, first subtract the fraction. Then subtract the whole number.

4. $\begin{array}{r} 5\frac{3}{4} \\ -\ 3\frac{1}{4} \\ \hline 2\frac{2}{4} = 2\frac{1}{2} \end{array}$ $\quad$ $\begin{array}{r} 6\frac{7}{8} \\ -\ 2\frac{1}{8} \\ \hline \end{array}$ $\quad$ $\begin{array}{r} 4\frac{5}{6} \\ -\ 3\frac{1}{6} \\ \hline \end{array}$ $\quad$ $\begin{array}{r} 12\frac{13}{16} \\ -\ 9\frac{3}{16} \\ \hline \end{array}$ $\quad$ $\begin{array}{r} 21\frac{11}{12} \\ -\ 14\frac{9}{12} \\ \hline \end{array}$

Subtracting Fractions from the Whole Number 1

- To subtract a fraction from 1, change 1 to a fraction. For the numerator and denominator of this new fraction, use the number that is the denominator of the fraction being subtracted.

Example 1:

$\begin{array}{r} 1 = \frac{5}{5} \\ -\ \frac{3}{5} = \frac{3}{5} \\ \hline \frac{2}{5} \end{array}$

Example 2:

$\begin{array}{r} 1 = \frac{8}{8} \\ -\ \frac{5}{8} = \frac{5}{8} \\ \hline \frac{3}{8} \end{array}$

5. $\begin{array}{r} 1 = \frac{3}{3} \\ -\frac{2}{3} \\ \hline \frac{1}{3} \end{array}$ $\quad$ $\begin{array}{r} 1 \\ -\ \frac{4}{8} \\ \hline \end{array}$ $\quad$ $\begin{array}{r} 1 \\ -\ \frac{6}{9} \\ \hline \end{array}$ $\quad$ $\begin{array}{r} 1 \\ -\ \frac{11}{16} \\ \hline \end{array}$ $\quad$ $\begin{array}{r} 1 \\ -\ \frac{3}{4} \\ \hline \end{array}$

6. As a hardware clerk, you want to know how many yards of screen are left on each roll listed below. To find out, subtract each present order from its in stock amount. Write your answers in the row labeled amount left.

	Roll A	Roll B	Roll C	Roll D	Roll E
in stock	$7\frac{11}{12}$	$6\frac{2}{3}$	$4\frac{1}{2}$	$12\frac{7}{8}$	1
present order	$4\frac{5}{12}$	$2\frac{1}{3}$	3	$\frac{5}{8}$	$\frac{11}{18}$
amount left					

7. Using the map at right, determine how much farther Jenny lives from the library than from the school.

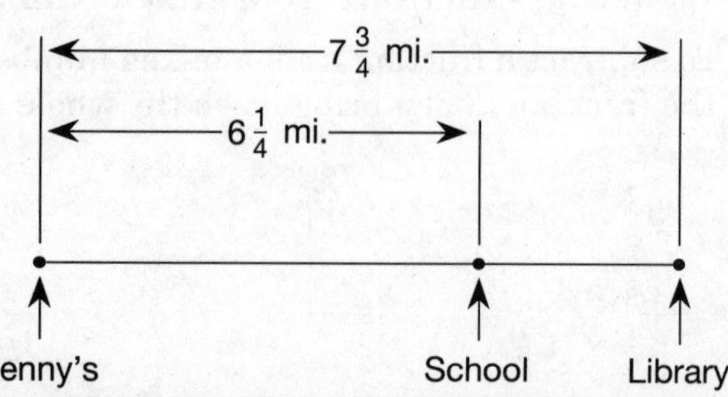

Subtracting Fractions from Whole Numbers

On Thursday you worked an 8-hour shift, minus $\frac{3}{4}$ hour for lunch. Your supervisor wants to know how many hours you actually worked. How do you subtract $\frac{3}{4}$ from 8?

- To subtract a fraction from a whole number:
  - *borrow* 1 from the whole number;
  - rewrite the 1 as a fraction with the same denominator as the fraction you are subtracting;
  - subtract as usual.

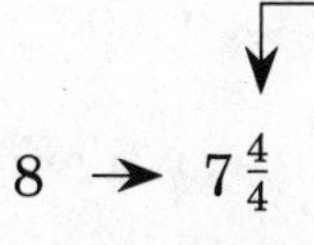

The borrowed 1 is written as $\frac{4}{4}$ and placed next to 7.

$$\begin{array}{r} 8 \\ -\frac{3}{4} \\ \hline \end{array} \rightarrow \begin{array}{r} 7\frac{4}{4} \\ -\frac{3}{4} \\ \hline 7\frac{1}{4} \end{array}$$

Answer: You worked $7\frac{1}{4}$ hours.

▼ Practice

In row 1, rewrite each whole number as shown. Write the correct numerator over each fraction bar.

1. $6 = 5\frac{}{3}$ $\quad 3 = 2\frac{}{4}$ $\quad 5 = 4\frac{}{2}$ $\quad 2 = 1\frac{}{8}$ $\quad 4 = 3\frac{}{16}$

For rows 2–4, subtract.

Skill Builders

2. $\begin{array}{r} 4 \\ -\frac{1}{2} \\ \hline \end{array} = \begin{array}{r} 3\frac{}{2} \\ -\frac{1}{2} \\ \hline \end{array}$ $\quad \begin{array}{r} 5 \\ -\frac{3}{4} \\ \hline \end{array} = \begin{array}{r} 4\frac{}{4} \\ -\frac{3}{4} \\ \hline \end{array}$ $\quad \begin{array}{r} 7 \\ -\frac{3}{8} \\ \hline \end{array} = \begin{array}{r} 6\frac{}{8} \\ -\frac{3}{8} \\ \hline \end{array}$ $\quad \begin{array}{r} 2 \\ -\frac{9}{16} \\ \hline \end{array} = \begin{array}{r} 1\frac{}{16} \\ -\frac{9}{16} \\ \hline \end{array}$

3. $\begin{array}{r} 4 \\ -\frac{2}{3} \\ \hline \end{array}$ $\quad \begin{array}{r} 2 \\ -\frac{1}{4} \\ \hline \end{array}$ $\quad \begin{array}{r} 3 \\ -\frac{1}{8} \\ \hline \end{array}$ $\quad \begin{array}{r} 6 \\ -\frac{3}{4} \\ \hline \end{array}$ $\quad \begin{array}{r} 7 \\ -\frac{7}{10} \\ \hline \end{array}$

4. $\begin{array}{r} 7 \\ -\frac{3}{5} \\ \hline \end{array}$ $\quad \begin{array}{r} 8 \\ -\frac{5}{16} \\ \hline \end{array}$ $\quad \begin{array}{r} 2 \\ -\frac{3}{8} \\ \hline \end{array}$ $\quad \begin{array}{r} 6 \\ -\frac{7}{12} \\ \hline \end{array}$ $\quad \begin{array}{r} 9 \\ -\frac{1}{3} \\ \hline \end{array}$

Subtracting Mixed Numbers by Borrowing

A customer at the building supply warehouse where you work says,

> "I already have $12\frac{5}{8}$ feet of wire at home. The job I'm doing requires a total of $15\frac{3}{8}$ feet. Can you tell me how much more wire I need to buy?"

You realize right away that you need to subtract $12\frac{5}{8}$ from $15\frac{3}{8}$.

- To subtract when the bottom fraction is larger than the top fraction, you must borrow. The borrowed 1 is changed to a fraction and combined with the top fraction.

Example:

	Step 1.	*Step 2.*	*Step 3.*
$15\frac{3}{8}$	$14\frac{8}{8} + \frac{3}{8}$	$14\frac{11}{8}$	$14\frac{11}{8}$
$-\ 12\frac{5}{8}$	$-\ 12\frac{5}{8}$	$-\ 12\frac{5}{8}$	$-\ 12\frac{5}{8}$
			$2\frac{6}{8} = 2\frac{3}{4}$ feet of wire

Step 1. You can't subtract $\frac{5}{8}$ from $\frac{3}{8}$,

so borrow 1 ($\frac{8}{8}$) from 15. Write $15 = 14\frac{8}{8}$.

Step 2. Combine the top fractions: $\frac{8}{8} + \frac{3}{8} = \frac{11}{8}$.

Step 3. Subtract the fraction column: $\frac{11}{8} - \frac{5}{8} = \frac{6}{8} = \frac{3}{4}$.

Then subtract the whole numbers: $14 - 12 = 2$.

▼ Practice

Subtract. First complete the row of partially worked Skill Builders.

Skill Builders

1. $6\frac{1}{4} - 4\frac{3}{4}$ → $5\frac{4}{4} + \frac{1}{4} - 4\frac{3}{4}$ → $5\frac{5}{4} - 4\frac{3}{4}$ $\qquad$ $4\frac{1}{3} - 1\frac{2}{3}$ → $3\frac{3}{3} + \frac{1}{3} - 1\frac{2}{3}$ → $3\frac{4}{3} - 1\frac{2}{3}$

2. $5\frac{2}{4} - 1\frac{3}{4}$ $\qquad$ $6\frac{3}{5} - 4\frac{4}{5}$ $\qquad$ $8\frac{1}{3} - 3\frac{2}{3}$ $\qquad$ $6\frac{3}{8} - 4\frac{5}{8}$ $\qquad$ $2\frac{1}{4} - 1\frac{2}{4}$

IN YOUR LIFE

Working with Dimensions

Fractions and mixed numbers show up in many do-it-yourself projects around the home. Usually, they appear as **dimensions**—numbers that give the length, width (or depth), height, and other important distances that may describe an object. Questions often arise that involve adding or subtracting two or more of these dimensions.

Suppose you are building the bookcase pictured below. The dimensions shown are all given in inches (").

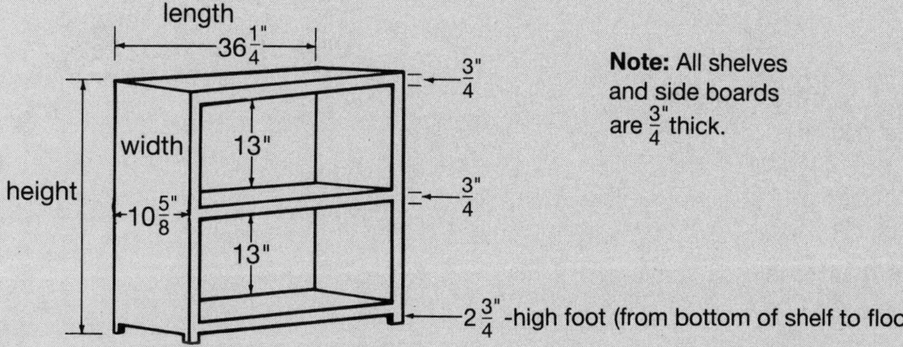

Note: All shelves and side boards are $\frac{3}{4}$" thick.

▼ Practice

Use the diagram to help you answer the following questions.

1. What is the total height of the bookcase?________
(Height = foot height + two 13" spaces + three $\frac{3}{4}$" shelf thicknesses.)

2. How much longer is the bookcase than it is high?________

3. How long is the middle shelf?________
(Middle shelf length = bookcase length − two side board thicknesses.)

4. If you place a $7\frac{9}{16}$" ceramic statue on the middle shelf, how much room will be above the statue?________

5. You designed the bookcase so that the height of the middle shelf is adjustable. Suppose you raise the middle shelf $\frac{7}{8}$" higher than it is now. How much room will now be . . .

a) *between* the lower and middle shelves?________

b) *above* the middle shelf?________

6. If you place the bookcase so that its back surface is $\frac{5}{8}$" from the wall, how far from the wall will the front edge be?________

Adding and Subtracting Unlike Fractions

If you have $\frac{2}{3}$ of a yard of wrapping paper on one roll and $\frac{1}{6}$ yard on another, do you have a full yard in all? To find out, you will need to add unlike fractions.

Unlike fractions—fractions that have different denominators—can be added or subtracted only after they are changed to like fractions.

- To change unlike fractions to like fractions, write all fractions so they have a common denominator—the same denominator.

  (To review raising fractions to higher terms in order to write fractions with a common denominator, reread page 15 at this time.)

To visualize fractions, think of a divided circle.

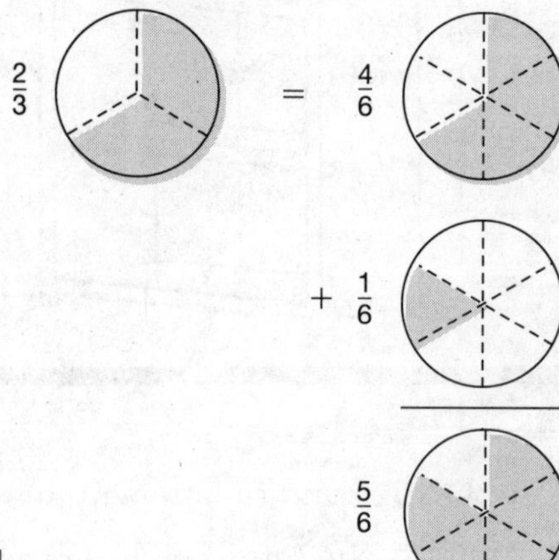

Example 1: Add $\frac{2}{3}$ and $\frac{1}{6}$.

Step 1. Choose 6 as a common denominator, and rewrite $\frac{2}{3}$ as sixths.

$$\frac{2}{3} = \frac{?}{6} \qquad \frac{2 \times 2}{3 \times 2} = \frac{4}{6}$$

Step 2. Add the like fractions.

$$\begin{array}{rcl} \frac{2}{3} & = & \frac{4}{6} \\ +\frac{1}{6} & = & \frac{1}{6} \\ \hline & & \frac{5}{6} \end{array}$$

Answer: $\frac{5}{6}$ yard. No, you would not have a full yard.

▼ MATH TIP

In Example 1, choose 6 as the common denominator because:
- one denominator is already 6;
- the second denominator (3) divides into 6 an even number of times.

Example 2: Subtract $\frac{1}{2}$ from $\frac{7}{8}$.

Step 1. Choose 8 as the common denominator. Rewrite $\frac{1}{2}$ as eighths.

$$\frac{1}{2} = \frac{?}{8} \qquad \frac{1 \times 4}{2 \times 4} = \frac{4}{8}$$

Step 2. Subtract $\frac{4}{8}$ from $\frac{7}{8}$.

$$\begin{array}{rcl} \frac{7}{8} & = & \frac{7}{8} \\ -\frac{1}{2} & = & \frac{4}{8} \\ \hline & & \frac{3}{8} \end{array}$$

Answer: $\frac{3}{8}$

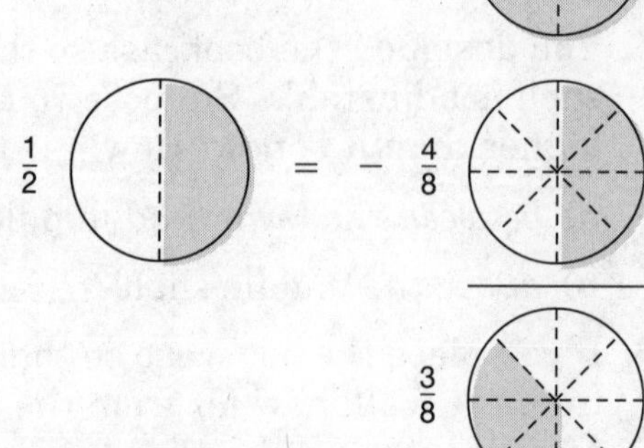

▼ Practice

Write the addition or subtraction of fractions represented by each picture.

1.  ____ + ____ = ____

2. 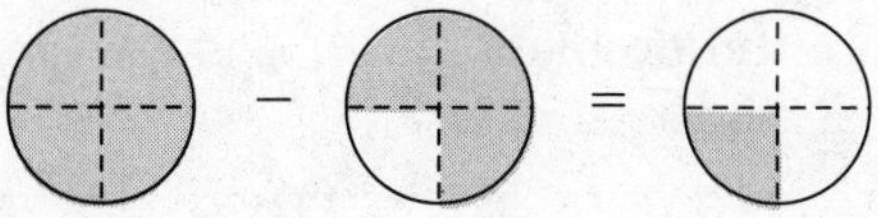 ____ − ____ = ____

For rows 3–4, raise each fraction to higher terms using the denominator given.

3. $\frac{1}{3} = \frac{}{6}$ $\frac{1}{2} = \frac{}{8}$ $\frac{2}{3} = \frac{}{9}$ $\frac{3}{4} = \frac{}{8}$ $\frac{2}{3} = \frac{}{12}$

4. $\frac{3}{5} = \frac{}{10}$ $\frac{3}{4} = \frac{}{12}$ $\frac{1}{4} = \frac{}{8}$ $\frac{7}{8} = \frac{}{16}$ $\frac{3}{4} = \frac{}{16}$

For rows 5–8, add or subtract as indicated. Use the largest denominator in each problem as a common denominator. Reduce answers.

Skill Builders

5. $\frac{1}{3} = \frac{}{6}$, $+\frac{3}{6} = \frac{}{6}$ $\frac{3}{5} = \frac{}{10}$, $-\frac{3}{10} = \frac{}{10}$ $\frac{7}{8} = \frac{}{8}$, $-\frac{3}{4} = \frac{}{8}$ $\frac{1}{2} = \frac{}{8}$, $\frac{1}{4} = \frac{}{8}$, $+\frac{3}{8} = \frac{}{8}$ $\frac{11}{12} = \frac{}{12}$, $\frac{5}{6} = \frac{}{12}$, $+\frac{1}{4} = \frac{}{12}$

6. $\frac{1}{2} + \frac{1}{6}$ $\frac{4}{5} - \frac{3}{10}$ $\frac{3}{4} + \frac{1}{2}$ $\frac{5}{6} - \frac{2}{3}$ $\frac{7}{8} - \frac{3}{4}$

7. $\frac{4}{7} + \frac{3}{14} =$ $\frac{7}{9} - \frac{2}{3} =$ $\frac{11}{12} + \frac{3}{4} =$ $\frac{5}{6} - \frac{7}{12} =$

8. $\frac{2}{6} + \frac{1}{3} + \frac{1}{6}$ $\frac{5}{8} + \frac{1}{4} + \frac{1}{2}$ $\frac{2}{5} + \frac{1}{5} + \frac{1}{10}$ $\frac{1}{2} + \frac{3}{4} + \frac{3}{8}$ $\frac{7}{12} + \frac{2}{3} + \frac{1}{4}$

Choosing a Common Denominator

In many problems, the largest denominator in the problem is not a common denominator.

Example: In the problem $\frac{1}{3} + \frac{1}{4}$, 4 is not a common denominator.

A common denominator must be a number that each denominator divides into evenly.

Multiplying Denominators Gives a Common Denominator

In most cases, the easiest way to choose a common denominator is to multiply the denominators in a problem by each other.

Example: In the problem $\frac{1}{3} + \frac{1}{4}$, 12 (3 × 4) can be used as a common denominator.

$$\begin{array}{rcccl} & \frac{1}{3} & = & \frac{1 \times 4}{3 \times 4} & = \frac{4}{12} \\ + & \frac{1}{4} & = & \frac{1 \times 3}{4 \times 3} & = \frac{3}{12} \\ \hline & & & & \frac{7}{12} \end{array}$$

Use the method of multiplying denominators when:

- the largest denominator does not work as a common denominator;
- there are two or more denominators.

▼ Practice

In each problem, multiply denominators to find a common denominator. Then add or subtract as indicated.

Skill Builders

1.

$$\begin{array}{rcl} & \frac{1}{2} & = \frac{}{6} \\ - & \frac{1}{3} & = \frac{}{6} \\ \hline \end{array} \qquad \begin{array}{rcl} & \frac{2}{3} & = \frac{}{12} \\ + & \frac{1}{4} & = \frac{}{12} \\ \hline \end{array} \qquad \begin{array}{rcl} & \frac{4}{5} & = \frac{}{20} \\ - & \frac{3}{4} & = \frac{}{20} \\ \hline \end{array} \qquad \begin{array}{rcl} & \frac{1}{2} & = \frac{}{30} \\ & \frac{1}{3} & = \frac{}{30} \\ + & \frac{1}{5} & = \frac{}{30} \\ \hline \end{array} \qquad \begin{array}{rcl} & \frac{3}{4} & = \frac{}{24} \\ & \frac{2}{3} & = \frac{}{24} \\ + & \frac{1}{2} & = \frac{}{24} \\ \hline \end{array}$$

(Hint: 2 × 3 = 6)

(Hint: 2 × 3 × 5 = 30)

2.

$$\begin{array}{rc} & \frac{2}{3} \\ + & \frac{1}{2} \\ \hline \end{array} \qquad \begin{array}{rc} & \frac{4}{5} \\ - & \frac{1}{2} \\ \hline \end{array} \qquad \begin{array}{rc} & \frac{3}{4} \\ - & \frac{1}{3} \\ \hline \end{array} \qquad \begin{array}{rc} & \frac{1}{2} \\ & \frac{1}{3} \\ + & \frac{1}{4} \\ \hline \end{array} \qquad \begin{array}{rc} & \frac{2}{3} \\ & \frac{1}{2} \\ + & \frac{2}{5} \\ \hline \end{array}$$

ON THE JOB

Working with Small Quantities

Ace Concrete Company delivers ready-to-pour concrete to construction sites. Ace receives several orders each day from do-it-yourselfers who need only a fraction of a cubic yard.

Part of your job at Ace is to keep track of the total amount of small deliveries. To do this, you must add fractions of a cubic yard. When adding fractions, here are a couple of things to try.

- First, try using 8 as a common denominator. Often, 8 works because most orders are for half, fourth, or eighth cubic yards, and 8 is divisible by both 2 and 4.
- If 8 doesn't work as a common denominator, try 12 or 24. 12 is divisible by 2, 3, 4, and 6, and 24 is divisible by 2, 3, 4, 6, and 8.

Suppose you wrote the following table for deliveries made last week.

PARTIAL CUBIC YARD DELIVERIES

Driver	Monday	Tuesday	Wednesday	Thursday	Friday
Fraser	$\frac{3}{4}$	$\frac{5}{8}$	$\frac{1}{2}$	$\frac{5}{6}$	$\frac{2}{3}$
Helzer	$\frac{7}{8}$	$\frac{1}{2}$	$\frac{3}{4}$	$\frac{2}{3}$	$\frac{5}{6}$
Macy	$\frac{1}{2}$	$\frac{3}{4}$	$\frac{3}{8}$	$\frac{3}{4}$	$\frac{7}{8}$
Totals:					

▼ Practice

Answer the questions based on the table above.

1. Complete the Totals row by adding each day's deliveries.
2. On Monday, how much more concrete did Helzer deliver than Macy?__________
3. How much more concrete did Fraser deliver on Monday than on Friday?__________
4. How much total concrete did Macy deliver during the 5-day week shown?__________ (Add from left to right across the row to the right of Macy.)
5. How much more concrete was delivered on Friday than on Wednesday?__________

Adding and Subtracting Mixed Numbers

Suppose you work as an assistant plant manager. The manager asks you to collect her staff's time cards and to add up the number of hours actually worked on Monday. You put together the following information.

Employee	Monday	Tuesday	Wednesday	Thursday	Friday
K. Silvieus	$8\frac{2}{3}$	$8\frac{1}{3}$	$10\frac{2}{3}$	8	$6\frac{2}{3}$
R. Huntington	$4\frac{1}{2}$	$5\frac{1}{2}$	5	$5\frac{1}{2}$	$4\frac{1}{2}$
P. Fineman	$5\frac{1}{4}$	$5\frac{1}{4}$	$5\frac{1}{4}$	$5\frac{1}{4}$	$5\frac{1}{4}$

The numbers you need to add are $8\frac{2}{3}$, $4\frac{1}{2}$, and $5\frac{1}{4}$. What's your first step?

- To add or subtract mixed numbers, change all fractions to **like fractions**. Then add or subtract as indicated, working with fractions first, then with whole numbers.

$$\begin{aligned} 8\tfrac{2}{3} &= 8\tfrac{8}{12} \\ 4\tfrac{1}{2} &= 4\tfrac{6}{12} \\ 5\tfrac{1}{4} &= +\,5\tfrac{3}{12} \\ \hline & 17\tfrac{17}{12} = 18\tfrac{5}{12} \text{ hours} \end{aligned}$$

▼ Practice

Add. First complete the row of partially worked Skill Builders.

Skill Builders

1. $\begin{aligned} 2\tfrac{1}{4} &= 2\tfrac{}{8} \\ +1\tfrac{5}{8} &= 1\tfrac{5}{8} \\ \hline \end{aligned}$ $\quad\begin{aligned} 4\tfrac{1}{2} &= 4\tfrac{}{6} \\ +2\tfrac{2}{3} &= 2\tfrac{}{6} \\ \hline \end{aligned}$ $\quad\begin{aligned} 5\tfrac{3}{4} &= 5\tfrac{}{12} \\ 3\tfrac{1}{3} &= 3\tfrac{}{12} \\ +1\tfrac{5}{12} &= 1\tfrac{}{12} \\ \hline \end{aligned}$ $\quad\begin{aligned} 4\tfrac{2}{3} &= 4\tfrac{}{12} \\ +3\tfrac{5}{6} &= 3\tfrac{}{12} \\ +1\tfrac{1}{4} &= 1\tfrac{}{12} \\ \hline \end{aligned}$

2. $\begin{array}{r} 3\frac{3}{8} \\ +1\frac{1}{4} \\ \hline \end{array}$ $\quad\begin{array}{r} 2\frac{1}{3} \\ +2\frac{1}{6} \\ \hline \end{array}$ $\quad\begin{array}{r} 5\frac{1}{2} \\ +3\frac{1}{6} \\ \hline \end{array}$ $\quad\begin{array}{r} 4\frac{5}{8} \\ +2\frac{1}{4} \\ \hline \end{array}$ $\quad\begin{array}{r} 7\frac{1}{12} \\ +5\frac{3}{4} \\ \hline \end{array}$

3. Look at the example and the chart at the top of the page. Add up the total hours worked for the following days.

Tuesday: ____________ Thursday: ____________

Wednesday: ____________ Friday: ____________

Subtracting Mixed Numbers

- When subtracting, rewrite unlike fractions as like fractions *before* doing any needed borrowing.

Subtract. First complete the row of partially worked Skill Builders.

Skill Builders

4. $\begin{array}{r} 6\frac{2}{3} = 6\frac{}{12} \\ -3\frac{1}{4} = 3\frac{}{12} \\ \hline \end{array}$ $\qquad$ $\begin{array}{r} 9\frac{3}{4} = 9\frac{}{16} \\ -5\frac{5}{16} = 5\frac{}{16} \\ \hline \end{array}$ $\qquad$ $\begin{array}{r} 7\frac{3}{4} = 7\frac{15}{20} = 6\frac{}{20} \\ -4\frac{4}{5} = 4\frac{16}{20} = 4\frac{}{20} \\ \hline \end{array}$

5. $\begin{array}{r} 9\frac{3}{4} \\ -6\frac{2}{3} \\ \hline \end{array}$ $\qquad$ $\begin{array}{r} 8\frac{4}{9} \\ -5\frac{1}{3} \\ \hline \end{array}$ $\qquad$ $\begin{array}{r} 6\frac{4}{5} \\ -2\frac{1}{4} \\ \hline \end{array}$ $\qquad$ $\begin{array}{r} 3\frac{5}{6} \\ -2\frac{3}{4} \\ \hline \end{array}$ $\qquad$ $\begin{array}{r} 7\frac{1}{2} \\ -5\frac{2}{5} \\ \hline \end{array}$

6. $\begin{array}{r} 11\frac{1}{2} \\ -8\frac{3}{4} \\ \hline \end{array}$ $\qquad$ $\begin{array}{r} 9\frac{3}{8} \\ -5\frac{7}{16} \\ \hline \end{array}$ $\qquad$ $\begin{array}{r} 3\frac{1}{4} \\ -1\frac{2}{5} \\ \hline \end{array}$ $\qquad$ $\begin{array}{r} 12\frac{5}{6} \\ -9\frac{7}{8} \\ \hline \end{array}$ $\qquad$ $\begin{array}{r} 17\frac{1}{2} \\ -12\frac{2}{3} \\ \hline \end{array}$

7. For birthday presents, Ardis makes fancy dinner place mats. She makes two styles as pictured below.

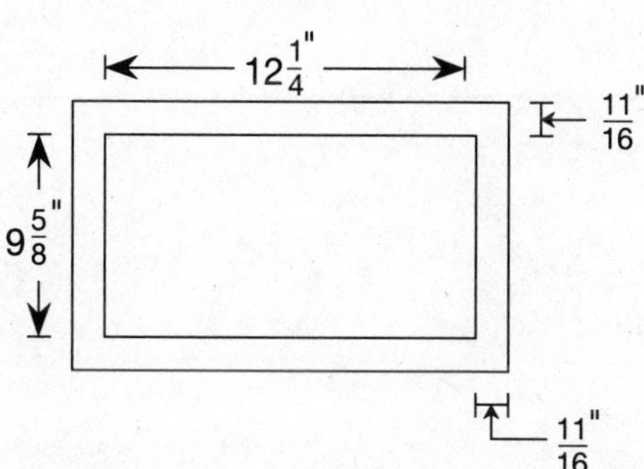

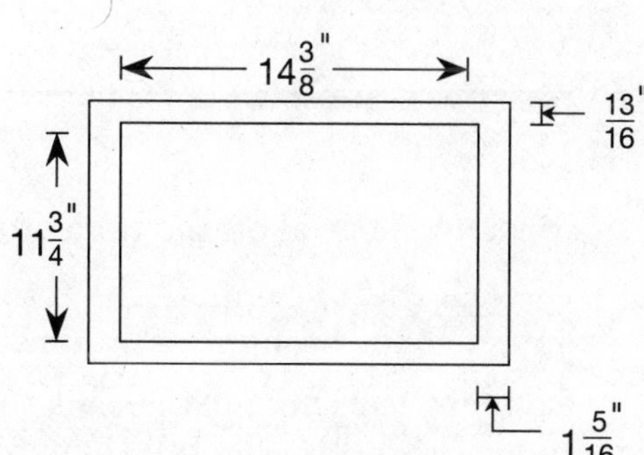

a) What is the total length and width of each place mat?

Style A: length ________ width ________

Style B: length ________ width ________

b) How much does Style B differ from Style A in . . .

total length? ________

total width? ________

IN YOUR LIFE

Working with Weight Limits

Imagine that you are a volunteer helper for a Boy Scout troop. For next weekend's overnight camping trip, you told each Scout to be sure to pack "no more than 22 pounds total" of food and gear—including the weight of the pack! As you might expect, each Scout showed up Saturday morning ready to go but with an overloaded pack.

To help the boys learn to follow instructions more carefully, you had each one unpack his gear and weigh each item being packed. You wrote out the list below as each boy weighed his gear on a bathroom scale. Weight was measured to the nearest $\frac{1}{4}$ pound.

	Weight of Gear						
Scout	Pack	Food	Extra Clothes	Sleeping Bag	Utensils	Personal Items	Total
Bobby	$3\frac{1}{4}$	$15\frac{3}{4}$	$3\frac{1}{2}$	$2\frac{1}{2}$	1	1	____
Matthew	$2\frac{3}{4}$	$14\frac{1}{2}$	$3\frac{1}{4}$	$1\frac{3}{4}$	1	1	____
Timothy	$3\frac{1}{2}$	$13\frac{3}{4}$	3	$2\frac{1}{2}$	$\frac{3}{4}$	1	____
Jimmy	$2\frac{3}{4}$	$14\frac{1}{4}$	$3\frac{1}{2}$	2	1	$\frac{3}{4}$	____

▼ Practice

Answer the questions based on the table above.

1. Add across each row to compute the total amount of weight that each boy brought with him.
2. You tell each boy that he must get his total weight down to 22 pounds. To do this, you tell them to remove food supplies until the total weight of all gear is 22 pounds. You tell them, "We'll share all our food anyway!"
   a) How much food will each boy need to leave behind?
   Bobby: ________ Matthew: ________ Timothy: ________ Jimmy: ________
   b) What is the total weight of food being left behind? ________
   c) How much food will each boy be carrying?
   Bobby: ________ Matthew: ________ Timothy: ________ Jimmy: ________
   d) What is the total weight of food that you allow the boys to take on the trip? ________

ON THE JOB

Recording Changes in Growth

Alisa Chambers works as a preschool assistant for Supercare Preschool. At the beginning and end of each school year, Alisa records the height of each student who attends on a full-time basis.

During the last two years, Alisa has kept a record of the growth rates of five children who have attended full-time both years. She's written the height information on the partially filled-in table below. To compute the amount of growth for each year, she subtracts a student's height at the beginning of the year from his or her height at the end of that year.

Example: Marnie's growth during the first year is computed at right.

End:	$42\frac{5}{8}$	→	$42\frac{5}{8}$	
Beginning:	$-40\frac{1}{4}$	→	$-40\frac{2}{8}$	
			$2\frac{3}{8}$"	

STUDENT HEIGHT
(in inches)

Student's Name	First Year: Beginning	First Year: End	First Year: Amount of Growth	Second Year: Beginning	Second Year: End	Second Year: Amount of Growth
Marnie Casper	$40\frac{1}{4}$	$42\frac{5}{8}$	**$2\frac{3}{8}$**	$42\frac{7}{8}$	$45\frac{1}{2}$	______
James Lynde	$39\frac{3}{8}$	$41\frac{1}{2}$	______	$41\frac{3}{4}$	$43\frac{1}{4}$	______
Susan Moore	$40\frac{9}{16}$	$42\frac{11}{16}$	______	$43\frac{1}{8}$	$45\frac{3}{4}$	______
Isabel Gonzalez	$41\frac{3}{16}$	$43\frac{1}{8}$	______	$43\frac{1}{2}$	$45\frac{15}{16}$	______
Alonso White	$38\frac{15}{16}$	$40\frac{7}{8}$	______	$41\frac{1}{4}$	$43\frac{1}{16}$	______

▼ Practice

The following questions apply to the table above.

1. Complete the table above: compute the *amount of growth* for each student for each year.
2. Which student grew the most during each of the two years indicated?
   first year: ____________ second year: ____________

Multiplying Fractions

Suppose you give a friend a recipe that serves 8 people.

> "But I'm serving only four people," he tells you.
>
> "No problem," you reply. "Just multiply all the amounts by $\frac{1}{2}$."

Drop Biscuits

$\frac{1}{4}$ teaspoon salt	$\frac{1}{2}$ teaspoon baking soda
$\frac{3}{4}$ cup flour	$\frac{2}{3}$ cup milk

To multiply by a fraction is to take a part of something.

As shown at right, $\frac{1}{2}$ of $\frac{1}{4}$ is $\frac{1}{8}$.

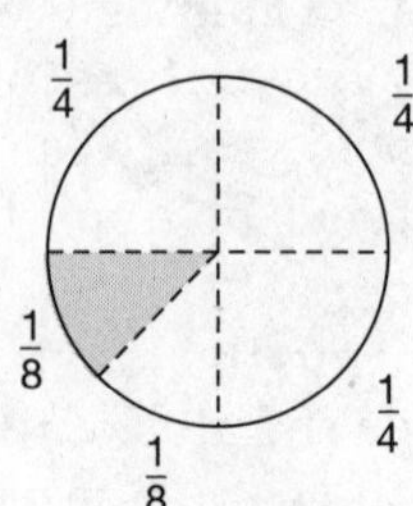

$\frac{1}{2}$ of $\frac{1}{4}$ is $\frac{1}{8}$

or $\frac{1}{2} \times \frac{1}{4} = \frac{1}{8}$

The rule for multiplying fractions is easy to learn.

- Multiply the numerators of the fractions to find the numerator of the answers.
- Multiply the denominators of the fractions to find the denominator of the answer.

Example 1: Multiply $\frac{3}{4}$ cup flour by $\frac{1}{2}$.

Step 1. Multiply the top numbers to find the numerator of the answer. $\frac{3}{4} \times \frac{1}{2} = \frac{3}{}$

Step 2. Multiply the bottom numbers to find the denominator of the answer. $\frac{3}{4} \times \frac{1}{2} = \frac{3}{8}$

Answer: $\frac{3}{8}$ cup flour

Example 2: Multiply $\frac{2}{3}$ cup milk by $\frac{1}{2}$.

Step 1. Multiply.

$\frac{2}{3} \times \frac{1}{2} = \frac{2}{6}$ ← top times top ← bottom times bottom

Step 2. Reduce the answers.

$\frac{2}{6} = \frac{2 \div 2}{6 \div 2} = \frac{1}{3}$

Answer: $\frac{1}{3}$ cup milk

▼ Practice

Multiply. Reduce your answers.

1. $\frac{1}{2} \times \frac{1}{3} = \frac{1}{6}$ $\quad \frac{2}{3} \times \frac{1}{5} =$ $\quad \frac{3}{4} \times \frac{1}{3} =$ $\quad \frac{2}{5} \times \frac{2}{9} =$ $\quad \frac{3}{8} \times \frac{1}{2} =$

2. $\frac{2}{3} \times \frac{1}{7} = \frac{2}{21}$ $\quad \frac{1}{2} \times \frac{1}{2} =$ $\quad \frac{2}{3} \times \frac{4}{5} =$ $\quad \frac{3}{7} \times \frac{3}{10} =$ $\quad \frac{5}{6} \times \frac{3}{4} =$

3. $\frac{1}{3} \times \frac{3}{4} \times \frac{2}{5} = \frac{6}{60}$ $\quad \frac{2}{3} \times \frac{1}{2} \times \frac{3}{4} =$ $\quad \frac{3}{2} \times \frac{2}{3} \times \frac{4}{5} =$

$= \frac{1}{10}$

Using Canceling to Simplify Multiplication

When you multiply fractions, you can often use a shortcut called **canceling.**

- To cancel, divide both a top number and a bottom number by the same number. Cancel before you multiply.

Canceling is similar to reducing a fraction. However, when you cancel, you simplify fractions *before* you multiply.

Example 1: Multiply $\frac{2}{9} \times \frac{6}{7}$

Step 1. Look at the fractions to see if opposite numerators and denominators can be divided by the same number. (9 and 6 can be divided by 3.)

$$\frac{2}{\textcircled{9}} \times \frac{\textcircled{6}}{7}$$

Step 2. Divide: 9 ÷ 3 = 3 and 6 ÷ 3 = 2. Write the results next to the original numbers. Multiply the new numerators and denominators.

$$\frac{2}{\cancel{9}_{3}} \times \frac{\cancel{6}^{2}}{7} = \frac{4}{21}$$

In Example 2, notice how canceling can be used more than once in the same problem.

Example 2: Multiply $\frac{4}{9} \times \frac{3}{8}$

Step 1. Divide both the 4 and the 8 by 4.

Step 2. Divide both the 3 and the 9 by 3.

$$\frac{\cancel{4}^{1}}{\cancel{9}_{3}} \times \frac{\cancel{3}^{1}}{\cancel{8}_{2}} = \frac{1}{3} \times \frac{1}{2} = \frac{1}{6}$$

Skill Builders

4. $\frac{5}{6} \times \frac{3}{4}$

$= \frac{5}{\cancel{6}_{2}} \times \frac{\cancel{3}^{1}}{4}$

$=$

$\frac{4}{7} \times \frac{10}{12}$

$= \frac{\cancel{4}^{1}}{7} \times \frac{10}{\cancel{12}_{3}}$

$=$

$\frac{12}{9} \times \frac{3}{4} =$

$= \frac{\cancel{12}^{3}}{\cancel{9}_{3}} \times \frac{\cancel{3}^{1}}{\cancel{4}_{1}}$

$=$

$\frac{7}{8} \times \frac{16}{14} =$

$= \frac{\cancel{7}^{1}}{\cancel{8}_{1}} \times \frac{\cancel{16}^{2}}{\cancel{14}_{2}}$

$=$

5. $\frac{7}{8} \times \frac{5}{7} =$ $\frac{4}{5} \times \frac{3}{8} =$ $\frac{5}{9} \times \frac{4}{15} =$ $\frac{3}{4} \times \frac{12}{7} =$

6. $\frac{7}{4} \times \frac{16}{14} =$ $\frac{3}{8} \times \frac{2}{9} =$ $\frac{12}{5} \times \frac{25}{36} =$ $\frac{2}{7} \times \frac{14}{18} =$

Multiplying with Fractions and Whole Numbers

To multiply a fraction by a whole number:

- Place the whole number over the number 1.
- Multiply just as you multiply any two fractions.

Example: Multiply $\frac{3}{4} \times 5$

whole number over 1

$= \frac{3}{4} \times \frac{5}{1} = \frac{15}{4}$ ← top times top ← bottom times bottom

$= 3\frac{3}{4}$

Skill Builders

7. $\frac{3}{9} \times 5$ $\quad$ $4 \times \frac{3}{8}$ $\quad$ $\frac{12}{7} \times 3$ $\quad$ $8 \times \frac{11}{12}$

$= \frac{3}{9} \times \frac{5}{1}$ $\quad$ $= \frac{4}{1} \times \frac{3}{8}$ $\quad$ $= \frac{12}{7} \times \frac{3}{1}$ $\quad$ $= \frac{8}{1} \times \frac{11}{12}$

8. $\frac{4}{5} \times 6$ $\quad$ $7 \times \frac{7}{8}$ $\quad$ $\frac{3}{4} \times 12$ $\quad$ $4 \times \frac{5}{8}$ $\quad$ $\frac{13}{16} \times 12$

9. Multiply weight by time (per pound) to find the cooking time of each roast listed in the table below.

Example: To cook a 3-lb. roast rare, multiply 3 by $\frac{1}{2}$:
cook for $3 \times \frac{1}{2} = \frac{3}{2} = 1\frac{1}{2}$ hours

Cooking Times

	Style		
Weight	**Rare**	**Medium**	**Well Done**
per pound	$\frac{1}{2}$ hr.	$\frac{5}{8}$ hr.	$\frac{3}{4}$ hr.
3 lb.	$1\frac{1}{2}$	____	____
4 lb.	____	____	____
5 lb.	____	____	____
6 lb.	____	____	____

Multiplying with Mixed Numbers

A co-worker tells you she used $2\frac{3}{4}$ pounds of packing materials to ship an electronic board. An item you want to ship is only one-third the size of the board, and you want to determine how much your packing material will weigh.

To figure this out, you'll need to multiply $2\frac{3}{4}$ by $\frac{1}{3}$.

- To multiply one or more mixed numbers, the first step is to change all mixed numbers to improper fractions.

First change $2\frac{3}{4}$ to an improper fraction:

Step 1. Change 2 to an improper fraction with a denominator of 4.

$$2 = \frac{8}{4}$$

Step 2. Add $\frac{8}{4}$ and $\frac{3}{4}$.

$$2\frac{3}{4} = 2 + \frac{3}{4} = \frac{8}{4} + \frac{3}{4}$$
$$= \frac{11}{4}$$

Now to determine the amount of packing material you need, multiply $\frac{11}{4}$ by $\frac{1}{3}$.

$$\frac{11}{4} \times \frac{1}{3} = \frac{11}{12} \text{ pound}$$

▼ MATH TIP

Many people like to use this shortcut for changing a mixed number to an improper fraction:

Numerator:
Multiply the whole number by the denominator and add the numerator.

(labels: denominator, whole number, numerator)

$$2\frac{3}{4} = \frac{(4 \times 2) + 3}{4} = \frac{11}{4}$$

(label: denominator)

Denominator remains the same.

▼ Practice

Multiply. First complete the row of partially worked Skill Builders.

Skill Builders

1. $1\frac{2}{3} \times 4$ $= \frac{5}{3} \times \frac{4}{1}$ $5 \times 3\frac{3}{4}$ $= \frac{5}{1} \times \frac{15}{4}$ $4\frac{1}{2} \times \frac{3}{5}$ $= \frac{9}{2} \times \frac{3}{5}$ $2\frac{1}{2} \times 3\frac{1}{2}$ $= \frac{5}{2} \times \frac{7}{2}$

2. $\frac{3}{4} \times 1\frac{1}{4}$ $3 \times 4\frac{1}{2}$ $2\frac{3}{4} \times 3\frac{4}{5}$ $4\frac{1}{3} \times 2\frac{9}{12}$ $6\frac{1}{3} \times 4$

IN YOUR LIFE

Using Measurement in Home Projects

Home projects are an important part of Bonnie Reed's life. She loves to build things and fix up her house in her spare time. Two of the projects she did last month are described below. Use your math skills to answer the questions that Bonnie faced during each project.

Project #1 Building a Picnic Table

Bonnie built the picnic table shown below. Before nailing it together, Bonnie needed to compute the length of support A.

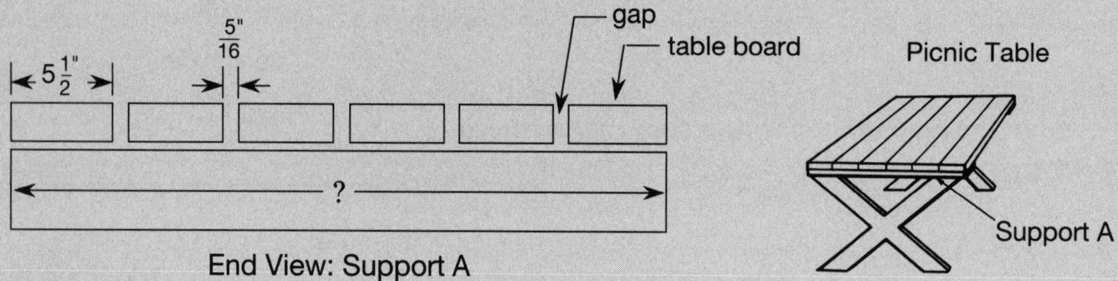

End View: Support A

What is the length of support A?__________
Hint: Length equals 6 table boards plus 5 gaps.

Project #2 Wallpapering Her Bedroom

Bonnie used 7 full strips of wallpaper to paper the wall in her bedroom. Seven full strips didn't quite complete the job, and she needed another partial strip.

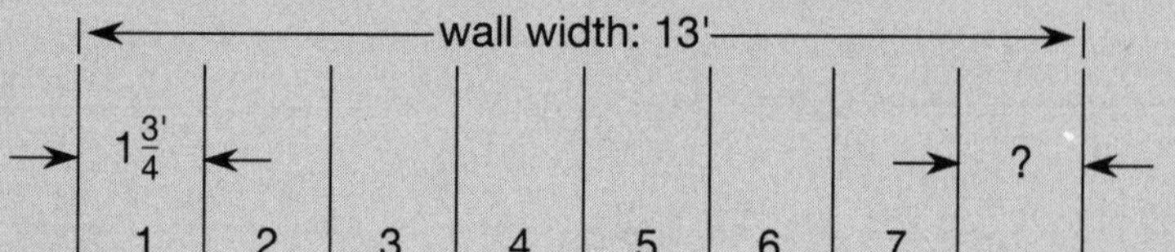

▼ **MATH TIP**

The symbol ' is used to stand for feet.

How wide is the partial strip that Bonnie needs?__________

ON THE JOB

Increasing a Recipe

Wilma Cabel is a cook at Sammy's Restaurant. She uses many of the recipes in her favorite cookbook. Trouble is, most of these recipes give amounts that serve only 4 or 6 people.

Here's how Wilma increases the servings of a recipe. Suppose Wilma has a recipe that feeds 4. If she wants to make 20 servings, Wilma thinks, "How many 4s are in 20?" Since $5 \times 4 = 20$, Wilma uses 5 times as much of each ingredient as called for in the recipe.

Below is Wilma's favorite recipe for split-pea soup. As written, this recipe makes 6 servings. For Thursday, though, Wilma wants to prepare 30 servings. On Friday, she wants to prepare 48 servings. Wilma has written the recipe as part of a table on which she can write her increased amounts.

- For Thursday's meal, Wilma multiplies each ingredient by 5 ($5 \times 6 = 30$).
- For Friday's meal, she multiplies by 8 ($8 \times 6 = 48$).

Example: To determine how many cups of peas to use in Thursday's meal, multiply $2\frac{1}{4}$ by 5.

$$2\tfrac{1}{4} \times 5 = \tfrac{9}{4} \times 5$$
$$= \tfrac{45}{4} = 11\tfrac{1}{4}$$

▼ Practice

Complete the table below for Wilma.

RECIPE FOR SPLIT-PEA SOUP

	Amount of Each Ingredient Needed		
Ingredients	**To Feed 6** (as Given)	**To Feed 30** (× 5)	**To Feed 48** (× 8)
green split peas	$2\frac{1}{4}$ cups	$11\frac{1}{4}$	______
broth	$2\frac{5}{8}$ cups	______	______
sliced onion	$1\frac{2}{3}$ cups	______	______
salt	1 teaspoon	______	______
pepper	$\frac{1}{2}$ teaspoon	______	______
dried marjoram	$\frac{1}{4}$ teaspoon	______	______
diced celery	$1\frac{1}{8}$ cups	______	______
diced carrot	$\frac{7}{8}$ cup	______	______

Dividing Fractions

When you divide, you are finding out how many times one number will go into a second number. This is also true for fractions.

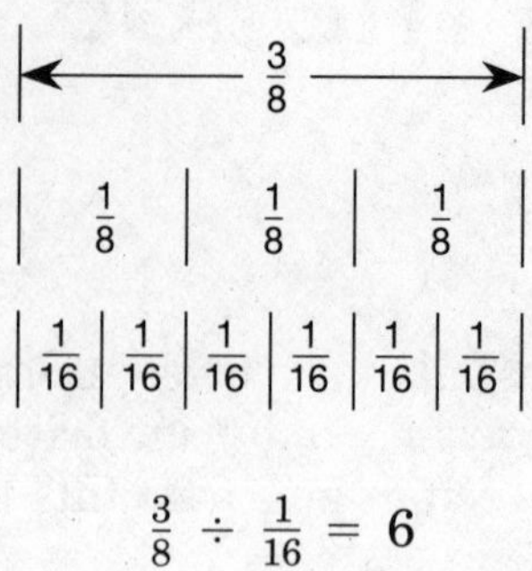

For example, if you want to know how many $\frac{1}{16}$-mile-long sections are in a stretch of road $\frac{3}{8}$ of a mile long, you divide $\frac{3}{8}$ by $\frac{1}{16}$.

As shown at right, there are six $\frac{1}{16}$s in $\frac{3}{8}$.

Dividing fractions involves just one more step than multiplying fractions.

- To divide fractions, *invert the divisor* (the number you're dividing by), and *change the division sign to a multiplication sign.* Then multiply to find the answer.

Inverting the Divisor

To **invert** means to turn a fraction upside down. When you invert a fraction, you switch the top and bottom numbers.

Inverting $\frac{2}{3}$

$\frac{2}{3} \rightarrow \frac{3}{2}$

- *Before inverting a divisor, you must first change it to a fraction if it's not one already.*
- Change a whole number divisor to a whole number over 1.
- Change a mixed number divisor to an improper fraction.

Type of Divisor	Example	Written as a Fraction ($\frac{a}{b}$)	Inverted ($\frac{b}{a}$)
proper fraction	$\frac{3}{4}$	$\frac{3}{4}$	$\frac{4}{3}$
improper fraction	$\frac{15}{12}$	$\frac{15}{12}$	$\frac{12}{15}$
whole number	7	$\frac{7}{1}$	$\frac{1}{7}$
mixed number	$3\frac{1}{4}$	$\frac{13}{4}$	$\frac{4}{13}$

▼ Practice

Invert each number below. The first problem in each row is done as an example.

1. $\frac{3}{4} \rightarrow \frac{4}{3}$ $\quad \frac{7}{8} \quad \frac{1}{2} \quad \frac{9}{16} \quad \frac{2}{3}$

2. $\frac{5}{3} \rightarrow \frac{3}{5}$ $\quad \frac{11}{8} \quad \frac{5}{2} \quad \frac{7}{3} \quad \frac{21}{16}$

3. $3 \rightarrow \frac{1}{3}$ $\quad 2 \quad 5 \quad 12 \quad 16$

4. $3\frac{1}{2} = \frac{7}{2} \rightarrow \frac{2}{7}$ $\quad 4\frac{2}{3} \quad 1\frac{3}{4} \quad 2\frac{3}{8} \quad 1\frac{9}{16}$

Dividing Fractions by Fractions

To divide one fraction by another:

- Invert the fraction *to the right* of the division sign.
- Change the division sign to a multiplication sign and multiply.

When you divide by a fraction, the answer may be *less than 1, equal to 1,* or *more than 1.*

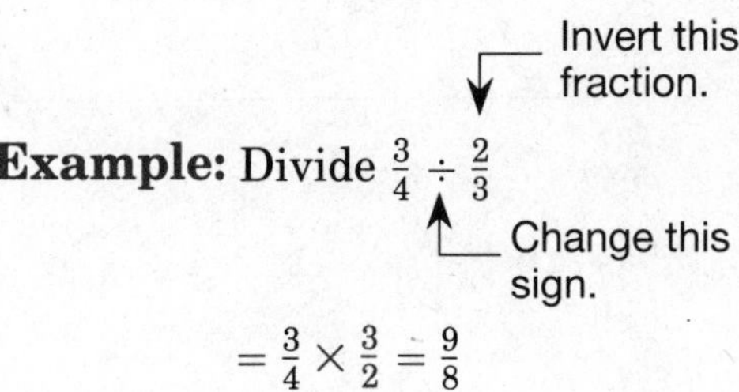

$= \frac{3}{4} \times \frac{3}{2} = \frac{9}{8}$

Answer: $\frac{9}{8} = 1\frac{1}{8}$

Skill Builders

5. $\frac{1}{2} \div \frac{3}{4} \rightarrow \frac{1}{2} \times \frac{4}{3}$ $\quad \frac{7}{8} \div \frac{7}{8} \rightarrow \frac{7}{8} \times \frac{8}{7}$ $\quad \frac{3}{4} \div \frac{1}{3} \rightarrow \frac{3}{4} \times \frac{3}{1}$

$=$ $\quad =$ $\quad =$

6. $\frac{2}{3} \div \frac{1}{2} =$ $\quad \frac{3}{4} \div \frac{2}{3} =$ $\quad \frac{1}{3} \div \frac{3}{8} =$ $\quad \frac{7}{8} \div \frac{1}{2} =$ $\quad \frac{11}{16} \div \frac{1}{3} =$

7. $\frac{2}{3} \div \frac{2}{3} =$ $\quad \frac{5}{8} \div \frac{4}{3} =$ $\quad \frac{12}{3} \div \frac{2}{4} =$ $\quad \frac{3}{6} \div \frac{1}{3} =$ $\quad \frac{12}{8} \div \frac{3}{2} =$

Dividing with Fractions and Whole Numbers

To divide a fraction by a whole number:

- Write the whole number as a fraction with a denominator of 1.
- Invert the whole number divisor, and multiply.

Dividing a fraction by a whole number gives an answer that is smaller than the fraction you start with.

Example:

Change sign.

$\frac{3}{8} \div 5 = \frac{3}{8} \div \frac{5}{1}$ Invert.

$= \frac{3}{8} \times \frac{1}{5}$

$= \frac{3}{40}$

Skill Builders

8. $\frac{5}{8} \div 2 = \frac{5}{8} \div \frac{2}{1}$
$= \frac{5}{8} \times \frac{1}{2}$
$=$

$\frac{11}{2} \div 3 = \frac{11}{2} \div \frac{3}{1}$
$= \frac{11}{2} \times$
$=$

$\frac{15}{12} \div 4 = \frac{15}{12} \div \frac{4}{1}$
$= \quad \times$
$=$

9. $\frac{3}{4} \div 6 =$ $\qquad$ $\frac{7}{8} \div 4 =$ $\qquad$ $\frac{9}{10} \div 5 =$ $\qquad$ $\frac{7}{2} \div 6 =$ $\qquad$ $\frac{8}{3} \div 2 =$

10. $\frac{12}{5} \div 4 =$ $\qquad$ $\frac{13}{2} \div 3 =$ $\qquad$ $\frac{10}{3} \div 5 =$ $\qquad$ $\frac{8}{2} \div 8 =$ $\qquad$ $\frac{9}{3} \div 5 =$

To divide a whole number by a fraction:

- Write the whole number over the number 1.
- Invert the fraction divisor, and multiply.

Dividing a whole number by a proper fraction gives an answer that is larger than the whole number you start with.

Example:

Change sign.

$6 \div \frac{2}{3} = \frac{6}{1} \div \frac{2}{3}$ Invert.

$= \frac{6}{1} \times \frac{3}{2}$

$= \frac{18}{2} = \mathbf{9}$

Skill Builders

11. $5 \div \frac{1}{3} = \frac{5}{1} \div \frac{1}{3}$ $\qquad$ $6 \div \frac{3}{4} = \frac{6}{1} \div \frac{3}{4}$ $\qquad$ $12 \div \frac{4}{3} = \frac{12}{1} \div \frac{4}{3}$

$=$ $\qquad$ $=$ $\qquad$ $=$

12. $7 \div \frac{2}{3} =$ $\qquad$ $3 \div \frac{1}{4} =$ $\qquad$ $6 \div \frac{3}{8} =$ $\qquad$ $12 \div \frac{4}{3} =$ $\qquad$ $15 \div \frac{3}{2} =$

Dividing with Mixed Numbers

To divide with mixed numbers:

- Change each mixed number to an improper fraction.
- Invert the divisor, and multiply.

Example 1:

$2\frac{1}{3} \div \frac{1}{2}$

$= \frac{7}{3} \div \frac{1}{2}$

$= \frac{7}{3} \times \frac{2}{1}$

$= \frac{14}{3}$

$= 4\frac{2}{3}$

Example 2:

$\frac{5}{8} \div 1\frac{2}{3}$

$= \frac{5}{8} \div \frac{5}{3}$

$= \frac{\cancel{5}^{1}}{8} \times \frac{3}{\cancel{5}_{1}}$

$= \frac{3}{8}$

Skill Builders

13. $1\frac{3}{4} \div \frac{7}{8}$ $\qquad$ $2\frac{1}{2} \div 1\frac{2}{3}$ $\qquad$ $5 \div 3\frac{1}{2}$ $\qquad$ $\frac{3}{5} \div 2\frac{5}{6}$

$= \frac{7}{4} \div \frac{7}{8}$ $\qquad$ $= \frac{5}{2} \div \frac{5}{3}$ $\qquad$ $= \frac{5}{1} \div \frac{7}{2}$ $\qquad$ $= \frac{3}{5} \div \frac{17}{6}$

$= \frac{7}{4} \times \frac{8}{7}$ $\qquad$ $= \frac{5}{2} \times \frac{3}{5}$ $\qquad$ $=$ $\qquad$ $=$

$=$ $\qquad$ $=$ $\qquad$ $=$ $\qquad$ $=$

14. $2\frac{2}{3} \div \frac{2}{3} =$ $\qquad$ $3\frac{1}{2} \div 1\frac{1}{2} =$ $\qquad$ $6 \div 4\frac{1}{3} =$ $\qquad$ $4\frac{3}{5} \div 5 =$ $\qquad$ $6\frac{3}{4} \div 2\frac{3}{8} =$

Buying Fabric

Standard-Size Fabrics

length

45" = width

Anne sews children's clothing to earn extra money. Girls' jumpers are her specialty.

For many of the dresses, she uses patterns that are available at fabric stores. On the back of each package that contains a pattern is information that tells how much fabric to purchase.

Fabric comes in two standard widths: 45 inches (45") and 60 inches (60"). When you buy fabric, you buy one or the other of these widths, and you buy a piece in the length given by the pattern you choose. The length is always given in yards and fractions of a yard.

length

60" = width

Here is an example of information on the back of a pattern for a girl's jumper.

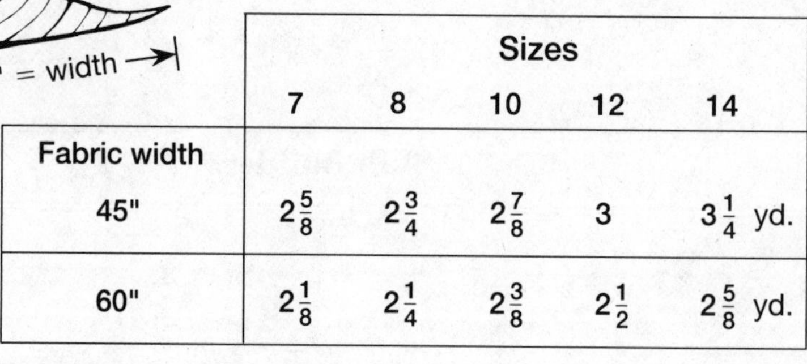

Fabric width	Sizes 7	8	10	12	14
45"	$2\frac{5}{8}$	$2\frac{3}{4}$	$2\frac{7}{8}$	3	$3\frac{1}{4}$ yd.
60"	$2\frac{1}{8}$	$2\frac{1}{4}$	$2\frac{3}{8}$	$2\frac{1}{2}$	$2\frac{5}{8}$ yd.

length of fabric

Example: Using 45"-wide fabric, it takes $2\frac{7}{8}$ yards to make a size 10 jumper.

▼ Practice

Solve the following problems using the table above. You will review many of the fraction skills you have learned in this chapter.

1. How many yards of 60" fabric does Anne need in order to make a size 10 jumper?

2. Using 45" fabric, how many yards will Anne need if she wants to make one size 7 jumper and one size 8 jumper?

3. How many more yards of 60" fabric are needed to make a size 12 jumper than a size 7 jumper?

Using Multiplication Skills

4. Determine how much material she will need in order to make each of the following:

a) 3 size 10 jumpers using 45" fabric
b) 4 size 8 jumpers using 60" fabric
c) 2 size 14 jumpers using 60" fabric

5. How many yards of fabric will be left on a 25-yard roll of 60" fabric if she buys enough material to make 6 size 14 jumpers?

Using Division Skills

6. How many size 10 jumpers can be made from a 16-yard roll of 45" fabric?

Hint: The answer is a whole number.

7. How many size 8 jumpers can be made from a 23-yard roll of 60" material?

8. Anne uses fabric remnants (leftover pieces) to make doll dresses. Complete the table below to determine how many dresses she can make from each remnant.

Hint: Each answer in the right-hand column is a whole number. Round each quotient down by discarding the proper fraction part of the answer.

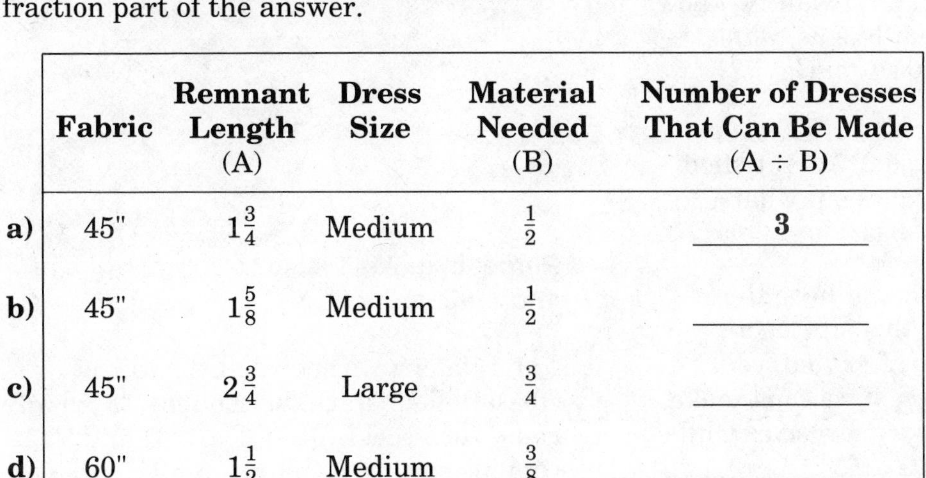

	Fabric	Remnant Length (A)	Dress Size	Material Needed (B)	Number of Dresses That Can Be Made (A ÷ B)
a)	45"	$1\frac{3}{4}$	Medium	$\frac{1}{2}$	3
b)	45"	$1\frac{5}{8}$	Medium	$\frac{1}{2}$	________
c)	45"	$2\frac{3}{4}$	Large	$\frac{3}{4}$	________
d)	60"	$1\frac{1}{2}$	Medium	$\frac{3}{8}$	________
e)	60"	$2\frac{1}{4}$	Large	$\frac{5}{8}$	________

Example:

a) $1\frac{3}{4} \div \frac{1}{2}$

$= \frac{7}{\cancel{4}_{2}} \times \frac{\cancel{2}^{1}}{1} = \frac{7}{2} = 3\frac{1}{2}$

↑ remainder not used

UNIT FOUR

Percents

It was Arturo's second week on the job. He was a sales trainee with a magazine distribution company, and before he went out on sales calls, he was learning all about what the company does.

"Arturo, here are all the responses from our survey," called Mr. Crow, his supervisor. "Please count up the number of letters, then separate them into piles: people who are satisfied with our service, people who are somewhat dissatisfied, and people who are very dissatisfied. Then count 'em up."

"OK. Should I give the numbers to you?"

"Yes, but not in that form. I want to know percents—what percent like us, what percent dislike us, and so on. Got it?"

"I think so. For example, if 1,000 people sent responses and I count 785 satisfied customers, I have to figure out what percent 785 out of 1,000 is?"

"That's right. See if you can have those figures on my desk by this afternoon. Then you and I will go after that 'very dissatisfied' pile and see if we can't make things right—and make a few sales while we're at it."

Percents make it easy to compare information.

Later, as Arturo stared at the tall "dissatisfied" stack, he thought, "Boy, if I could turn these into sales, with my 6% commission, I'd be doing great!"

Think About It

- In what two ways does Arturo's company use percents in this scene?
- What other uses of percents do you know of?

How Do Percents Play a Part in *Your* Life?

Like Arturo, perhaps you use percents on your job. Or, like many people, you may encounter percents in other parts of your everyday life. The following questions may make you more aware of what percents mean.

Think about a newspaper or magazine you've read lately, or pick up one now. How many times are percents used? Why do you think percents are used instead of decimals or fractions?

____

____

____

Do you have money in a savings account? What rate of interest is it earning?

____

Have you ever taken out a loan? What was the interest rate you paid?

____

When was the last time you bought something on sale? What was the percent off? How much money did you save?

____

____

____

Skills You Will Learn

Number Skills
- finding the part
- finding the percent
- finding the whole

Life and Workplace Skills
- marking sale items
- working for commissions
- understanding simple interest
- finding interest for part of a year
- learning about certificates of deposit
- understanding charge-card interest rates
- becoming familiar with repayment schedules

Thinking Skills
- working with the percent circle
- interchanging percents, decimals, and fractions

Calculator Skills
- finding the part
- finding the percent
- finding the whole
- increasing or decreasing a whole by a part

Identifying Numbers in Percent Problems

All percent problems involve three important numbers: the **percent**, the **whole**, and the **part**.

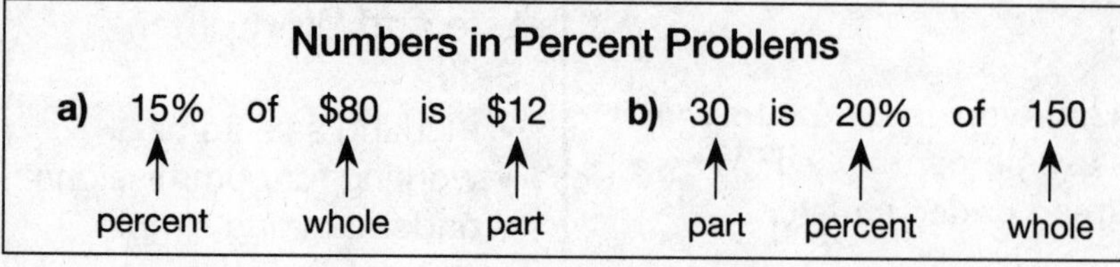

Percent problems ask you to find one of these numbers when you know the other two. In the rest of this unit, you'll learn to solve these three types of problems:

- Finding the **part**, knowing the percent and whole

  Example: What is 15% of $80?

  percent = 15% whole = $80

- Finding the **percent**, knowing the whole and part

  Example: What percent of $80 is $12?

  whole = $80 part = $12

- Finding the **whole**, knowing the percent and part

  Example: If 15% of a number is $12, what is the number?

  percent = 15% part = $12

▼ Practice

Identify the *part, percent,* and *whole* in each statement below.

1. 25% of 300 is 75.

part = ________

percent = ________

whole = ________

2. 54 is 60% of 90.

part = ________

percent = ________

whole = ________

Circle the letter of what you are asked to find in each problem below.

3. If 40% of a number is 200, what is the number? You have to find the ______.

a) part **b)** percent **c)** whole

4. What percent of 50 is 19? You have to find the ______.

a) part **b)** percent **c)** whole

The Percent Circle

Each type of percent problem is solved by multiplication or division. To remember whether to multiply or to divide, we'll use a memory aid called the **percent circle.** The symbols *P*, %, and *W* are used on this circle.

Percent Circle

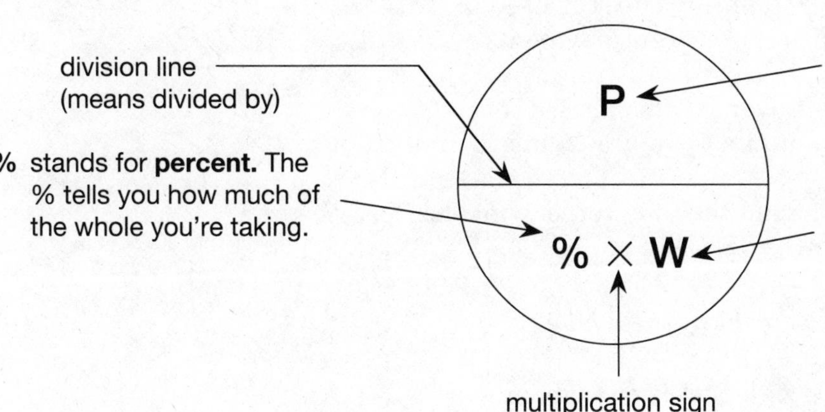

division line
(means divided by)
P
% stands for **percent.** The % tells you how much of the whole you're taking.
% × W
multiplication sign
P stands for **part.** The part is the number you get when you take a percent of the whole.
W stands for **whole.** The whole is the number you take a part of.

Example 1: Identify P, %, and W in the statement below:

25% of 200 is 50.

Answer: P = 50
% = 25%
W = 200

Example 2: Identify P, %, and W in the statement below:

15 is 30% of 50.

Answer: P = 15
% = 30%
W = 50

▼ Practice

Identify P, %, and W in each statement below.

1. 75 is 20% of 375.

P = ______

% = ______

W = ______

2. 85% of 300 is 255.

P = ______

% = ______

W = ______

Circle the symbol of what you are asked to find.

3. What percent of 75 is 25?
P % W

4. What is 18% of 150?
P % W

5. If 10% of a number is 9, what is the number?
P % W

6. 12 is what percent of 48?
P % W

Using the Percent Circle

To use the percent circle:
- Cover the symbol of the number you are trying to find.
- Do the math indicated by the uncovered symbols.

Example 1: Finding *part* of a whole

If 25% of your $800 monthly check is used to pay rent, how much is your rent payment?

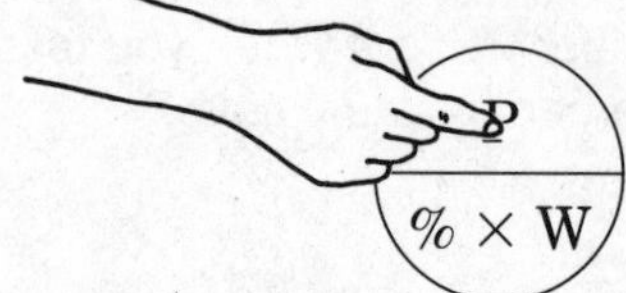

Step 1. Cover P (the part)—the number you are trying to find.

Step 2. Read the uncovered symbols: % × W
P = % × W

- *To find the part, multiply the percent by the whole.*

Example 2: Finding what *percent* a part is of a whole

If $250 of your monthly $800 check is used to buy food, what percent of your check is spent on food?

Step 1. Cover % (the percent)—the number you are trying to find.

Step 2. Read the uncovered symbols: $\frac{P}{W}$
$\% = \frac{P}{W}$ (means P ÷ W)

- *To find the percent, divide the part by the whole.*

Example 3: Finding a *whole* when a part is given

Suppose you buy a used car and make a 10% down payment of $250. What's the price of the car?

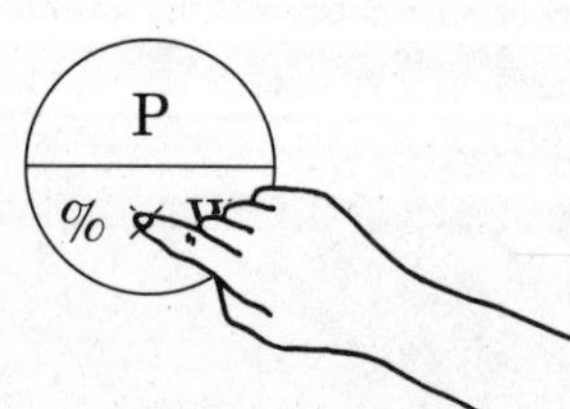

Step 1. Cover W (the whole)—the number you are trying to find.

Step 2. Read the uncovered symbols: $\frac{P}{\%}$
$W = \frac{P}{\%}$ (means P ÷ %)

- *To find the whole, divide the part by the percent.*

▼ Practice

Fill in the percent circle. Then complete the three sentences below with the words *multiply* or *divide*.

1. To find the part, ______________________________ .
2. To find the percent, ______________________________ .
3. To find the whole, ______________________________ .

Circle the symbol of what you're asked to find in each problem. Then place a check to indicate whether you solve the problem by multiplication or division. *Do not solve the problems*. The first one is done for you.

4. Suppose that you paid $.18 sales tax when you bought lunch for $3.50. What percent was the sales tax of the cost of the food? P (%) W

   ______ **multiplication** ___✓___ **division**

5. In 50 minutes, you completed 25% of your homework. At this rate, how long will all of your homework take? P % W

   ______ **multiplication** ______ **division**

6. When you bought a sofa, you made a down payment of $38, which is 10% of the sales price. What is the sales price of the sofa? P % W

   ______ **multiplication** ______ **division**

7. In 4 months, a friend lost 8 pounds. If her original weight was 136 pounds, what percent of her body weight did she lose? P % W

   ______ **multiplication** ______ **division**

8. Suppose that each month, 10% of your income is automatically placed in a savings account at work. If your monthly income is $765, how much goes into savings from each check? P % W

   ______ **multiplication** ______ **division**

FOCUS ON CALCULATORS

Percent

On the next six pages, we'll show how you can use a calculator to solve the three main types of percent problems.

Finding the Part

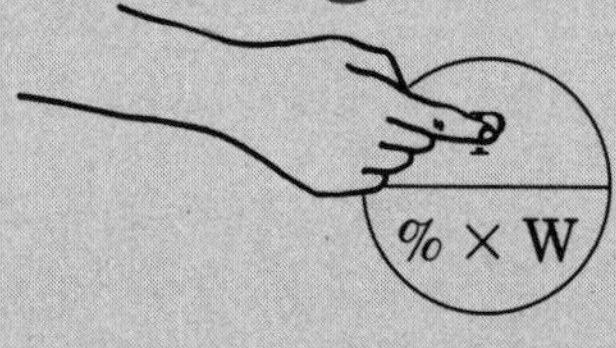

P = % × W

Percent Circle: To find part of a whole, multiply the percent by the whole.

Example 1: Find 32% of $400.

Step 1. Identify W and %.
W = 400 % = 32%

Step 2. Multiply 400 by 32%.
You must multiply in this order:

- Enter 400 (W).
- Press (×).
- Enter 32, the number of percent.
- Press (%).

(On most calculators, pressing (%) completes this calculation. On some calculators, though, you must press (%) and then (=).)

Press Keys	Display Reads
C	0.
4 0 0	400.
×	400.
3 2	32.
%	128.

Answer: $128

▼ Practice

A. Calculate the answer to each problem below.

1. Find 40% of $220.

2. What is 8% of 95?

3. What is 7.5% of $132?

4. Find 25% of 246 pounds.

5. If the tax rate is 5%, how much sales tax will be charged on a sweater on sale for $19.00?

6. Paying a commission of 6%, how much would a seller have to pay a real estate company if the house sold for $58,000?

Finding the Percent

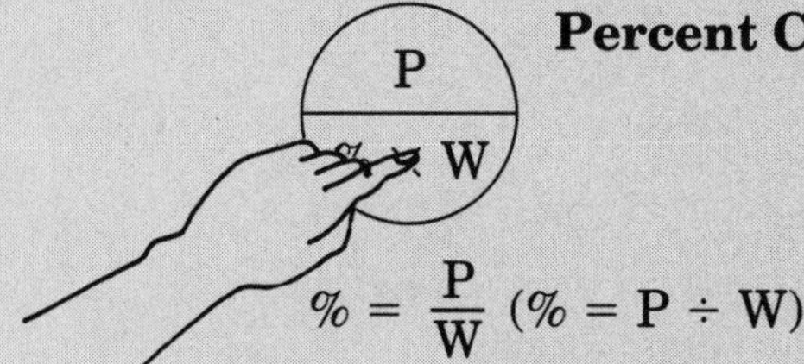

Percent Circle: To find the percent, divide the part by the whole.

$$\% = \frac{P}{W} \quad (\% = P \div W)$$

Example 2: 15 is what percent of 75?

Step 1. Identify P and W.
P = 15 W = 75

Step 2. Divide 15 by 75, pressing (%) as the final key.

- Enter 15.
- Press (÷).
- Enter 75.
- Press (%).

(On most calculators, pressing (%) completes this calculation—giving the answer as the percent. On some calculators, though, you must press (%) and then press (=).)

Press Keys	Display Reads
C	0.
1 5	15.
÷	15.
7 5	75.
%	20.

Answer: 20%

▼ Practice

B. Calculate the answer to each problem.

1. 10 is what percent of 50?

2. What percent of $90 is $15? (Round your answer to the hundredths place.)

3. $6.50 is what percent of $130?

4. What percent of 60 is 22.5?

5. Suppose that each month you put $50 in a savings account. If your take-home pay is $625, what percent do you place in savings?

6. 12 of the 30 students in a class are women. What percent of the class is women?

Finding the Whole

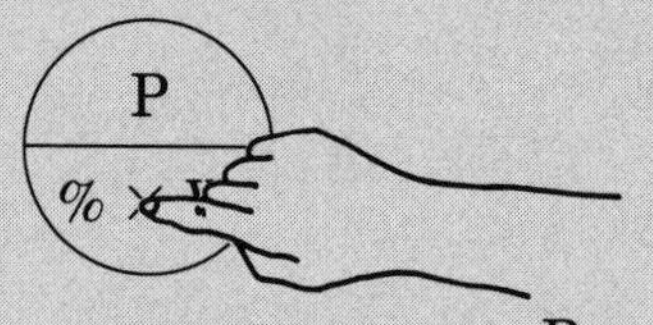

Percent Circle: To find the whole, divide the part by the percent.

$$W = \frac{P}{\%} \quad (W = P \div \%)$$

Example 3: 40% of what number is 32?

Step 1. Identify P and %.
P = 32 % = 40%

Step 2. Divide 32 by 40%.

- Enter 32.
- Press (÷).
- Enter 40, the number of percent.
- Press (%).

(On most calculators, pressing (%) completes this calculation. On some calculators, though, you must press (%) and then press (=).)

Press Keys	Display Reads
C	0.
3 2	32.
÷	32.
4 0	40.
%	80.

Answer: 80

▼ Practice

C. Calculate the answer to each problem.

1. 30% of what number is 27?

2. 50 is 25% of what number?

3. 60 is 7.5% of what number?

4. 25% of what amount is $1.76?

5. Imagine that a friend paid 15% down when he bought a used piano. If his down payment was $120, how much did the piano cost?

6. Suppose you pay 24% of your monthly take-home pay for rent. If your rent is $246, how much take-home pay do you receive each month?

Practicing Calculator Skills

D. 1. As a payroll clerk, you need to determine the amount of each deduction to be withheld from each employee's check. Suppose that a certain employee earns a gross monthly salary of $1,292.50.

- *Multiply* this employee's gross monthly salary by each withholding rate to determine each amount of deduction. (Round to the nearest penny.)

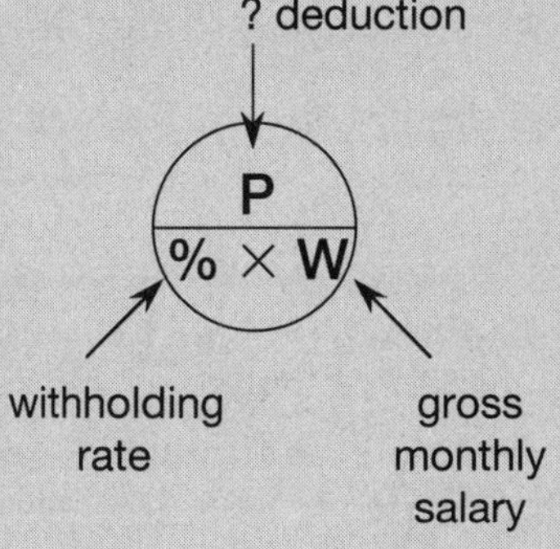

Type of Deduction	Withholding Rate	Amount of Deduction
a) F.I.C.A. (social security)	8.2%	________
b) federal income tax	21.0%	________
c) state income tax	4.5%	________
d) unemployment insurance	5.8%	________
e) health insurance	7.0%	________

2. When another employee got his paycheck, he noticed the deduction amounts listed below. Suppose this employee has a gross monthly salary of $1,418.95.

- *Divide* each of the deductions by his gross monthly salary to determine each withholding rate that applies to him. (Round each rate to the nearest .1 percent.)

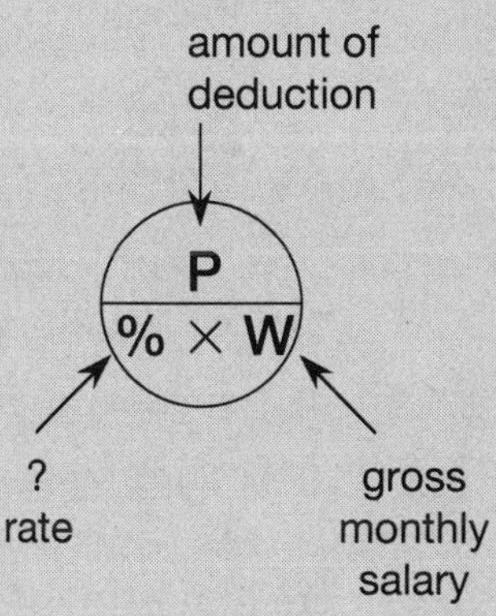

Type of Deduction	Amount of Deduction	Withholding Rate
a) F.I.C.A. (social security)	$135.22	________
b) federal income tax	$349.20	________
c) state income tax	$92.13	________
d) unemployment insurance	$86.56	________
e) health insurance	$76.62	________

3. As a salesclerk, you are asked by your boss to use the sale information below to determine the regular price of each item listed.

- *Divide* each saved amount by the percent saved to determine each regular price.

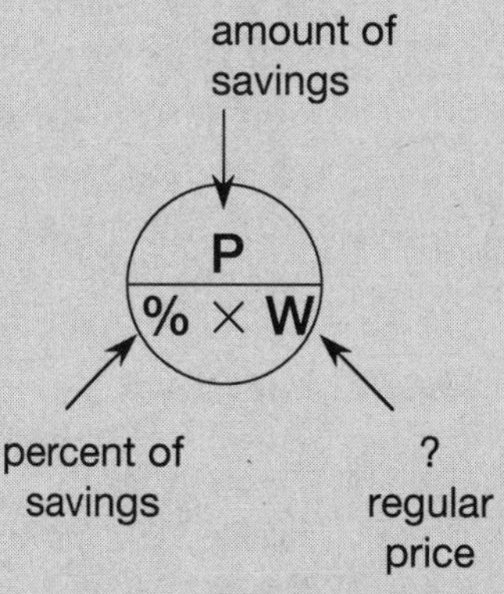

Item	Sale Information	Regular Price
a) long-sleeved shirts	25% off ($3.75 off)	________
b) dress pants	20% off ($12.40 off)	________
c) jackets	30% off ($19.50 off)	________

Increasing or Decreasing an Amount

Many percent problems involve increasing or decreasing a whole by a part. For example, you may want to find the total purchase price of a sweater in a state where there is a sales tax. Without a calculator, this takes two steps:

- First, you must find the amount of sales tax (the part).
- Second, you must add the sales tax to the selling price (the whole).

As the example shows, a calculator combines these two steps into a single step. This single step greatly simplifies these types of problems.

Example 4: In a state with a 6% sales tax, what is the total purchase price of a sweater selling for $32.50?

Step 1. Identify % and W.
% = 6%   W = 32.50

Step 2. On your calculator, add 32.50 plus 6% of 32.50 by pressing the keys as follows:

- Enter 32.50.
- Press (+).
- Enter 6, the number of percent.
- Press (%).

(On most calculators, pressing (%) completes this calculation. On some calculators, though, you must press (%) and then (=).)

Press Keys	Display Reads
C	0.
3 2 . 5 0	32.50
+	32.50
6	6.
%	34.45

Answer: $34.45

Calculator Discovery

When you press (3)(2)(.)(5)(0)(+)(6)(%),* your calculator automatically adds 32.50 and 6% of 32.50. The amount of tax, 1.95 (6% of 32.50), never appears on the display. This is pretty amazing.

If you want to subtract a percent from a whole (as you do in discount problems), press (−) instead of (+).

Example: Pressing (4)(0)(−)(2)(0)(%)* subtracts 20% of $40 from $40 and gives the answer, $32.

*On some calculators, you may need to press (=) to complete this calculation.

▼ Practice

Do the problems below with your calculator. Remember:

- To solve an increase problem, add the percent.
- To solve a decrease problem, subtract the percent.

RATE INCREASE: new amount = original amount + amount of increase

1. Last winter, a family spent an average of $175 per month to heat its home. This year, its heating bills have increased 20%. How much do the monthly heating bills average now?

2. Before she received a raise of 4%, Alice earned $1,140 per month. What is her new monthly salary?

RATE DECREASE: new amount = original amount − amount of decrease

3. To cut down on auto expenses, you plan to drive your car 30% fewer miles this year than last year. Last year you drove an average of 1,250 miles per month. To reach your goal, what monthly mileage must you average now?

4. By Thanksgiving, a friend plans to lose 8% of his body weight. If he weighs 275 pounds now, what weight does he hope to reach by Thanksgiving?

MARKUP: selling price = store's cost + markup

5. The Sport Shoppe places a 35% markup on every item it sells. If the Sport Shoppe pays $11.10 for Pro/Team footballs, how much would a customer be charged for a football?

6. At Marvi's Clothes for Women, Marvi buys wool sweaters for $32 each. If Marvi adds a 30% markup to her cost, at what price does she sell these sweaters?

DISCOUNT: sale price = original price − amount of discount

7. On Saturday, Auto Discount is holding its annual "25% Off Everything Sale." What could you expect to pay at this sale for a case of oil if the regular price is $13.80?

8. Wholesale Foods offers a 10% discount on any case of canned food. If the regular price of a can of peas is $.89, or $21.36 for a case of 24, what is the discount price on a full case?

Changing Percents to Decimals or to Fractions

The first step in solving a percent problem is to change the percent to either a decimal or a fraction. On this page, we'll strengthen the skills you partially learned on pages 22 and 23.

Changing Percents to Decimals

25% of

is

Can you tell why?

To change a percent to a decimal:

- Move the decimal point two places to the left, adding a zero if necessary.
- Drop the percent sign.
- Drop any unnecessary zeros.

▼ **MATH TIP**

Remember that the decimal point in a whole number is understood to be at the right of the number, even though it is not written.

Examples:

Percent	Move Decimal Point Two Places Left	Decimal
35%	.35	.35
80%	.80	.80 = .8 ← The zero can be dropped.
9%	.09 ← Add a 0.	.09
8.5%	.08.5 ← Add a 0.	.085

Changing Percents to Fractions

To change a percent to a fraction:

- Write the percent as a fraction with a denominator of 100.
- Reduce the fraction if possible.

Example: Change 45% to a fraction.

Step 1. Write 45% as 45 over 100. $45\% = \frac{45}{100}$

Step 2. Reduce $\frac{45}{100}$ by dividing top and bottom numbers by 5. $\frac{45 \div 5}{100 \div 5} = \frac{9}{20}$

Answer: $\frac{9}{20}$

ON THE JOB

Marking Sale Items

As a salesclerk, you are responsible for placing sale tags on items being discounted. You prepare three different kinds of tags:

Tag #1 gives the savings as a percent: **SALE: 25% OFF**

Tag #2 gives the savings as a decimal: **SALE: \$.25/\$1 OFF**

Tag #3 gives the savings as a fraction: **SALE: $\frac{1}{4}$ OFF**

On Tuesday, Carla—the store manager—asks you to prepare tags for an upcoming sale. She wants you to prepare all three types of tags for each sale item. She will decide later which tag (or two) to place on each.

To make the different tags, you change each percent to its equivalent decimal and fraction:

▼ MATH TIP

\$.25/\$1 off means \$.25 off per \$1.

Example: 25% off

Decimal

25% = .25

= .25

= \$.25/\$1 off
(since .25 of \$1 is \$.25)

Fraction

$25\% = \frac{25}{100}$

$= \frac{25 \div 25}{100 \div 25}$

$= \frac{1}{4}$ off

▼ Practice

Complete the list below. Write each sale amount (given as a %) both as a decimal (cents/\$1) and as a fraction.

	Sale Item	Discount (savings)	Cents/\$1 off	Fraction off
a)	handbags	25% off	\$.25/\$1	$\frac{1}{4}$
b)	blouses	35% off	______	______
c)	pants	15% off	______	______
d)	scarves	10% off	______	______
e)	bathrobes	40% off	______	______
f)	discontinued items	50% off	______	______

Changing Fractions to Percents

To change a fraction to a percent, multiply the fraction by 100%.

Look how simple this method is:

Example 1: Change $\frac{3}{4}$ to a percent.

$$\frac{3}{\not{4}_{1}} \times \frac{\overset{25\%}{\not{100\%}}}{1} = 75\%$$

Example 2: Change $\frac{5}{8}$ to a percent.

$$\frac{5}{8} \times \frac{100\%}{1} = \frac{500\%}{8} = 62.5\% = 62\tfrac{1}{2}\%$$

Example 3: Change $\frac{1}{3}$ to a percent.

$$\frac{1}{3} \times \frac{100\%}{1} = \frac{100\%}{3} = 33\tfrac{1}{3}\%$$

▼ **MATH TIP**

You can also change a fraction to a percent in this way:

- Change the fraction to a decimal.
- Change the decimal to a percent.

Isn't the shortcut at left much easier to remember?

▼ **MATH TIP**

The fractions $\frac{1}{3}$ and $\frac{2}{3}$ occur often in real-life problems, so you may want to memorize the following facts:

$\frac{1}{3} = 33\frac{1}{3}\%$ $\frac{2}{3} = 66\frac{2}{3}\%$

▼ Practice

1. Change each fraction below to a percent.

$\frac{2}{4}$ $\frac{3}{5}$ $\frac{10}{16}$ $\frac{9}{10}$ $\frac{5}{6}$

2. As a salesclerk, you've been asked to change sales tags on certain shoes. The boss wants the tags to tell the percent off rather than the fraction of the price off.

On the lines provided, write the changes you'd make. The first has been done for you.

Item	Is Marked	Will Be Marked
a) dress shoes	$\frac{1}{5}$ off	**20% off**
b) loafers	$\frac{1}{3}$ off	________
c) cowboy boots	$\frac{1}{4}$ off	________
d) discontinued shoes	$\frac{2}{3}$ off	________

Commonly Used Percents, Decimals, and Fractions

You have now seen how percents, decimals, and fractions can be changed from one to another. This skill is used throughout the remainder of this unit.

▼ Practice

1. Below is a partially completed chart of the most commonly used percents, decimals, and fractions. Complete this chart.

Percent	Decimal	Fraction	Percent	Decimal	Fraction
10%					$\frac{3}{5}$
	.2			$.66\frac{2}{3}$	
		$\frac{1}{4}$	70%		
30%					$\frac{3}{4}$
		$\frac{1}{3}$		.8	
	.4		90%		
50%					

Once you've checked the answer key for the right answers, you should memorize these commonly used percents, decimals, and fractions.

When working with money, you can think of percent as being "cents per dollar."

Example: A 6% sales tax means you pay 6¢ sales tax for every dollar you spend.

Thinking of percent this way gives you a feeling of about how much a stated percent is.

2. Complete the chart below, showing how many cents per dollar each percent, decimal, and fraction represents. You may want to change decimals and fractions to percents first if it's helpful.

Part	Cents per Dollar	Part	Cents per Dollar
a) $\frac{1}{10}$	10% = $.10	**e)** .9	
b) $\frac{1}{4}$		**f)** 20%	
c) $33\frac{1}{3}\%$		**g)** $\frac{2}{3}$	
d) .75		**h)** $\frac{1}{2}$	

Finding the Part

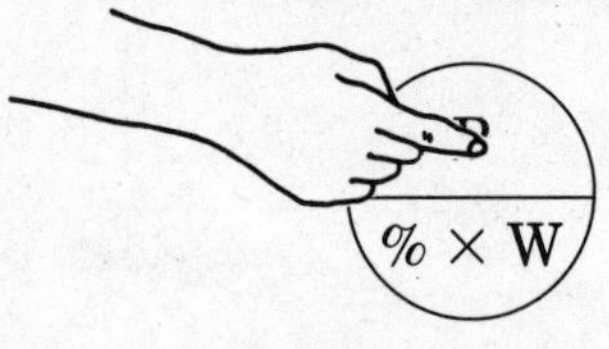

$P = \% \times W$

Percent Circle: To find part of a whole, multiply the percent by the whole.

How to Do It: Change the percent to either a decimal or a fraction, then multiply.

Example: The $92 wheelbarrow that you plan to buy will be 25% off tomorrow. You want to know if you'll save enough money to buy a $27 sprinkler system.

To determine this, find 25% of $92.

Method 1

Step 1. Change 25% to a decimal.
25% = .25

Step 2. Multiply 92 by .25.

$$\begin{array}{r} 92 \\ \times\ .25 \\ \hline 4\ 60 \\ 18\ 4 \\ \hline 23.00 \end{array} = 23$$

Answer: $23. No, you will not save enough money to buy the sprinkler system.

Method 2

Step 1. Change 25% to a fraction.
$25\% = \frac{25}{100} = \frac{1}{4}$

Step 2. Multiply 92 by $\frac{1}{4}$.
$\frac{1}{4} \times \frac{92}{1} = \frac{92}{4}$

$= 23$

Answer: $23

▼ MATH TIP

In most problems, Method 1 is easier. But when the percent is $33\frac{1}{3}\%$ ($= \frac{1}{3}$) or $66\frac{2}{3}\%$ ($= \frac{2}{3}$), Method 2 is easier.

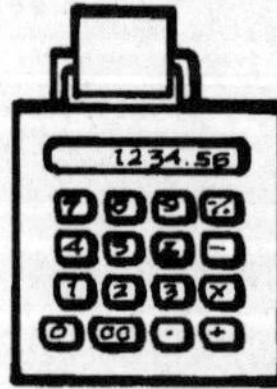

Calculator Solution of Example

Press Keys: C 9 2 × 2 5 %*

Answer: 23.

*On some calculators, you must press = after %.

▼ Practice

As a review, change each percent to a decimal *and* a fraction.

1.	75%	40%	5%	$66\frac{2}{3}\%$	$33\frac{1}{3}\%$
decimal	______	______	______	$.66\frac{2}{3}$	______
fraction	______	$\frac{4}{10} = \frac{2}{5}$	______	______	______

*2. Value-Mart is offering discounts on sale items listed below.

Each discount rate is given as a percent of the regular price. Find each discount and sale price. The first is worked as an example.

a) • Discount = Regular Price × Discount Rate

Example: sport shirt = $12.90 × 20% = $2.58

b) • Sale Price = Regular Price − Discount

Example: sport shirt = $12.90 − $2.58 = $10.32

Item	Regular Price	Discount Rate	Discount (a)	Sale Price (b)
sport shirt	$12.90	20%	**$2.58**	**$10.32**
dress pants	$32.60	15%	______	______
dress shoes	$49.96	25%	______	______
bathrobe	$24.00	$33\frac{1}{3}$%	______	______
tie	$6.60	50%	______	______
ring	$19.80	$66\frac{2}{3}$%	______	______

*3. Almost every state has a sales tax. A sales tax is computed as a percent of a price and varies from state to state.

Determine each sales tax and total purchase price. The first is worked as an example.

a) • Sales Tax = Price × Sales Tax Rate

Example: houseplant = $16.95 × 6% = $1.017 = $1.02

b) • Total Purchase Price = Price + Sales Tax

Example: houseplant = $16.95 + $1.02 = $17.97

Item	Price	Sales Tax Rate	Sales Tax (a)	Total Purchase Price (b)
houseplant	$16.95	6%	**$1.02**	**$17.97**
restaurant meal	$23.75	8%	______	______
coffee table	$84.90	5%	______	______
microwave oven	$279.00	4%	______	______
lawn mower	$189.50	7.5%	______	______
used car	$999.00	5.5%	______	______

*Round all amounts to the nearest penny.

Finding the Percent

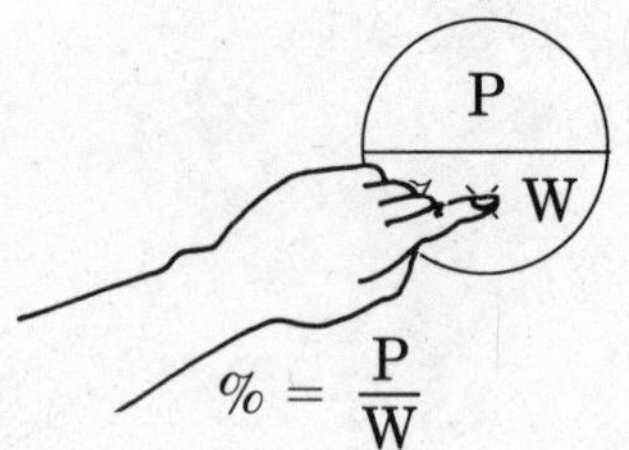

Percent Circle: To find the percent, divide the part by the whole.

How to Do It: Write a fraction $\frac{P}{W}$. Reduce this fraction, then change it to a percent.

Example: A co-worker tells you that 12 employees called in sick the day before the holiday. Of a total 60 employees, what percent called in sick?

Step 1. Write the fraction 12 (P) over 60 (W). Reduce this fraction. $\frac{P}{W} = \frac{12}{60} = \frac{1}{5}$

Step 2. Multiply $\frac{1}{5}$ by 100%.

$$\frac{1}{5} \times \frac{100\%}{1} = \frac{100\%}{5} = 20\%$$

Answer: 12 is 20% of 60.
20% of the employees called in sick.

▼ MATH TIP

Another way to ask the same question is:

"What percent of 60 is 12?"

Asked either way, 60 (the number following the word *of*) is the whole; 12 is the part.

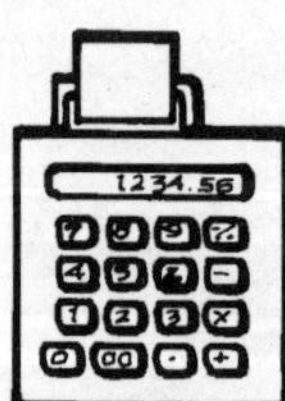

Calculator Solution of Example

Press Keys: C 1 2 ÷ 6 0 %*

Answer: 20.

*On some calculators, you must press = after %.

▼ Practice

Solve each problem below. Remember first to write $\frac{P}{W}$ as a fraction. Then reduce this fraction before multiplying by 100%.

1. 5 is what percent of 25?
2. $10 is what percent of $40?
3. What percent of $60 is $15?
4. What percent of 16 pounds is 2 pounds?

5. At the Super Bowl Sunday Sale at Armandi's, a customer bought the items listed below at the sale price. Determine each percent of savings and each sale price. An example is done for you.

a) percent of savings = (savings bonus ÷ regular price) × 100%

Example: gloves ($4 ÷ $20) × 100% = $\frac{1}{5}$ × 100% = 20%

b) sale price = regular price − savings bonus

Example: gloves $20 − $4 = $16

Item	Regular Price	Savings Bonus	Percent of Savings (Nearest 1%) (a)	Sale Price (b)
gloves	$20	$4	**20%**	**$16**
purse	$35	$5	______	______
coat	$117	$39	______	______
sweater	$40	$10	______	______
shoes	$47	$14	______	______
scarf	$12.50	$1.25	______	______

6. Imagine that you are taking a telephone poll to see how people plan to vote on 5 upcoming tax measures. Find each percent "yes," "no," and "undecided." Round each answer to the nearest percent. An example is done for you.

a) percent "yes" = ("yes" responses ÷ number of responses) × 100%

Example: Measure #1 (50 ÷ 200) × 100% = 25%

b) percent "no" = ("no" responses ÷ number of responses) × 100%

Example: Measure #1 (125 ÷ 200) × 100% = $62\frac{1}{2}$% ≈ 63%

c) percent "undecided" = 100% − percent "yes" − percent "no"

Example: Measure #1 100% − 25% − 63% = 12%

Measure Number	Number of Responses	"Yes" Responses	"No" Responses	Percent "Yes" (a)	Percent "No" (b)	Percent "Undecided" (c)
1	200	50	125	**25%**	**63%**	**12%**
2	400	150	225	______	______	______
3	300	50	175	______	______	______
4	300	150	100	______	______	______
5	500	175	230	______	______	______

Finding the Whole

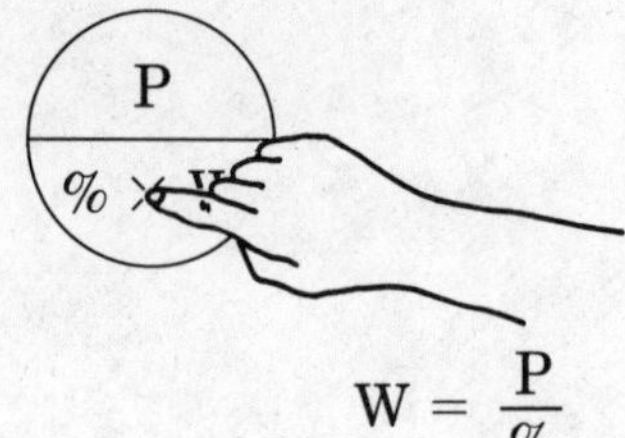

$W = \frac{P}{\%}$

Percent Circle: To find the whole, divide the part by the percent.

How to Do It: Change the percent to either a decimal or a fraction, then divide.

Example: Your supervisor announces, "20% of the circuit boards assembled today are defective." He shows you a tray of 17 defective boards. How many circuit boards in all were produced that day?

In other words, 20% of what number is 17?

Method 1

Step 1. Change 20% to a decimal.
20% = .20

Step 2. Divide 17 by .20.
(or divide by .2).

$$\begin{array}{r} 85. \\ .2\overline{)17.0} \\ -16 \\ \hline 10 \\ -10 \\ \hline \end{array}$$

Answer: 85 circuit boards were produced that day.

Method 2

Step 1. Change 20% to a fraction.
$20\% = \frac{20}{100} = \frac{1}{5}$

Step 2. Divide 17 by $\frac{1}{5}$.

$17 \div \frac{1}{5} = \frac{17}{1} \times \frac{5}{1}$

$= \frac{85}{1} = 85$

Answer: 85 circuit boards

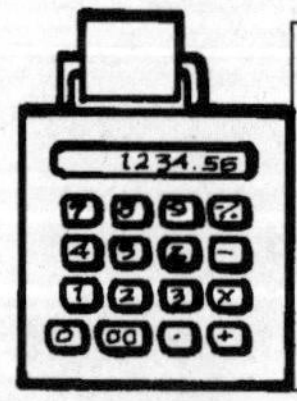

Calculator Solution of Example

Press Keys: (C) (1) (7) (÷) (2) (0) (%)*

Answer: (85.)

*On some calculators, you must press (=) after (%).

▼ Practice

Using either method, solve the following problems.

1. 50% of what number is 19?

2. 75% of what amount is $27?

3. $11.75 is 25% of what amount?

4. 125 is $33\frac{1}{3}\%$ of what number?
Hint: Use the fraction form of $33\frac{1}{3}\% = \frac{1}{3}$

5. Divide *savings amount* by *% savings* to find the *original price* of each item listed below.

Item	Savings Amount (a)	% Savings (b)	Original Price (a ÷ b)
a) lawn chair	$13.50	25%	**$54**
b) water hose	$4.75	20%	______
c) sprinkler	$4.00	40%	______
d) bench	$7.50	15%	______
e) table	$28.00	$33\frac{1}{3}$%	______

▼ MATH TIP

Always use the fraction form of $33\frac{1}{3}$% when multiplying or dividing.

Remember: $33\frac{1}{3}\% = \frac{1}{3}$

6. Compute the purchase price that each customer paid by dividing the *down payment amount* by the *down payment percent.*

Example: Garcia: $28.50 ÷ 10% = $285.00

Customer	Down Payment Percent	Down Payment Amount	Purchase Price
a) Garcia	10%	$28.50	**$285**
b) Hershner	15%	$45.00	______
c) McNeil	5%	$13.85	______
d) Schuck	20%	$136.75	______
e) Trotta	$33\frac{1}{3}$%	$87.83	______

7. As part of his service to customers, Joe test-drives each car he tunes up. On the table below, he's listed the number of miles he drove during the test *and* the percent of a full tank of gas he used for the test.

Divide to determine how far each customer can expect to drive on a full tank of gas.

Example: '87 Chevy: 45 ÷ 10% = 450 miles

Car	Test Miles Driven	% of Full Tank Used for Test	Full-Tank Mileage
a) '87 Chevy	45	10%	**450 miles**
b) '88 Honda	48	12%	______
c) '76 Ford	124	$33\frac{1}{3}$%	______
d) '81 VW	42	14%	______

ON THE JOB

Working for Commissions

Imagine that you work as a salesperson for Engman Furniture. You are paid a salary of $5.00 per hour *plus* commissions.

- A **commission** is calculated as a percent of sales.

Your commissions are based on the price of furniture you sell. Engman's pays you a larger commission for sales of higher-priced furniture.

Below are listed the sales you made last week. You calculated your commission for the sale of the lounger as follows:

commission = sale price × commission rate
= $399 × 4% = $399 × .04
= $15.96

Item	Sale Price	Commission Rate	Amount of Commission
a) lounger	$399	4%	**$15.96**
b) lamp	$49	3%	________
c) sofa and love seat	$789	5%	________
d) oak end table	$149	4%	________
e) dining room set	$1,289	6%	________

▼ Practice

Use the information in the table above to help you answer the questions.

1. Compute the amount of each of your other commissions. Write each answer on the line provided in the table.

2. Suppose you worked 40 hours last week.
a) How much did you earn in direct salary (at $5.00/hr.)? ________
b) How much did you earn in commissions? ________
c) What total amount did you earn during the week? ________
d) To the nearest percent, what percent of your total earnings was made up of commissions? ________

3. On Tuesday of this week, you sold a bedroom set for which you were paid a 6% commission of $107.94. What was the sale price of the bedroom set? ________

IN YOUR LIFE

Making Sure of Percent

As you've seen, percent problems are not too difficult to solve once you answer the question, "What am I trying to find—the part, the percent, or the whole?"

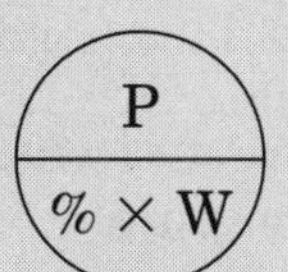

For a fun and quick review of the uses of the percent circle, read each tag below. Write the correct amount or percent on each blank line. Good luck!

1.

Ties on Sale

40% Off

Regular Price: $12.00

You Save: $ ______

4.

Belts on Sale

Regular Price: $16.50

Now $33\frac{1}{3}$% Off

You Pay: $______

Hints:

$33\frac{1}{3}\% = \frac{1}{3}$

$66\frac{2}{3}\% = \frac{2}{3}$

2.

Blouses

Save $5.00

Regular Price: $25.00

You Save: ______ %

5.

Sweaters on Sale

Pay just $66\frac{2}{3}$% of the regular price.

Regular Price: $45

You Save: ______ %

You Pay Only: $ ______

3.

Pajamas

Save $6.00

That's 15% of the original price.

Original Price: $ ______

6.

Pants

Save 20%

Take $15 off the regular price.

Regular Price: $ ________

You Pay Only $ ________

Understanding Simple Interest

Interest is money that is earned (or paid) for the use of money.

- If you deposit money in a savings account, *the bank pays you interest* for the use of your money.
- If you borrow money, *you pay the lender interest* for the use of its money.

Interest is earned (or paid) on **principal**—the amount that is deposited (or borrowed).

- **Simple interest** is interest earned (or paid) on the amount of principal only. (Additional interest is not paid on any amount of interest that gets added to the principal.)

To compute simple interest, we use the **simple-interest formula.**

In words: Interest equals Principal times Rate times Time
In symbols: I = PRT (which means P × R × T)

Interest (I)	=	Principal (P)	×	Rate (R)	×	Time (T)
Expressed in dollars		Expressed in dollars		Expressed as a percent		Expressed in years

▼ **MATH TIP**

Be sure not to confuse the use of the letter *P* in the simple-interest formula with its use in the percent circle. In I = PRT, *P* stands for *principal.* In the percent circle, *P* stands for *part.*

Example: How much interest is earned on \$400 deposited for 2 years in a bank that pays 5% simple interest?

Step 1. Identify P, R, and T.
P = \$400 R = 5% = .05 T = 2

Step 2. Replace the letters in PRT with the values given in Step 1.
I = PRT = \$400 × .05 × 2

$$\begin{array}{r} \$400 \\ \times\ .05 \\ \hline 20.00 \end{array} = \$20 \rightarrow \begin{array}{r} \$20 \\ \times\ 2 \\ \hline \$40 \end{array}$$

Answer: \$40

▼ **MATH TIP**

5% could also be written $\frac{5}{100} = \frac{1}{20}$.

In that case, we would do the math as follows:

$I = \$400 \times \frac{1}{20} \times 2$

$I = \overset{20}{\cancel{\$400}} \times \frac{1}{\underset{1}{\cancel{20}}} \times 2$

$= \$40$

▼ Practice

Answer the following questions about interest.

Interest Earned

1. Part of Sandra's job is to compute interest earned in simple-interest savings accounts at Ace Credit Union. Deposits for less than $1,000 earn 5%, while larger deposits earn 6%.

   Complete the chart for her at right.

	Principal	Interest Rate	Time (Years)	Interest
a)	$400	5%	1	______
b)	$500	5%	3	______
c)	$650	5%	2	______
d)	$1,500	6%	2	______
e)	$2,000	6%	3	______
f)	$5,000	6%	1	______

2. How much would you earn on a deposit of $1,500 in 2 years if the simple interest rate was 5.5%?

3. You deposited $700 in a savings account that earns 6.5% interest.

   a) How much interest will you earn in 2 years?

   b) What will be the total in your account at the end of 2 years?

   total = principal + interest

▼ MATH TIP

Change a decimal percent such as 5.5% to a decimal in the same way you change a whole number percent to a decimal:

- Move the decimal point two places to the left, then drop the % sign.

5.5% = 0 5 5 = .055

Interest Paid

Solve problems 4–5 by using the chart at right.

4. If a customer of United Bank borrows $8,500 to buy a used car, how much interest will she owe if she repays the entire loan at the end of 1 year?

5. Suppose you borrowed $4,500 from United Bank to buy a boat. The bank agreed to let you pay the entire principal plus interest at the end of two years.

   a) How much interest will you owe at the end of 2 years?

   b) What total amount will you owe the bank at that time?

   total owed = principal + interest

United Bank Simple-Interest Loans	
new car	10.5%
used car	12.5%
boat	15.0%
personal	18.0%

ON THE JOB

Interest for Part of a Year

Although interest is earned (or paid) at a yearly rate, not all deposits or loans are made for whole years. Some are made for part of a year.

- To use the simple-interest formula for part of a year, write the time either as a decimal or as a fraction.

In Example 1, both the interest rate and the time are written as fractions, and canceling is used to simplify the multiplication.

Example 1: How much interest will you earn on a deposit of $600 if you are paid an interest rate of 5% and you leave your money in the bank for 9 months?

Step 1. Identify P, R, and T.
$P = \$600 \quad R = 5\% = \frac{5}{100} \quad T = \frac{9}{12} = \frac{3}{4}$

Step 2. Replace the letters in I = PRT with the values given in Step 1.

$$I = PRT = 600 \times \frac{5}{100} \times \frac{3}{4}$$
$$= \overset{6}{\cancel{600}} \times \frac{5}{\underset{1}{\cancel{100}}} \times \frac{3}{4}$$
$$= \frac{90}{4}$$
$$= 22.5$$

Answer: $22.50

In Example 2, time is given as a mixed decimal. In this problem, it looks easier to work with decimals than to change to fractions.

Example 2: How much interest will you pay on a loan of $599 borrowed for 2.5 years at a 12% simple interest rate?

P = $599 R = 12% = .12 T = 2.5
I = PRT = 599 × .12 × 2.5

```
  599            71.88
×  .12        ×    2.5
 1198          35940
 599          14376
 71.88 ──→    179.700 = 179.70   written to the nearest cent
```

Answer: $179.70

▼ MATH TIP

Time can be written in different forms:

- **fraction**
  6 months =
  $\frac{6}{12}$ year = $\frac{1}{2}$ year
- **mixed fraction**
  1 year and 3 months =
  $1\frac{3}{12} = 1\frac{1}{4}$ years
- **decimal**
  $2\frac{1}{2}$ years = 2.5 years

▼ Practice

1. Write each time period as a proper fraction. Reduce if possible.

   3 months = 8 months = 10 months =

2. Write each time period as a decimal fraction. Round long answers to the hundredths place.

   a) 6 months = 3 months = 9 months =

   b) 4 months = 8 months = 11 months =

3. United Bank advertised the special savings plan shown at right.

   As a customer service representative, you must determine how much each of the following customers will earn in this special plan. Fill in the correct amounts on the lines provided.

Give us your money for 6 months, and we'll give you a great deal!

Amount of Deposit	Interest Rate
\$100–\$499	6%
\$500–\$999	6.5%
\$1,000–\$4,999	7%

Customer	Amount Deposited	Interest (6 months)
a) Johnson	\$250	________
b) Laurence	\$800	________
c) Murphy	\$3,750	________

4. Brennan's Furniture ran the following advertisement:

BRENNAN FURNITURE BONANZA!!

Saturday Only Sale
- No money down!
- You pick the interest rate!

Plan A: Pay balance at end of 6 months, pay 6%.
Plan B: Pay balance at end of 12 months, pay 8%.
Plan C: Pay balance at end of 18 months, pay 10%.

As a clerk in the accounting office, determine how much each of these customers will owe at the end of the chosen loan period. Fill in the correct amounts on the lines provided.

Customer	Amount Financed	Payment Plan	Total Interest	Total Due at Payment Time (Amount Financed + Total Interest)
a) Burkle	\$500	Plan B	________	________
b) Hanks	\$699	Plan C	________	________
c) White	\$249	Plan A	________	________

IN YOUR LIFE

Learning about Certificates of Deposit

One of the first things Samantha sees when she enters her bank is a sign similar to the one at right. Out of curiosity one day, Samantha asked the teller, "What is a CD?"

New **CD** rates!

Earn up to 8%.

Save and earn with us!

Samantha learned that a CD is a **certificate of deposit**—a special type of savings program. A CD pays a higher rate of interest than a savings account. However, you must leave your money with the bank for a specified length of time. You pay a penalty for early withdrawal.

There are three things to consider about a CD:

- the dollar amount you need to give the bank;
- the length of time until **maturity**—the time at which you cash in a CD (withdraw your principal plus interest);
- the interest rate you're earning.

The table below gives typical CD information.

United Bank: Certificates of Deposit	
Time	Interest Rate
3 months	7.0%
6 months	7.5%
1 year	7.8%
2 years	8.0%

▼ MATH TIP

The interest rate quoted for a CD is a *yearly* rate.

Don't forget this when you want to find interest actually earned.

▼ Practice

Use the table above to answer the following questions. Assume that United Bank is paying a 6% savings account rate.

1. Samantha wants to place $500 in a savings fund for 6 months.

  a) How much interest can she earn in her savings account? ____________

  b) How much interest can she earn by buying a 6-month CD? ____________

2. Suppose Samantha has $1,000 to place in a CD for 6 months. How much more interest can she earn by buying a $1,000 6-month CD than by buying two $1,000 3-month CDs in a row? ____________

IN YOUR LIFE

Understanding Charge-Card Interest Rates

Like millions of other people, Alex Rudman has a charge card. He received this card after answering an advertisement in the mail. The card sounded like a bargain, offering an interest rate of 1.5%, a rate that sounded very low to Alex. After all, he'd heard about car interest rates of 12% and higher.

After running up a bill of $600 the first month, Alex made his minimum monthly payment of $60. The statement he received the next month showed that Alex owed $540 ($600−$60) *plus* a finance charge of $8.10! Alex was quite surprised. The interest rate had seemed so low!

What Alex didn't realize was that the 1.5% interest rate was being charged *each month* on any unpaid balance. Here's how his monthly finance charge was calculated:

Step 1. Change 1.5% to a decimal.
1.5% = 0 15 = .015

Step 2. Multiply $540 times .015.
$540 × .015 = $8.10

If Alex had read his application carefully, he would have learned that a 1.5% monthly rate is equal to an **annual percentage rate** (APR) of 18.8%!

▼ MATH TIP

You can think of a charge card as a high-interest personal loan. Smart shoppers use charge cards very carefully!

▼ Practice

Solve the following problems.

1. Calculate the monthly finance charge Alex will pay for each month shown at right. Write your answers on the lines provided. **Hint:** Finance charge = 1.5% × unpaid balance.

2. Suppose Alex charged $2,000 on his charge card (the maximum his card allows) and made no monthly payments for 1 year.

a) How much interest (finance charge) would Alex be charged for that year? ___________
Hint: Interest = APR × $2,000.

b) How much in all would Alex owe the charge-card company? ___________ **Hint:** Total = $2,000 + interest.

Month	Unpaid Balance	Finance Charge
March	$300.00	________
April	$550.00	________
May	$125.00	________

IN YOUR LIFE

Becoming Familiar with Repayment Schedules

Cleo White wants to borrow money from the County Employees' Credit Union. He wants to buy a good used car. Cleo is told that credit union loans must be paid back according to a **loan repayment schedule.** This means that—rather than paying a loan back in a lump sum at some later date—Cleo must begin paying it back immediately by making equal month-by-month payments. He is informed that most bank loans are also of this type.

While applying for his loan, Cleo learns that the amount of his monthly payment will depend on two things:

- the **APR** (annual percentage rate being charged); and
- the total length of the repayment period.

The higher the APR, the larger the monthly payment. The longer the repayment period, the smaller the monthly payment, but the greater the total interest he'll pay.

The credit union manager gave Cleo a copy of the information shown below. Cleo sees that the APR depends on the type of loan he wants to take out.

TYPE OF LOAN	APR
new car	10%
used car	12%
signature (can be used for anything)	14%

MONTHLY PAYMENTS

APR	Loan Amount	Repayment Period: 24 months	36 months	48 months
10%	$2,500	$116	$81	$64
	$5,000	$231	$161	$127
	$7,500	$346	$242	$191
12%	$2,500	$118	$83	$66
	$5,000	$235	$166	$131
	$7,500	$353	$249	$197
14%	$2,500	$120	$86	$69
	$5,000	$240	$171	$137
	$7,500	$360	$257	$206

Example: → 10%

To determine the total amount of his payments, Cleo must multiply his monthly payment by the repayment period.

Example: For a 12% loan of $2,500 taken out for 24 months, Cleo would pay: $118 × 24 = **$2,832**

Total interest paid on this loan is found by subtraction: $2,832 − $2,500 = **$332**

▼ Practice

Use the table on page 136 to solve the following problems.

1. Suppose Cleo borrows $7,500 to buy a used car.

a) What APR will Cleo pay?

b) What will Cleo *pay each month* if he decides to repay the loan in . . .

24 months? ________

36 months? ________

48 months? ________

c) How much will Cleo *repay in all* if his loan repayment period is . . .

24 months? ________

36 months? ________

48 months? ________

Hint: Total repayment = monthly payment × repayment period.

d) How much *total interest* will Cleo end up paying if he repays the loan in . . .

24 months? ________

36 months? ________

48 months? ________

Hint: Total interest = total repayment − loan amount.

2. Suppose that Cleo decides instead to buy a new car.

a) What APR will Cleo pay?

b) How much total interest will Cleo pay for a 48-month $7,500 loan?

c) How much interest money would Cleo save with a 48-month $7,500 loan by buying a new car rather than a used car?

3. Why do you think that new-car loans have a lower APR than used-car loans? Also, why do **signature loans**—which can be used for any purpose you want—have the highest APR?

Hint: Loan interest rates are partly determined by the risk that the lender takes on.

Choosing a Purchase Plan

19" Color TV
Save 20%
Sale Price: $300

26" Color TV
Save 25%
Sale Price: $490

After reading the ad at Jones Furniture Mart, Donna decided to buy a new color television. There were two sets on sale that interested Donna, and Jones offered three different purchase plans:

Purchase Plan I

- Pay cash.
- Receive an additional 5% discount off sale price.

Purchase Plan II

- Pay 20% down.
- Pay balance + simple interest of 18% as a single payment at the end of 18 months.

Purchase Plan III

- Pay 10% down.
- Pay balance and interest charges according to the following repayment schedule:

TABLE OF MONTHLY PAYMENTS

	Repayment Period	
Model	12 months	24 months
19"	$24.75	$14.50
26"	$40.50	$23.75

Before she decides which set to buy and which purchase plan to choose, Donna would like to compare information. Answer the questions on page 139 to get an idea of the comparisons Donna wants to make.

▼ Practice

In this exercise, you will review what you have learned about percents.

1. What is the original price of each TV set?
Hint: First determine what percent each sale price is of each original price.

a) Original price of 19" set: ________

b) Original price of 26" set: ________

2. Suppose Donna chooses Purchase Plan I.

a) How much additional cash discount would Donna receive on each set?

19" set: ________ 26" set: ________

b) What price would Donna actually pay for each set?

19" set: ________ 26" set: ________

3. Suppose Donna chooses Purchase Plan II.

a) How much down payment would Donna be required to make on each set?

19" set: ________ 26" set: ________

b) What total (principal + interest) would Donna be required to pay Jones at the end of 18 months?

Hint: Principal = sale price − down payment

19" Set:		26" Set:	
Principal:	________	Principal:	________
Interest:	________	Interest:	________
Total:	________	Total:	________

4. Suppose Donna chooses Purchase Plan III.

a) How much down payment would Donna be required to make on each set?

19" set: ________ 26" set: ________

b) If Donna buys the 19" set and pays it off in 12 months, what total will she have paid Jones?

Hint: Total = 10% down payment + amount of monthly payments

c) If Donna buys the 26" set and pays it off in 24 months, how much interest will she have paid Jones?

Hint: Interest = total − sale price

UNIT FIVE

Topics in Measurement

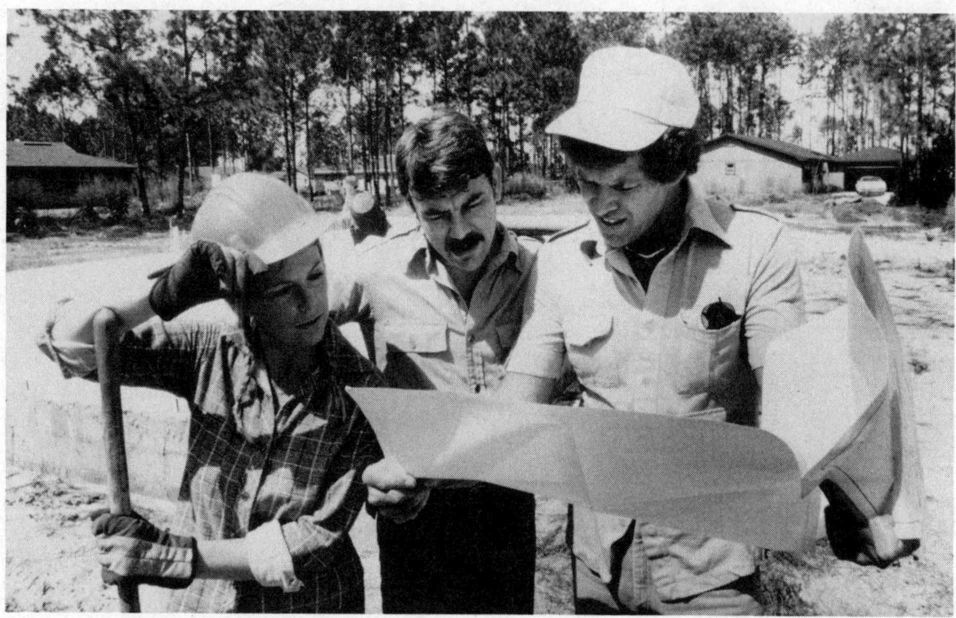

A construction site is just one of many places where measurement plays an important role.

Listen to some fragments of conversation on a construction site:

"How many feet wide is this lot?"

"I've got $6\frac{1}{2}$ pounds of this cement mix. How many gallons of water should I mix with it?"

"That space will never house a 36.9-cubic-foot refrigerator."

"The deck will be 250 square feet, and about $4\frac{1}{2}$ feet above ground level."

"Pick up a couple pounds of nails while you're out, would you?"

"I think you'd better take about 10 or 12 centimeters off the edge here."

"Man, it must be 90 degrees out here!"

Think About It

- What do all these fragments of conversation have in common?
- How many different types of measurement are being discussed? Can you think of others that might be discussed on this site?

How Does Measurement Play a Part in *Your* Life?

Think about all the things you've measured in your day-to-day life and on the job. Why do we measure? How does measurement improve our lives? Answer the following questions to help you find out.

Make a list of all the things you have measured in the past month or so. Then jot down why you did each measurement. Don't forget less obvious measuring such as time and temperature.

____

____

____

____

Have you ever had trouble changing from one unit of measurement to another, such as feet to inches or cups to gallons? What made it difficult?

____

____

____

Have you ever estimated a measurement? Why was an exact measurement not necessary?

____

____

____

Skills You Will Learn

Number Skills

- recognizing English and metric units
- becoming familiar with area
- becoming familiar with volume

Life and Workplace Skills

- measuring with an English ruler
- measuring with a centimeter ruler
- working with metric tools
- weighing on a market scale
- using a postage scale
- weighing on a metric scale
- becoming familiar with a kitchen scale
- working with liquid measure
- reading a weather thermometer
- tiling a room
- buying soil for a lawn

Thinking Skills

- estimating distances
- estimating weights

Introducing Measurement

Measurement is an important part of daily life. In this unit, we'll study examples of the measurement of distance, weight, liquid volume, and temperature.

A measurement is given as a number and a label. The label is called a **measurement unit**. In the length 23 yards, yards is the measurement unit.

Two types of measurement units are used in the United States: the familiar **English system** (or U.S. Customary System) and the **metric system.** Make yourself familiar with the comparison of units pictured below. Then answer the questions on the next page.

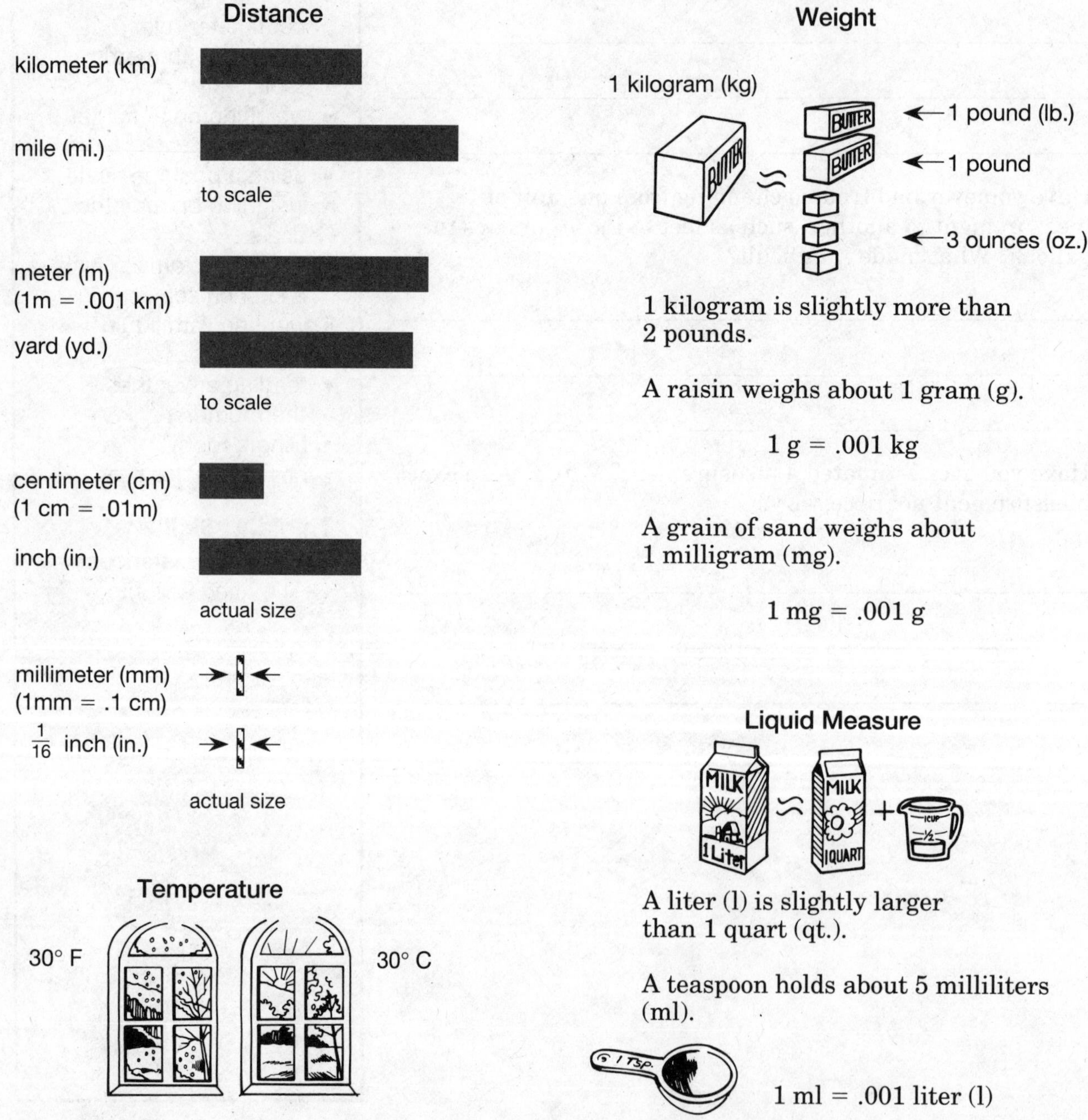

1 kilogram is slightly more than 2 pounds.

A raisin weighs about 1 gram (g).

1 g = .001 kg

A grain of sand weighs about 1 milligram (mg).

1 mg = .001 g

A liter (l) is slightly larger than 1 quart (qt.).

A teaspoon holds about 5 milliliters (ml).

1 ml = .001 liter (l)

Most of us are not familiar with the metric system. However, we may encounter it in our work.

▼ Practice

Fill in each blank with one of the choices in parentheses.

1. A meter is ________________ than a yard. (longer, shorter)
2. A kilogram is ________________ than a pound. (heavier, lighter)
3. A liter is ________________ than a quart. (larger, smaller)
4. A speed of 50 kilometers per hour is ________________ than a speed of 50 miles per hour. (greater, less)

Below each picture, circle the symbol of the metric unit that would be used to make the indicated measurement.

Distance

5.

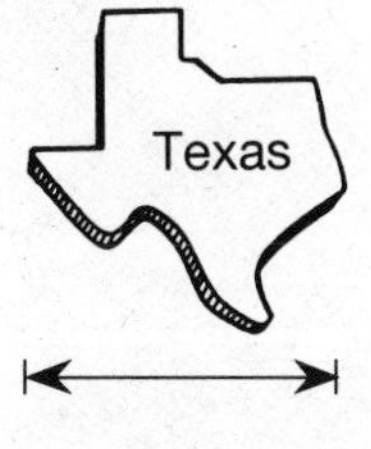

cm m km

6.

cm m km

7.

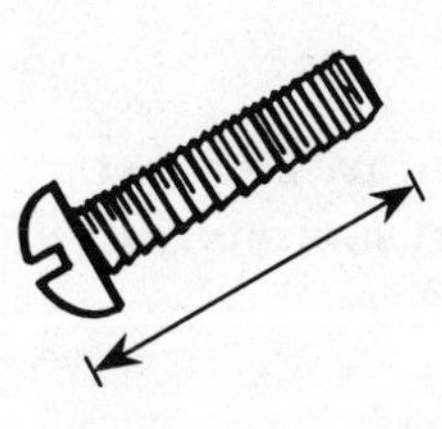

mm cm m

8.

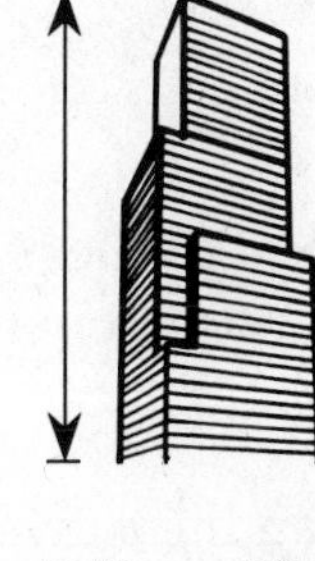

mm cm m

Weight

9.

mg g kg

10.

mg g kg

11.

mg g kg

12.

mg g kg

Liquid Volume (capacity)

13.

ml l

14.

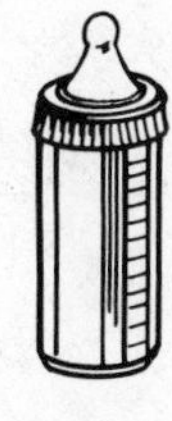

ml l

15.

ml l

16.

ml l

Measuring with an English Ruler

Probably the most commonly used measuring tool found around most homes is the **ruler.** Pictured below is the familiar 6-inch English ruler.

- Each inch is divided into . . .

  sixteenth inches (from one line to the next)

  eighth inches (every 2 lines) $\frac{1''}{8} = \frac{2''}{16}$

  quarter inches (every 4 lines) $\frac{1''}{4} = \frac{4''}{16}$

  half inches (every 8 lines) $\frac{1''}{2} = \frac{8''}{16}$

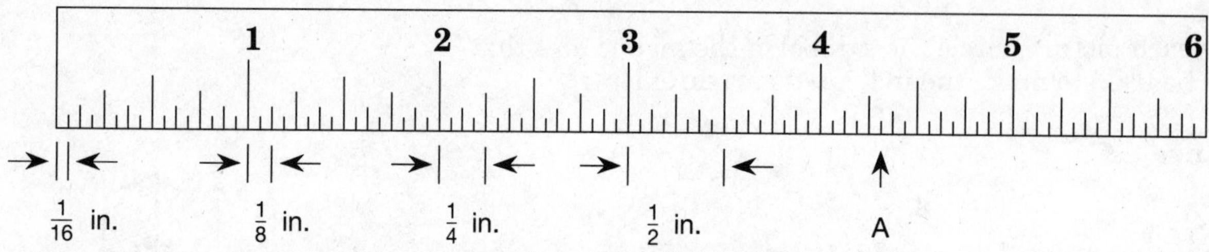

You read a ruler from left to right. To make reading easier, each fraction of an inch is represented by a line of different height.

- When measuring, always reduce fraction answers when possible.

Example: How far is point A from the left end of the ruler?

First notice that point A is between 4 and 5 inches from the left end.

Because point A is at a $\frac{1}{16}$-inch line, count the number of sixteenths that point A is beyond 4. Point A is 5 sixteenths to the right of the 4.

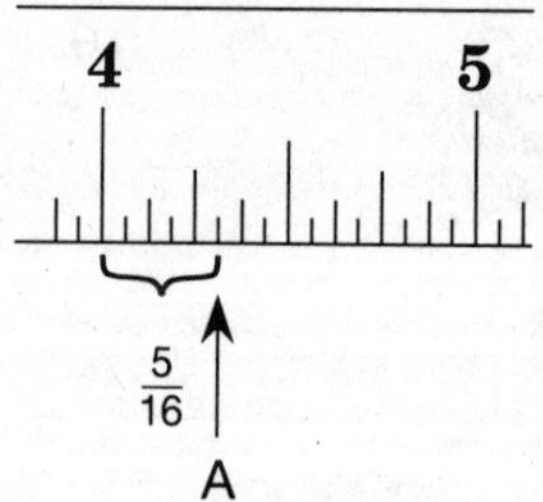

Answer: $4\frac{5}{16}$ inches

▼ Practice

What distance is represented in each ruler pictured below? Reduce fraction answers.

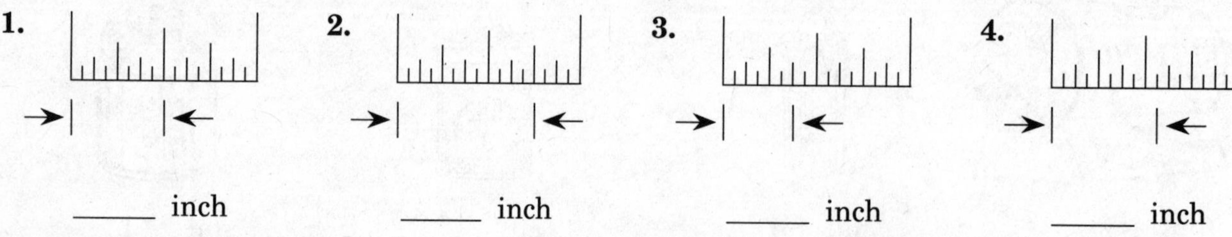

1. _____ inch

2. _____ inch

3. _____ inch

4. _____ inch

▼ Practice

What is the length of each object pictured below? Reduce the fraction part of each answer to lowest terms.

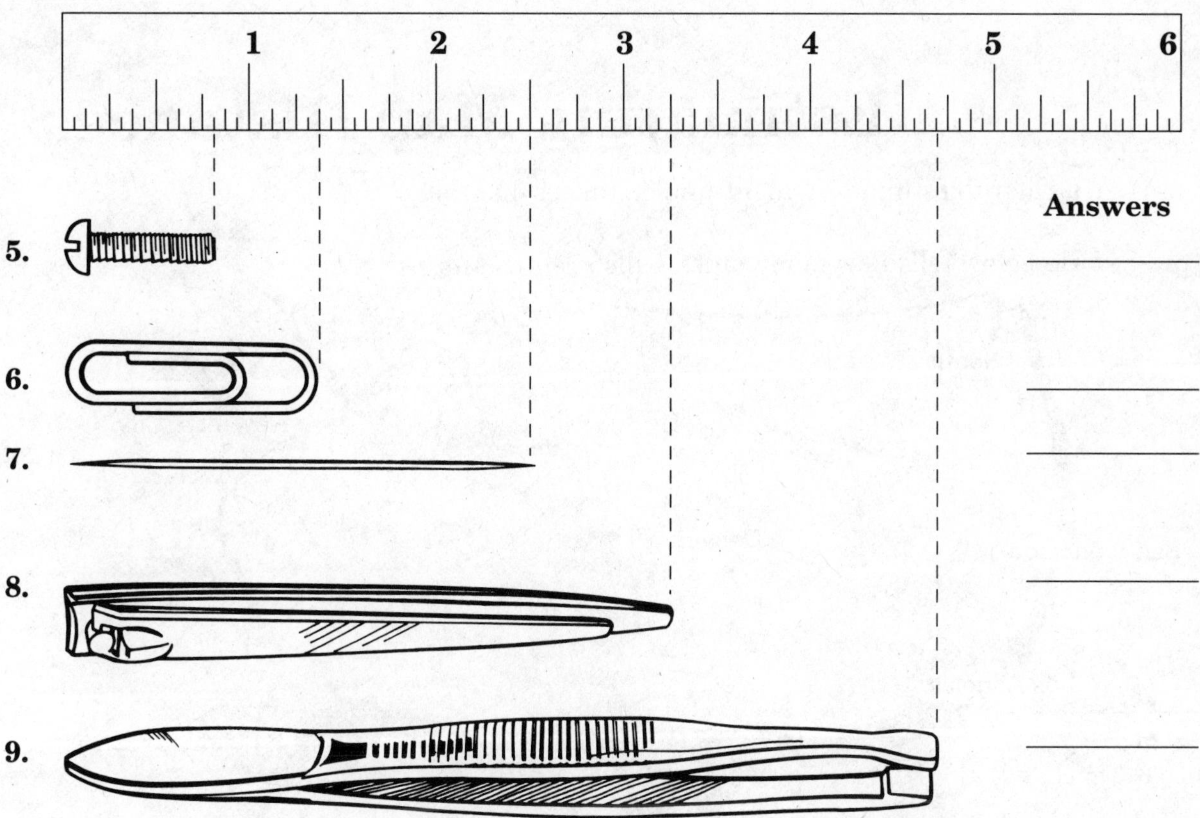

Problems 10–12 refer to the pencil pictured below. Choose each answer from the choices given.

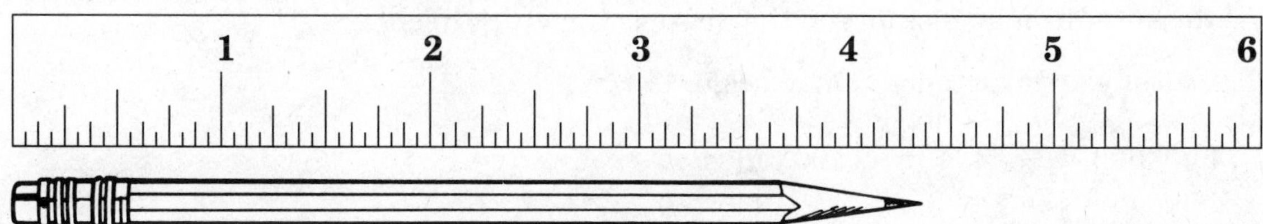

10. What is the length of the pencil to the nearest $\frac{1}{16}$ inch?

a) $4\frac{3}{8}$"
b) $4\frac{7}{16}$"
c) $4\frac{1}{2}$"

11. What is the length of the pencil to the nearest $\frac{1}{8}$ inch?

a) $4\frac{1}{4}$"
b) $4\frac{3}{8}$"
c) $4\frac{1}{2}$"

12. What is the length of the pencil to the nearest $\frac{1}{4}$ inch?

a) $4\frac{1}{4}$"
b) $4\frac{1}{2}$"
c) $4\frac{3}{4}$"

IN YOUR LIFE

Estimating Map Distances

You can use a ruler to estimate straight-line distances on a map.

The **map scale** below tells how many miles 1 inch represents.

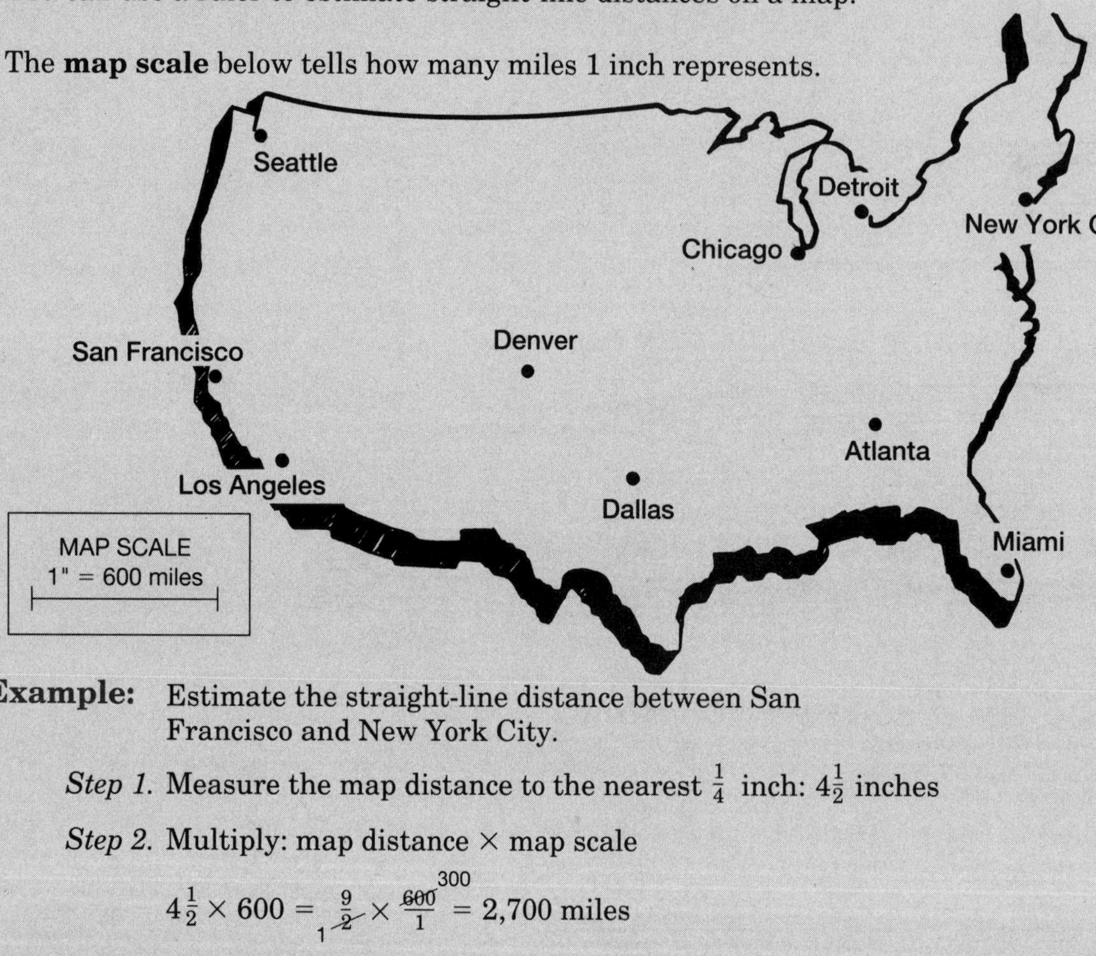

Example: Estimate the straight-line distance between San Francisco and New York City.

Step 1. Measure the map distance to the nearest $\frac{1}{4}$ inch: $4\frac{1}{2}$ inches

Step 2. Multiply: map distance × map scale

$$4\frac{1}{2} \times 600 = \frac{9}{\cancel{2}_{1}} \times \frac{\cancel{600}^{300}}{1} = 2{,}700 \text{ miles}$$

▼ Practice

Use the map above to help you answer the questions. Round your answers to the nearest mile.

1. Use a ruler or the map scale to estimate the distance between . . .

a) Seattle and Los Angeles ________
b) Denver and Chicago ________
c) New York and Miami ________
d) Atlanta and Detroit ________

2. Suppose you take a round-trip flight from Los Angeles to Atlanta.

a) Approximately how many total miles will you fly? ________
b) If your airplane flies at an average speed of 550 miles per hour, about how many total hours (to the nearest $\frac{1}{2}$ hour) will you be in the air? ________

Measuring with a Centimeter Ruler

Pictured below is a **15-centimeter ruler.** One-centimeter units are numbered 1 to 15. Each centimeter is divided into 10 millimeters.

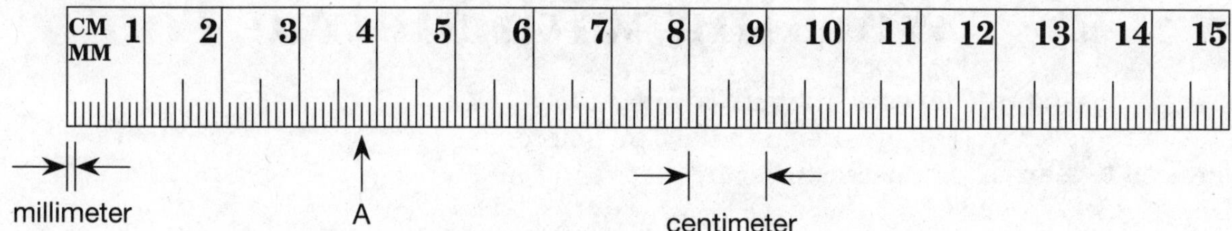

On a centimeter ruler, no fractions are used. Instead, you read a distance as a number of centimeters (cm) plus a number of millimeters (mm). For example, point A is 3 cm 8 mm from the left end of the ruler.

Because 1 cm = 10 mm, each millimeter = .1 centimeter.

3 cm 8 mm = 3.8 cm

▼ MATH TIP

To write a distance in centimeters only, write millimeters as the first number to the right of the decimal point.

Example 1: Write 4 cm 9 mm as centimeters only.

Answer: 4 cm 9 mm = 4.9 cm

Example 2: Write 7.5 cm as a number of centimeters and millimeters.

Answer: 7.5 cm = 7 cm 5 mm

▼ Practice

What is the length of each object pictured below? Express each answer on the lines provided.

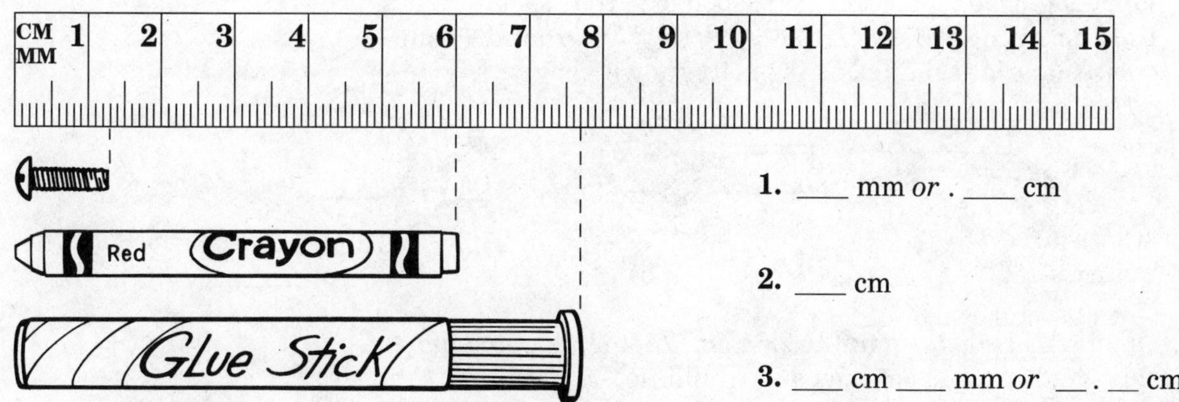

1. ____ mm *or* . ____ cm

2. ____ cm

3. ____ cm ____ mm *or* ___ . ___ cm

ON THE JOB

Working with Metric Tools

You have just been hired to work at SouthTowne Auto Repair. You've never worked on foreign-made cars before, and you need to learn about metric tools and metric nut and bolt sizes.

Your boss shows you that metric tools and nut and bolt sizes are measured in millimeters instead of fractions of an inch. The most common metric sizes are from 3 mm to 19 mm in 1 mm increments, which is about the same range of sizes as the English sizes $\frac{1}{8}$ inch to $\frac{3}{4}$ inch.

To help you gain experience, your boss has asked you to measure the following bolt heads and to label them according to size. You learn that the correct labeling of metric sizes consists of writing sizes in millimeters only. For example, a bolt head that measures 16 millimeters across is labeled 16 mm, *not* 1.6 cm.

▼ Practice

Answer the following questions.

1. Using a centimeter ruler, measure the width of each bolt head below. Write your answers on the lines provided.

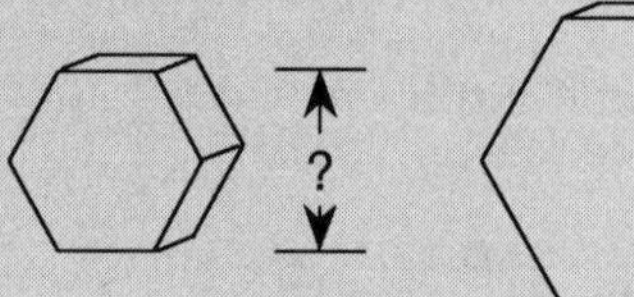

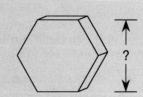

Widths: ________ ________ ________ ________ ________

2. To compare metric sizes with English sizes, try the following. Determine the metric bolt size that each English wrench below can "most closely" fit around. (Your choices **are not** limited to the bolts shown above.)

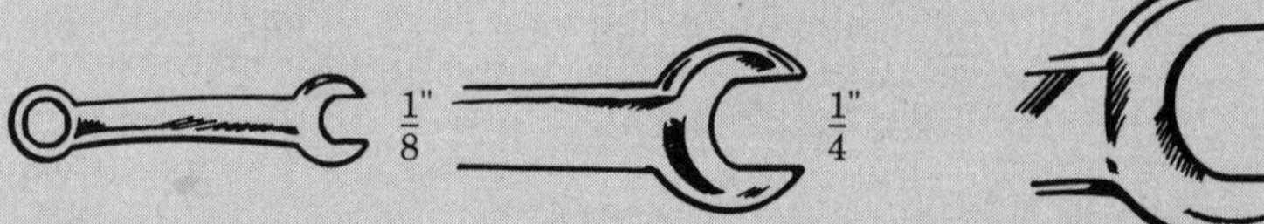

"Closest fit" metric size: **a)** ______ **b)** ______ **c)** ______

3. One inch is *exactly* equal to 2.54 cm (25.4 mm). Knowing this, determine about how many millimeters are in a distance of one foot. ____________

IN YOUR LIFE

Weighing on a Market Scale

Many people who shop for vegetables and other unpackaged foods use a **market scale** to weigh the food they're selecting. The scale pictured below may be similar to one you've seen or used.

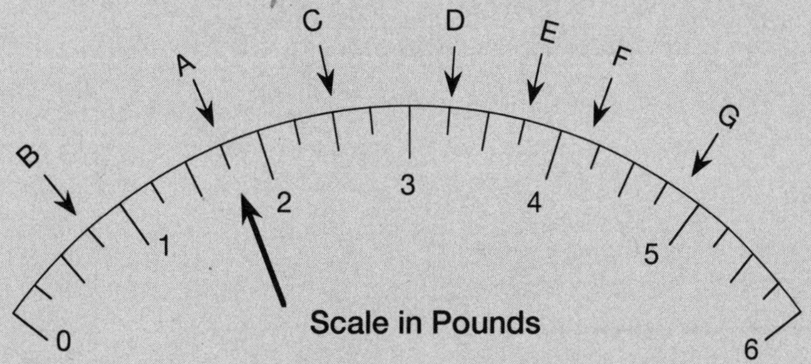

- A market scale shows weight in pounds and fractions of a pound.

On the scale above, the distance between divisions is $\frac{1}{4}$ pound. Since 1 pound = 16 ounces, each quarter pound can also be written as 4 ounces. ($\frac{1}{4} \times 16 = 4$)

Example: What weight is represented by point A?
Point A is 3 division lines, or $\frac{3}{4}$ of a pound, beyond 1 pound.

Answer: Point A is $1\frac{3}{4}$ pounds ***or*** 1 pound 12 ounces.

▼ Practice

Refer to the scale shown above to solve the following problems.

1. What weight is represented by each of the following points? Write each answer as a mixed number of pounds *and* as pounds and ounces.

B = ______ lb. or ______ oz. D = ______ lb. or ______ lb. ______ oz.

C = ______ lb. or ______ lb. ______ oz. E = ______ lb. or ______ lb. ______ oz.

2. *Estimate* the cost of each purchase below to the nearest dollar.

a) a bag of apples, whose weight is represented by point F, selling at a price of $1.12 per pound

b) several tomatoes, represented by point G, selling for $1.79 per pound

ON THE JOB

Using a Postage Scale

Curt James works at Emerson Mail Order Gifts. Part of Curt's job is to determine the postage (mailing cost) of each gift. Curt then adds the postage to the purchase price of the gift. The purchaser is billed for both the gift cost and the postage.

To determine postage, Curt weighs each wrapped gift on the postage scale below. Next, he looks at the Third-Class Rates table and reads the amount of postage. Then he adds the postage to the cost of the gift and writes the total on the customer's bill.

Postage Scale

Third-Class Rates	
0 to 1 oz.	$0.29
over 1 to 2 oz.	0.52
over 2 to 3 oz.	0.75
over 3 to 4 oz.	0.98
over 4 to 6 oz.	1.21
over 6 to 8 oz.	1.33
over 8 to 10 oz.	1.44
over 10 to 12 oz.	1.56
over 12 to 14 oz.	1.67
over 14 but less than 16 oz (1lb.)	1.79

Example: How much should a customer be billed when buying a \$3.89 mechanical pencil if the weight of the pencil is indicated by letter A?

Step 1. Read the weight represented by A, and find the postage.
Weight = $1\frac{3}{4}$ oz. (The distance between one mark and the next is $\frac{1}{4}$ oz.)
Postage = \$.52 ($1\frac{3}{4}$ oz. is "over 1 to 2 oz.")

Step 2. Add \$3.89 and \$.52.
\$3.89 + \$.52 = \$4.41

Answer: A customer would be billed \$4.41.

▼ Practice

Find the letter for each item on the scale above. Then use the scale and postage rates to complete the table. The first one has been done as an example.

Customer Billing Amounts

Item	Cost (a)	Weight	Postage (b)	Total Cost (a + b)
A. mechanical pencil	\$3.89	**$1\frac{3}{4}$ oz.**	**\$.52**	**\$4.41**
B. pocket watch	\$15.99	______	______	______
C. hand calculator	\$7.29	______	______	______
D. French perfume	\$18.75	______	______	______
E. pocket dictionary	\$12.50	______	______	______

ON THE JOB

Weighing on a Metric Scale

Tuan Yan works in an import food store. Most of the food products he sells are from countries that use the metric system. Because of this, the weight of his products is usually given in kilograms and grams.

Part of Tuan's job is to package oriental fruits and vegetables. He then weighs each package and labels it with its metric weight. This enables shoppers to compare prices with similarly weighted imported canned goods.

Tuan uses a metric scale similar to the one shown below.

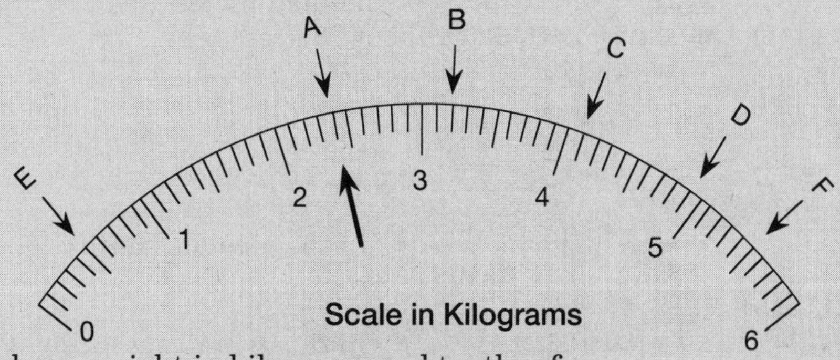

- A metric scale shows weight in kilograms and tenths of a kilogram.

On the scale above, the distance between divisions is .1 kilogram. Since 1 kilogram = 1,000 grams, .1 kilogram can also be written as 100 grams (1,000 × .1 = 100).

Example: What weight is represented by point A?
Point A is 4 division lines beyond 2 kilograms.
Four division lines are .4 kilogram.

Answer: Point A is read as 2.4 kilograms or as
2 kilograms 400 grams.

Practice

Use the scale above to help you answer the following questions.

1. What weight is represented by each of the following points? Write each answer as a mixed decimal number of kilograms *and* as kilograms and grams.

B = ______ kg or ______ kg ______ g   D = ______ kg or ______ kg ______ g

C = ______ kg or ______ kg ______ g   E = ______ kg or ______ g

2. Point F represents the weight of a bag of Asian pears. If Asian pears sell for $3.49 per kilogram, what price should Tuan charge for the bag?

IN YOUR LIFE

Using a Kitchen Scale

Pictured below is a kitchen scale—also called a diet (or dietetic) scale. This scale is used to measure the weight of a small amount of food. Many people use a kitchen scale to measure out food that's called for in a recipe. Or people on special diets use this scale to weigh food to determine the number of calories it contains.

Most kitchen scales, such as the one pictured, read a weight both in ounces (oz.) and in grams (g). Remember that a gram is equal to $\frac{1}{1,000}$ kilogram. One ounce is equal to about 28 grams.

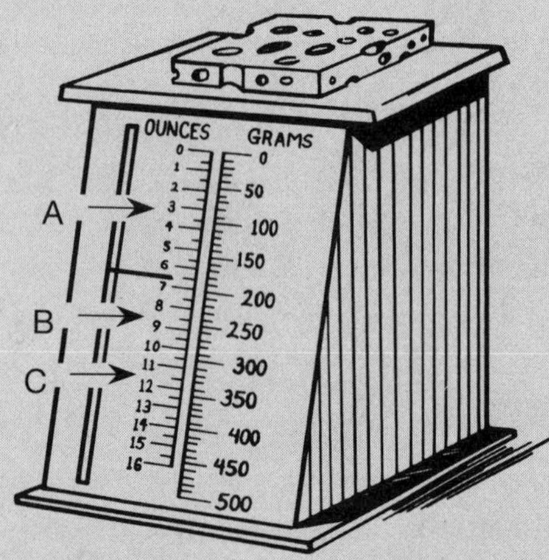

Note:

- On the **ounces scale** (left), the distance from one line to the next is $\frac{1}{2}$ ounce.
- On the **grams scale** (right), the distance from one line to the next is 10 grams.

Example: The weight of the piece of Swiss cheese can be read on both scales:

Weight: approximately $6\frac{1}{2}$ oz. or 185 grams (between 180 and 190)

▼ Practice

Use the scale above to help you answer the following questions.

1. To the nearest 50 grams, what weight in grams is equivalent to 1 pound (16 ounces)? ________

2. What weight is represented by each arrow to the left of the scale? The easiest way to read the scale for these weights is to use a ruler or piece of paper to see where each arrow would be on the scale.

A = ____ oz. or ____ g B = ____ oz. or ____ g C = ____ oz. or ____ g

3. If 1 ounce of Swiss cheese has 95 calories, how many calories are contained in the piece pictured on the scale above? Round your answer to the nearest calorie. ________

Reading a Weather Thermometer

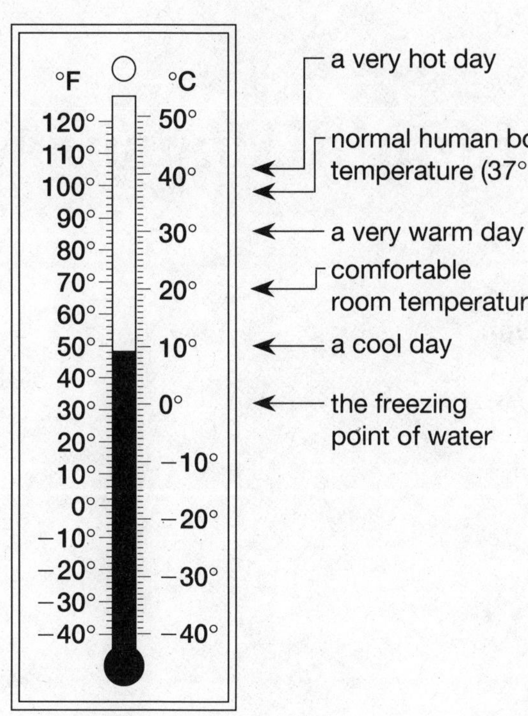

The most common type of weather thermometer is a **vertical scale** type such as the one pictured at left. This thermometer contains both **Fahrenheit** (English system) and **Celsius** (metric system) readings.

You are probably most familiar with Fahrenheit readings. However, many TV and radio weather reports now give temperatures in both degrees Fahrenheit (°F) and degrees Celsius (°C).

This page will give you a chance to become more familiar with both temperature-measuring systems.

- Not shown on the thermometer at left is the fact that water boils at 212° F which is 100° C.

▼ Practice

Circle the temperature reading that you think is correct for each activity pictured below.

1.

35° F   75° F   125° F

2.

25° F   56° F   88° F

3.

53° F   71° F   95° F

4.

0° C   25° C   40° C

5.

1° C   50° C   100° C

6.

55° F   105° F   212° F

ON THE JOB

Working with Liquid Measure

Mick Jones works at Ernie's Elm Street Service Station. A few days ago, Ernie told Mick that the station would begin to use products labeled with metric measurement. In particular, Ernie plans to sell oil by the liter instead of by the quart. And he eventually wants to sell gasoline by the liter instead of by the gallon.

To prepare Mick for these changes, Ernie wants Mick to become familiar with how the liter and milliliter compare with the gallon, quart, and fluid ounce.

Ernie said to Mick, "You'll need to understand these units pretty well. A lot of customers will know nothing about metric units! You'll probably get a lot of questions."

Ernie gave the following information to Mick. "Study this stuff," Ernie said. "This should answer at least some of your questions."

In the English system, liquid is measured in 3 main units: the **gallon,** the **quart,** and the **fluid ounce.** Here's how these units are related:

- 1 gallon = 4 quarts or 1 gal. = 4 qt.
- 1 quart = 32 fluid ounces or 1 qt. = 32 fl. oz.

Another unit, called the **pint**, is also used sometimes.

- 1 pint = $\frac{1}{2}$ quart = 16 fl. oz.

In the metric system, liquid is measured in 2 main units: the **liter** and the **milliliter**.

- 1 liter = 1,000 milliliters or 1 l = 1,000 ml

To compare the two types of measurement, it is best to compare the liter with the quart. A liter is slightly larger than a quart.

1 liter ≈ 1.06 quarts (about 6% larger than a quart)

This means that 4 liters is what you compare with a gallon.

4 liters ≈ 4.2 quarts = 1.06 gallons

A milliliter is a small amount of liquid, about $\frac{1}{30}$ of a fluid ounce.

1 fluid ounce ≈ 30 milliliters

Ernie also showed Mick the following examples:

- To change liters to quarts, multiply by 1.06.

Example 1: If a car takes 3 liters of oil for an oil change, how many quarts of oil is this equal to?

Multiply $3 \times 1.06 \approx 3.2$ quarts

- To change liters to gallons, multiply by .26.

Example 2: How many gallons of gas were put in a tank that was filled with 50 liters of gas?

Multiply $50 \times .26 = 13$ gallons

- To change milliliters to fluid ounces, divide by 30.

Example 3: How many fluid ounces of cleanser are in a 750-milliliter bottle of windshield cleaner?

Divide $750 \div 30 = 25$ fluid ounces
or 1 pint 9 fluid ounces

After several months, Ernie had made the changes, and Mick did get a lot of questions from customers.

▼ Practice

Use the information on page 154 and above to answer each of the following questions from Ernie's customers.

1. "It says here that you put 5 liters of oil in my truck. How many quarts is that?" __________
2. "75 liters of gas! My car only holds about 20 gallons when the tank is empty. How many gallons of gas did you put in there?" __________
3. "I asked for one of those 16-fluid-ounce cans of gas additive. How much does this 500-milliliter can hold?" __________
4. "Oil for $1.59 per liter! I don't even know what that means. Just tell me how much I'm paying per quart." __________
   Hint: Divide $1.59 by 1.06.
5. "When gas sells for $.38 per liter, what am I really paying for each gallon?" __________
   Hint: Multiply $.38 by 4, then divide the product by 1.06.

Becoming Familiar with Area

Area is a measure of surface. For example, to measure the size of a floor, you determine its area. The symbol for area is A.

Sample Area Unit

1 square foot

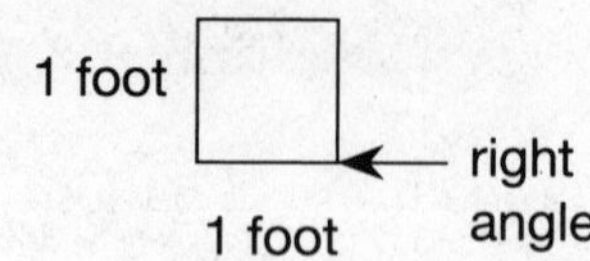

To measure area, you use an **area unit** in the shape of a square.

- A **square** has equal sides that meet at right angles.

The most common area you'll ever work with is that of a rectangle.

- A **rectangle** has two pairs of equal sides, with each two sides meeting at a right angle.

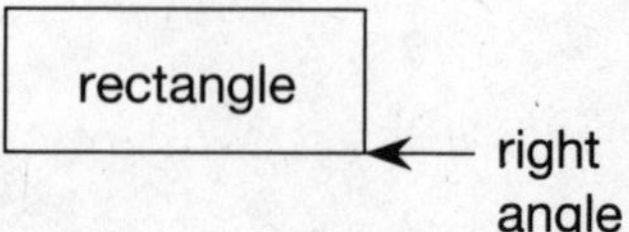

Dividing the rectangle below into 1-foot squares, you can see that its area is 24 square feet. Notice that we can get this area most easily by multiplying the length (6 feet) by the width (4 feet).

length = 6 feet

width = 4 feet

Area = length × width
Area = 6 ft. × 4 ft. = 24 square feet

- To find the area of a rectangle, multiply length by width.

▼ MATH TIP

In the English system, the common area units are the *square inch* (sq. in.), *square foot* (sq. ft.), and *square yard* (sq. yd.).

In the metric system, the common area units are the *square centimeter* (cm^2) and the *square meter* (m^2).

▼ Practice

Determine the area of each figure below. Be sure to include the correct area unit label as part of each answer. The area unit that each figure is divided into is indicated on each figure.

1. A = ____________

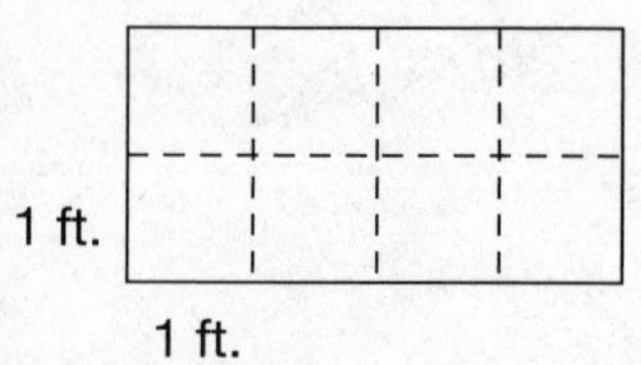

2. A = ____________

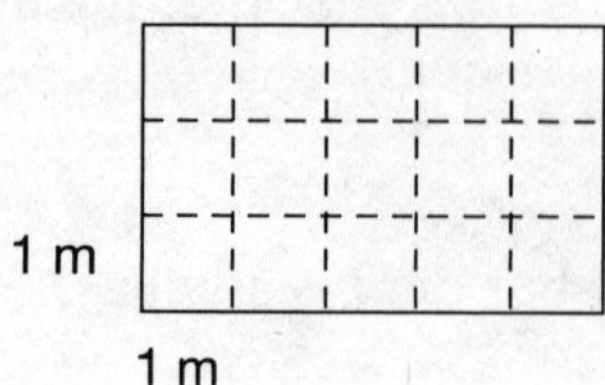

3. A = ____________

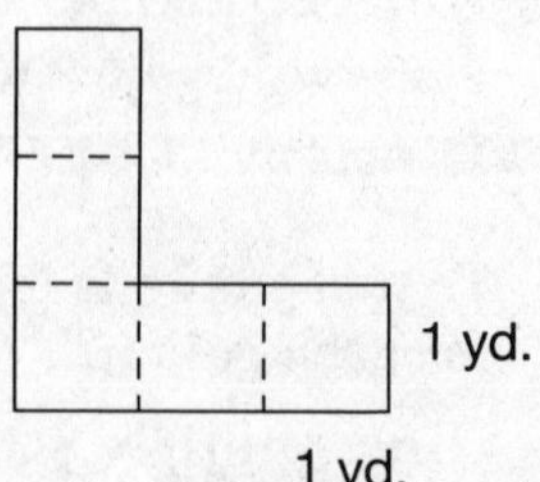

IN YOUR LIFE

Tiling a Room

Tiling a room is a home-improvement project that many people do themselves. No professional skills are needed, and tiles can be laid in a short time. Particularly easy to use are self-stick vinyl tiles that can be laid over old tile or old linoleum. Self-stick vinyl tiles cost about $1.00 per square foot.

Suppose you want to tile two rooms in your house: the spare bedroom and the family room. Sketches of these rooms are shown below.

Spare Bedroom

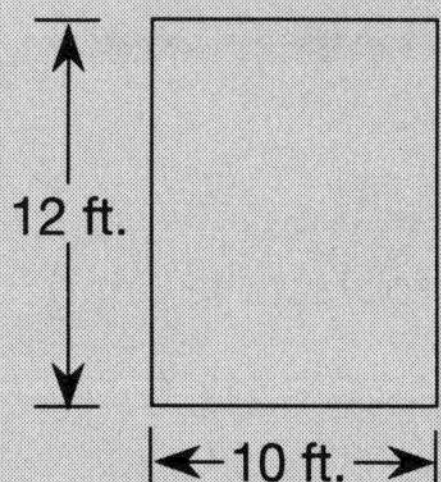

Family Room

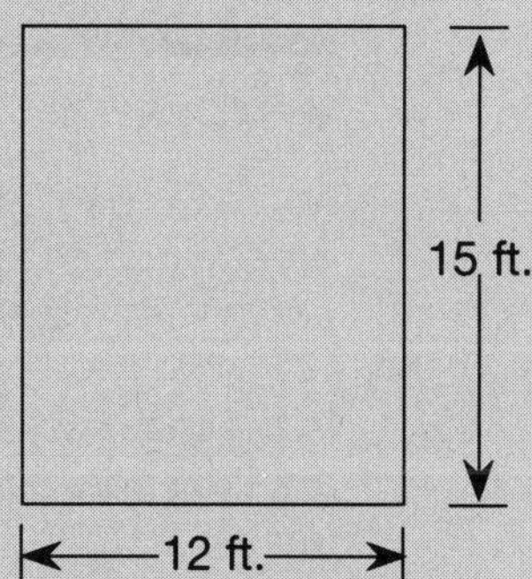

▼ Practice

Use the sketches to help you answer the questions.

1. Determine the cost of tiling the spare bedroom by answering the following questions.
   a) What is the area of floor to be tiled?____________
   b) If you use tiles that are each 1 square foot in area, how many tiles will you need?____________
   c) If you choose a tile that costs $1.09 per square foot, how much will you spend on tiles?____________
2. Determine the cost of tiling the family room by answering these questions.
   a) What is the area of flóor to be tiled?____________
   b) For this room you have chosen a tile that measures 9" by 9". How many tiles will you need?____________
   Hint: Since 9" = $\frac{3}{4}$ ft., each tile has an area of $\frac{3}{4} \times \frac{3}{4} = \frac{9}{16}$ sq. ft.
   c) If you pay $.98 for each tile, how much will it cost you to tile the family room?____________

▼ MATH TIP

To determine how many tiles are needed, divide the area of the floor to be tiled by the area of a single piece of tile being used.

9 in. = $\frac{3}{4}$ ft.

$\frac{3}{4}$ ft.

$\frac{3}{4}$ ft.

Area

$\frac{9}{16}$ sq. ft.

Becoming Familiar with Volume

Volume is a measure of space. For example, volume is the space taken up by a solid object such as a brick. Volume is also the space enclosed by a solid surface. The volume of a box is the space enclosed by its top, its sides, and its bottom. The symbol for volume is V.

To measure volume, you use a **volume unit** in the shape of a cube.

- A **cube** has 6 surfaces called faces. Each face is a square.

Sample Volume Unit

1 cubic yard

1 yd.
1 yd.
1 yd.

The most common volume you'll ever work with is that of a **rectangular solid**—a fancy name for familiar shapes such as boxes, suitcases, books, and rooms!

Below is a rectangular solid divided into 24 cubic feet. Notice that we can find this volume most easily by multiplying the length (4 feet) by the width (2 feet) by the height (3 feet).

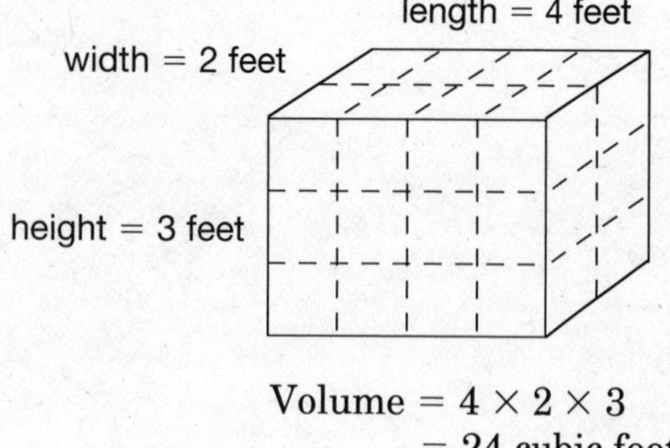

Volume $= 4 \times 2 \times 3$
$= 24$ cubic feet

▼ MATH TIP

In the English system, the common volume units are the *cubic inch* (cu. in.), *cubic foot* (cu. ft.), and *cubic yard* (cu. yd.).

In the metric system, the common volume units are the *cubic centimeter* (cm^3) and the *cubic meter* (m^3).

- **To find the volume of a rectangular solid, multiply the length by the width by the height.**

▼ Practice

Determine the volume of each figure below. Be sure to include the correct volume unit label as part of each answer. The volume unit that each figure is divided into is indicated on each figure.

1. V = ___________

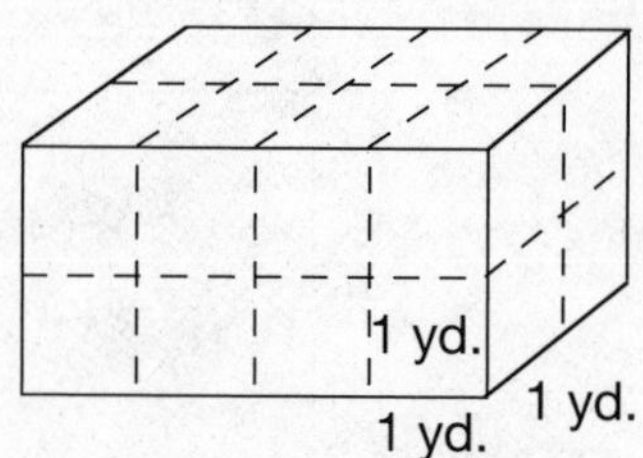

2. V = ___________

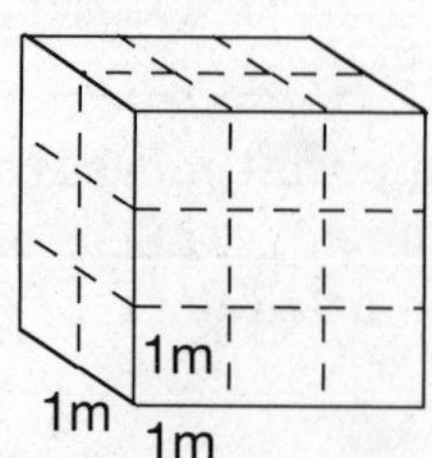

3. V = ___________

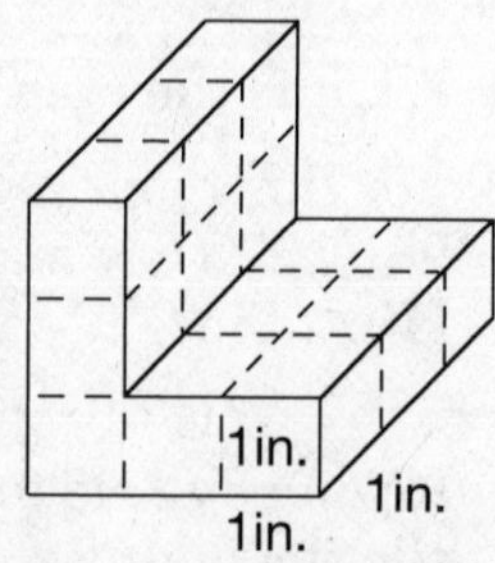

IN YOUR LIFE

Buying Soil for a Lawn

Lin Li is going to put a lawn around her house. To do this, she must put a 4-inch layer of topsoil on the dirt that is there now.

Lin learns that soil is sold by the cubic yard. Before she orders, she must estimate the total number of cubic yards of topsoil she needs.

A sketch of Lin's property is shown below.

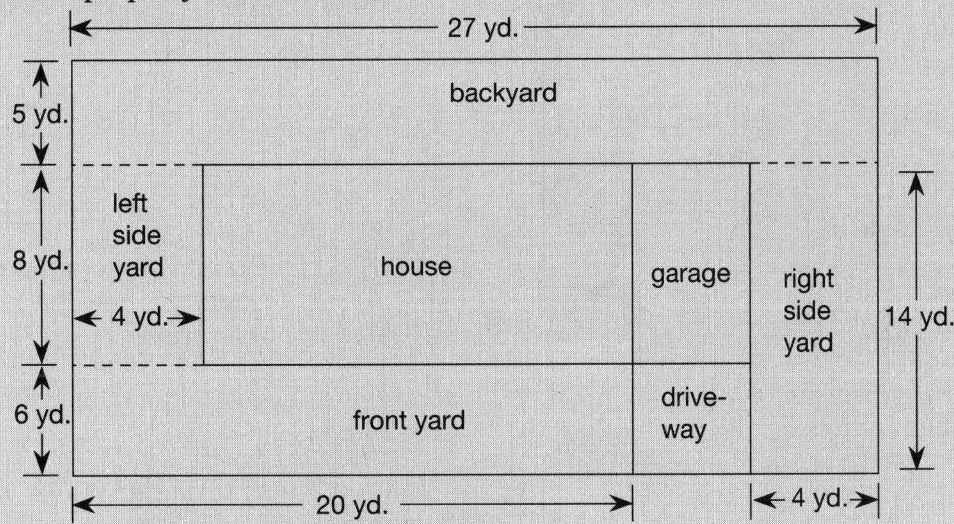

Example: To compute how much topsoil she needs for the left side yard, Lin multiplies as follows:

left side yard = length × width × depth

$= 8 \text{ yd.} \times 4 \text{ yd.} \times \frac{1}{9} \text{ yd.}$ (since 4 in. $= \frac{4}{36}$ yd. $= \frac{1}{9}$ yd.)

$= \frac{8}{1} \times \frac{4}{1} \times \frac{1}{9} = \frac{32}{9}$

$= 3\frac{5}{9}$

Answer: She needs $3\frac{5}{9}$ cubic yards.

▼ Practice

Use the sketch to help you answer the questions.

1. Complete the list at right started by Lin to determine the total amount of topsoil she needs to order.

2. If she pays $9 per cubic yard of topsoil (including delivery), how much will Lin pay for the topsoil she needs?__________

Volume of Soil Needed

left side yard	$3\frac{5}{9}$
right side yard	______
front yard	______
backyard	______
TOTAL:	______

UNIT SIX

Data Analysis

Graphs and charts frequently appear in newspapers and magazines.

"Look at what it says in today's paper, Ed. The town referendum results are in, and it looks like people have finally decided to make recycling mandatory."

Ed peered over his brother David's shoulder and studied the newspaper carefully. "Where does it say that? I read the paper this morning, and all it said was that people voted on a lot of different issues. The results weren't given."

"You must not have looked at these charts and graphs on page two. It shows right here that 72% of the voters voted in favor of the recycling plan. It's about time. Now maybe the town can save some money on waste removal."

"Wait a minute. How did you get 72% in favor of recycling from that graph?"

"You just find where the recycling issue is listed on the graph, find which bar indicates yes votes, and follow that bar up and across to the percentage marks."

"Got it. So that means that, according to the graph, people also voted in favor of the wage increase for fire fighters. I knew the town would support them," said Ed.

Think About It

- Why didn't Ed know the referendum results?
- How did Ed figure out the result of the vote on the fire fighters' wages?
- Why do you think the newspaper printed a graph instead of including all the numbers in the article?

How Do Graphs and Data Play a Part in *Your* Life?

"Data" simply refers to a collection of numbers. A graph is just a picture of those numbers that usually makes the numbers easier to understand. Answer the following questions to learn more about the data and graphs in your day-to-day life.

Think about where you usually see graphs and charts. Give two or three reasons why these formats might be used instead of just words.

____

____

____

____

____

Open a newspaper or magazine and find a graph or chart. What is the title of the graph or chart? ________________

What values does the graph or chart show (time, years, percents, etc.)? ________________________

Why do you think the graph or chart is used there? __________

____

Take a few minutes and try constructing a graph of your own.

1. Plot a point above each day listed on the graph. Each point should show how many hours you slept each night last week.

2. Connect all the data points with a line.

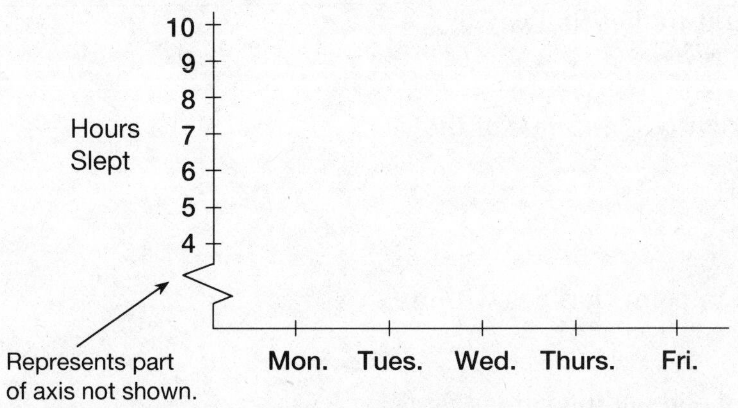

Now take some time to think about the information you have graphed. Can you draw any interesting conclusions?

Skills You Will Learn

Data Analysis Skills

- interpolating
- extrapolating
- computing the mean
- determining the median
- computing a ratio

Reading Graphs

- reading tables
- reading a bar graph
- reading a line graph
- reading a circle graph

Life and Workplace Skills

- choosing clothes from a catalog
- bar graphs in business
- using a line graph at home
- thinking about a family budget
- drawing a bar graph

Thinking Skills

- using more than one data source
- drawing conclusions from data
- constructing graphs

Numerical Data

Data analysis is the study and use of **numerical data.**

- Numerical data is a group (often called a **set**) of numbers (called **data points**) that are related in some way.

Example 1: the set of numbers that stand for the ages of all the students in a math class

The table at right consists of a set of six data points.

Data Points

Men	Women
23 years	19 years
34 years	29 years
57 years	43 years

Data analysis is used in home life, schools, businesses, and government agencies. You use data analysis yourself when you count the change in your pocket to see how much you can spend for lunch.

Interpolation

Sometimes you want information not specifically given by data points. However, the number you want may fall *between* two given data points.

When this happens, you **interpolate.**

- To interpolate is to *estimate* the value of a data point that lies between two known data points.

Example 2: Referring to the table at right, determine the *approximate* temperature at 3:30 P.M. on Monday.

To estimate the 3:30 temperature, notice that 3:30 lies halfway between 3:00 and 4:00. Ask yourself, "What temperature lies halfway between 92° F and 88° F?"

The answer, 90° F, is your *best estimate* of the 3:30 temperature.

Answer: estimate—90° F.

Monday Afternoon Temperatures

1:00	2:00	3:00	4:00	5:00
93° F	95° F	92° F	88° F	84° F

Interpolation is used to estimate a data point that lies within the **range** of your given data points.

- The range consists of the beginning and ending values that make up your data.

In Example 2, the range is from 84°–95° Monday afternoon.

Extrapolation

Sometimes you may want to know a number that falls *outside* the range of your given data points.

When this happens, you **extrapolate**.

- To extrapolate is to *estimate* the value of a data point that lies outside the range of your given data.

Example 3: Refer again to the table in Example 2. What is the approximate temperature at 6:00 P.M. on Monday?

To estimate the 6:00 temperature, look at the temperature pattern during the time from 3:00–5:00. As shown at right, *the pattern is a decrease of 4° F each hour.*

Ask yourself, "If this pattern continues, what will be the temperature at 6:00 P.M.?" To find out, subtract 4° F from 84° F.

The answer, 80° F, is your *best estimate* of the 6:00 temperature.

Answer: estimate—80° F

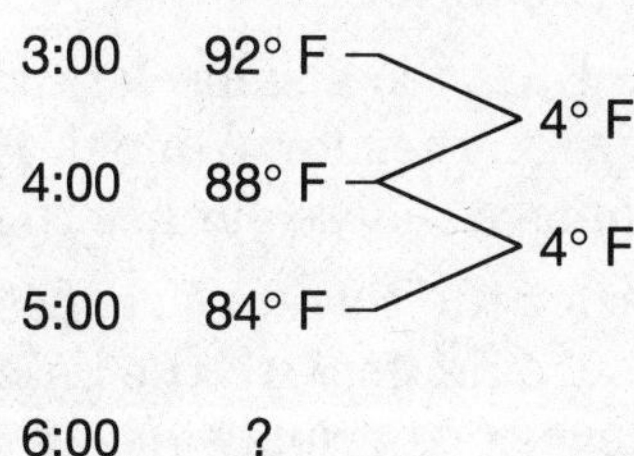

▼ Practice

Problems 1–4 refer to Table 1 at right.

1. What is the most desirable weight for a 5'8" man of average build? _________
2. Using interpolation, determine the most desirable weight for a 6'1" man of small build. _________
3. What is the height range for men for which data points are given? ____' ____" to ____' ____"
4. Using extrapolation, determine the most desirable weight for a 6'4" man of average build. _________

TABLE 1

Desirable Weight for Men
(pounds, without clothing)

Height	Small Build	Average Build	Large Build
5'4"	122	133	145
5'6"	130	142	155
5'8"	139	151	166
5'10"	147	159	174
6'	154	167	183
6'2"	162	175	192
6'4"	170		

Problems 5–8 refer to Table 2 at right.

5. What is the most desirable weight for a 5'6" woman of large build? _________
6. Using interpolation, determine the most desirable weight for a 5'1" woman of average build. _________
7. What is the height range for women for which data points are given? ____' ____" to ____' ____"
8. Using extrapolation, determine the most desirable weight for a 6'2" woman of large build. _________

TABLE 2

Desirable Weight for Women
(pounds, without clothing)

Height	Small Build	Average Build	Large Build
5'	100	109	118
5'2"	107	115	125
5'4"	113	122	132
5'6"	120	129	139
5'8"	126	136	146
5'10"	133	144	156
6'	141	152	166

ON THE JOB

Choosing Clothes from a Catalog

Elsie Busby is a salesclerk in the catalog department of Joan's Clothes for Women. Part of Elsie's job is to help customers choose clothes that fit comfortably.

To order the correct size, Elsie compares a woman's measurements with the listed catalog sizes shown below. However, experience has taught Elsie that women tend to have measurements that are not exactly those listed. For best fit, Elsie always recommends a size in which no single measurement is too small—even if one or more measurements are slightly large. Elsie knows that it is the tight-fitting clothes that get returned!

Women's Regular—fits 5'4" to 5'7"

	X-Small	Small		Medium		Large		X-Large
Sizes →	4	6	8	10	12	14	16	18
bust	32	33	34	35	36	38	40	42
waist	24	25	26	27	28	30	32	34
hips	35	36	37	38	39	41	43	45
sleeve	28	29	29	30	30	31	31	32

Women's Petite—fits 4'11" to 5'3"

	X-Small	Small		Medium		Large
Sizes →	4	6	8	10	12	14
bust	32	33	34	35	36	38
waist	24	25	26	27	28	30
hips	35	36	37	38	39	41
sleeve	26	27	28	28	29	29

▼ Practice

Use the tables above to help you answer the questions.

1. Jennie, who is 5'6" tall, wants to order a dress.

a) Should she order petite or regular?__________

b) Given Jennie's measurements at right, what size would Elsie recommend?__________

2. Sandi, who is 5'3$\frac{1}{2}$" tall, is also ordering a dress. What size would Elsie recommend? (Choose the size and whether Sandi should order petite or regular.)______________

Jennie
Bust: 36
Waist: 29$\frac{1}{2}$
Hips: 41
Sleeve: 31

Sandi
Bust: 36
Waist: 27$\frac{1}{2}$
Hips: 38
Sleeve: 29$\frac{1}{2}$

The Language of Data Analysis

Three words that are often used in data analysis are *mean, median,* and *ratio.* We'll discuss the definition and use of each word on these next three pages.

Mean

Mean is another word for **average.** You may already know the two steps used to find the average of a set of numbers:

- First, compute the sum of the set.
- Second, divide this sum by the number of numbers in the set.

Example: Find the mean (average) of the following amounts: $74.50, $68.90, $71.35, $77.85

Step 1. Compute the sum of the set.

```
 $74.50
  68.90
  71.35
+ 77.85
-------
$292.60
```

Step 2. Divide this sum by 4.

```
      $ 73.15
   4)$292.60
   ↑ - 28
   |    12
   |  - 12
   |     0 6
   |     - 4
   |      20
   |    - 20
numbers in the set
```

Answer: $73.15

▼ Practice

A. You are working as a nurse's aide in a hospital. You've been asked to solve the following problems.

1. Find and record the average temperature of each patient during the 3-hour period listed on the chart below. Round your answers to the nearest tenth.

2. Estimate what Stacey's temperature was at 11:30 A.M. __________

3. Estimate what Bill's temperature will most likely be at 1:00 P.M. Assume his temperature continues to decrease at the same rate it has been decreasing. __________

Temperature Chart

Name	9:00 A.M.	10:00 A.M.	11:00 A.M.	12:00 Noon	Average (nearest .1° F)
Frank	101.6° F	102.8° F	103.4° F	102.0° F	________
Janessa	99.7° F	100.2° F	101.5° F	101.4° F	________
Stacey	102.9° F	103.1° F	102.4° F	100.6° F	________
Bill	104.4° F	103.2° F	102.0° F	100.8° F	________

Median

The **median** of a set of numbers is the middle value.

- **If a set contains an odd number of numbers, the median is the middle number.**
- **If a set contains an even number of numbers, the median is the average of the two middle numbers.**

Example 1: Find the median of the following amounts: $1.25, $1.10, $1.38, $1.19, $1.63

Step 1. Arrange the numbers in order, with the smallest number first.

Step 2. Since there is an odd number (5) of numbers, the median is the middle number.

$1.10
$1.19
$1.25 ← middle number = median
$1.38
$1.63

Answer: median = $1.25

Example 2: What is the median of the following weights: 12 lb., 9 lb., 11 lb., 8 lb.

Step 1. Arrange the numbers in order, with the smallest number first.

8, 9, 11, 12

Step 2. Since there is an even number (4) of numbers, the median is the average of the two middle numbers.

Median is the average of the two middle numbers.
9 + 11 = 20
20 ÷ 2 = 10 ← median

Answer: median = 10 lb.

▼ Practice

B. You are working as a teacher's aide in a 7th-grade class. You've been asked to solve the following problems.

1. Find the median test score for the group of 4 or 5 students who took each test indicated below.

2. a) For comparison, compute the average score of the math test.

b) Does this answer tell you why the teacher would rather know the median than the average?

Name	Math	Science	Social Studies	English
Lola	28	32	38	
Fran	30		41	37
Jess	29	31	40	38
Arnie	32	38	39	41
Louise	50	48	45	47
MEDIAN	_____	_____	_____	_____

Ratio

A **ratio** is a comparison of two numbers. For example the ratio of *women to men* on the list at right is 4 to 3.

Class List	
Women	Men
Joyce	Alan
Mary	Ben
Alicia	Abe
Lucina	

A ratio can be written in symbols in two ways:

- With a colon, the ratio 4 to 3 is written 4:3.
- As a fraction, the ratio 4 to 3 is written $\frac{4}{3}$.

In words, a ratio is always read with the word *to*. The ratios 4:3 and $\frac{4}{3}$ are both read as "4 to 3."

▼ **MATH TIP**

A ratio is usually reduced to lowest terms. However, a ratio that is an improper fraction like $\frac{4}{3}$ is not changed to a mixed number.

When you write a ratio, write the numbers in the same order as asked for in the question.

- Although the ratio of women to men is 4 to 3, the ratio of *men to women* is 3 to 4 (3:4 or $\frac{3}{4}$).

Example: A new car gets 24 miles per gallon during city driving and 36 miles per gallon during highway driving. What is the ratio of highway mileage to city mileage?

Step 1. Write highway mileage as the numerator of the ratio fraction because it is mentioned first in the question.

$$\frac{36}{24} = \frac{\text{highway mileage}}{\text{city mileage}}$$

Step 2. Reduce the ratio fraction $\frac{36}{24}$.

$$\frac{36 \div 12}{24 \div 12} = \frac{3}{2}$$

Answer: 3:2 or $\frac{3}{2}$

▼ Practice

C. You are working at Friendly Shoe Store. Your supervisor asks you to solve the following problems.

1. Compute the profit made on each model of running shoe.

2. Compute the average profit of the 5 models listed.

3. Determine the median profit of the 5 models listed.

4. Determine the ratio of the selling price of model A to that of model B.

5. Determine the ratio of the profit of model B to that of model E.

6. Determine the ratio of the profit of the most profitable shoe to that of the least profitable shoe.

Running Shoes

Model	Selling Price (a)	Store's Cost (b)	Profit (a − b)
A	$60.00	$40.00	______
B	$52.00	$36.00	______
C	$48.00	$34.00	______
D	$40.00	$25.00	______
E	$30.00	$18.00	______

Reading a Bar Graph

A **graph** is a visual display of information. As a picture, a graph lets you get a quick idea about the data being shown. It also lets you compare data points quickly.

A **bar graph** gets its name from the bars that it uses to show data. These bars may be drawn vertically (up and down) or horizontally (across).

Numerical values are read along numbered **axes** that make up the sides of the graph.

- You read a value for each bar by finding the number on the **axis** that is across from the end of the bar.

Example: Below is a bar graph showing the growth of the population of the United States.

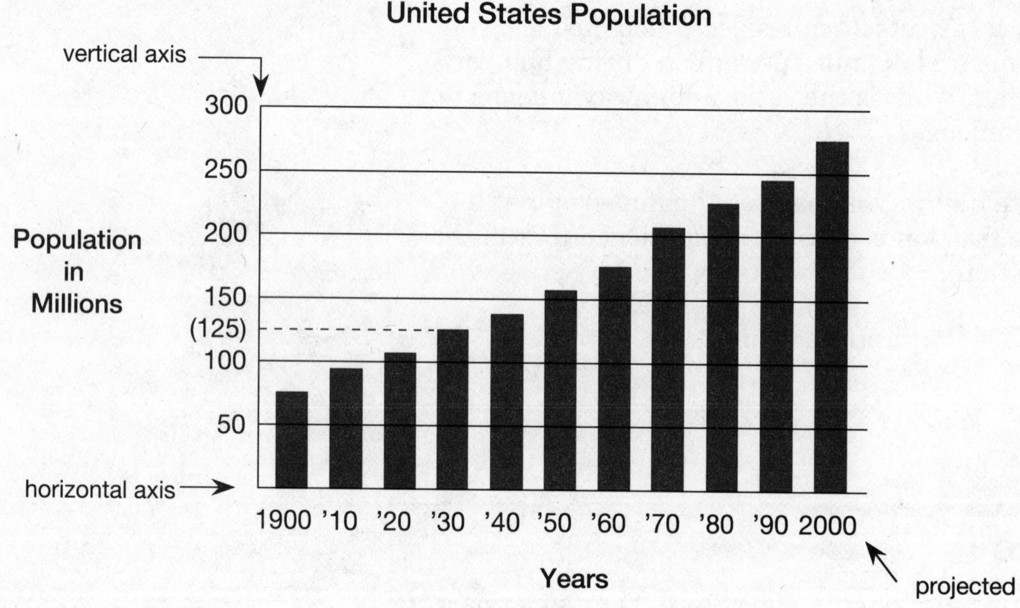

Questions about bar graphs usually ask you to find a specific value or to compare one value with another.

Sample Questions	**Answers**
1. What was the population of the United States in 1930?	**1.** First, locate the bar that is above the year 1930. Then look directly left from the top of the bar. On the vertical axis, you'll read that the 1930 population is between 100 and 150 million, or **about 125 million.**
2. What is the approximate ratio of the 1990 population to the 1900 population?	**2.** To compute this ratio, divide the approximate 1990 population (250) by the approximate 1900 population (75). **Ratio** $= \frac{250}{75} = \frac{10}{3}$ **or 10:3**

ON THE JOB

Bar Graphs in Business

Imagine that you work in an office at Blue Dolphin Toy Company. At the end of each year, you take the monthly sales figures for the year and construct a bar graph. You then give the graph to your boss, who's very interested in the overall sales picture.

Here is the graph you constructed to show last year's sales.

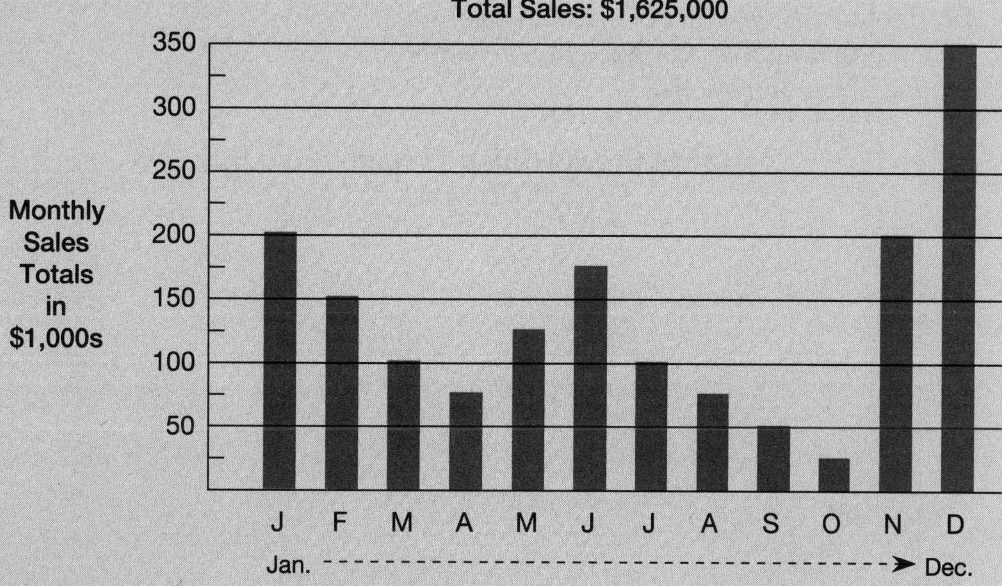

▼ Practice

Use the graph to help you answer the questions.

1. To the *nearest $1,000*, what is the *mean* monthly sales amount? __________
   Hint: Mean monthly sales = total sales ÷ 12.
2. What are the monthly sales totals for the best and the worst months?
   Best month: __________ **Worst month:** __________
3. To the *nearest $1,000*, what is the *mean* monthly sales amount during the 3-month Christmas season of November, December, and January? __________
4. What two months are the peak sales months for the two main sales seasons?
   Christmas Season: __________ **Summer Season:** __________
5. What is the *ratio* of December sales to June sales? __________
6. What is the *median* monthly sales amount for the entire year? __________

Reading a Line Graph

A **line graph** gets its name from the thin line that it uses to show data.

- Because every point on the line has a value, a line graph can be used to show continuous changes in data.

Like a bar graph, a line graph has numbered **axes.** The value of each point on the line is read as two numbers, one taken from each axis.

Example: Below is a growth chart that shows how the weight of an averaged-size boy changes between birth and age 10.

Dotted lines drawn from a point on the line indicate that an average-sized 5-year-old boy weighs about 35 pounds.

▼ **MATH TIP**

Use the corner of a piece of paper to help determine where points on the line are to be read on each scale.

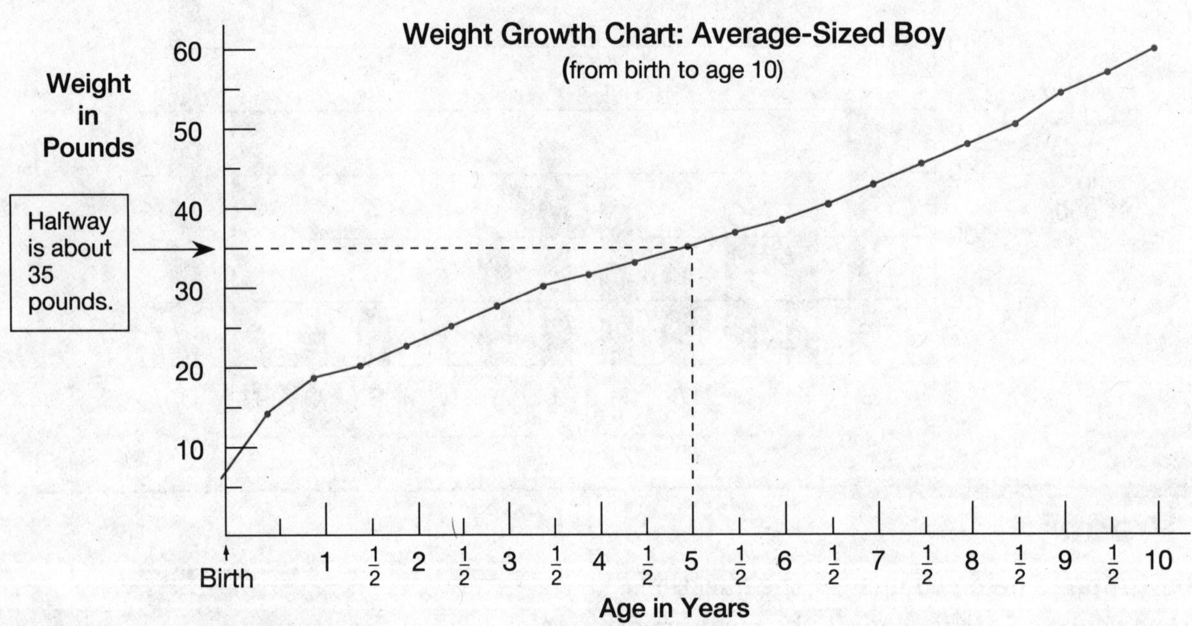

Questions about line graphs usually are concerned with changes in data as you move from left to right across the graph.

Sample Questions	**Answers**
1. During which year does a boy's weight increase most rapidly?	**1.** Look for the year during which the line on the graph is rising most rapidly (is the steepest). **Answer:** from birth to age 1
2. What is the approximate ratio of a boy's weight at age 1 to his birth weight?	**2.** To compute this ratio, put the weight at age 1 over the birth weight. **Answer:** ratio $= \frac{18}{6} = \frac{3}{1}$ or 3:1

IN YOUR LIFE

Recording Growth

On his daughter's birthday each year, Marty records Angelina's height on a line graph. The line graph is part of a medical file that Marty was given at the time of Angelina's first visit to the baby doctor.

The dots shown on the graph stand for the only heights Marty actually measured. However, by connecting each pair of dots with a straight line, Marty has made a continuous record of Angelina's growth. Marty can estimate Angelina's height at any age simply by reading a point on the line above that age. (This is an example of interpolation on a line graph.)

Example: As the dotted lines on the graph show, Angelina's height at age $3\frac{1}{2}$ is approximately 40 in.

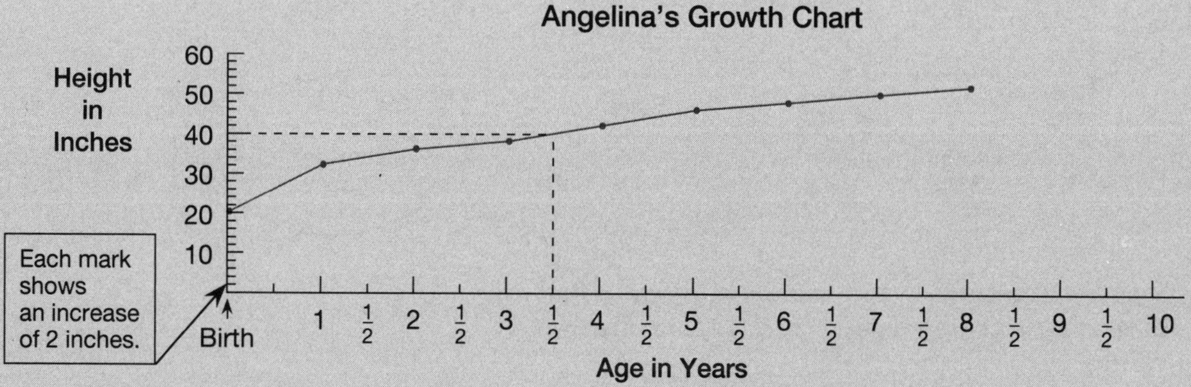

▼ Practice

Use the graph to answer the following questions.

1. To the nearest inch, how tall was Angelina on her 8th birthday? ___________
2. To the nearest inch, how much did Angelina grow between the day she was born and the day she turned 6? ___________
3. To the nearest inch, what was Angelina's height at age 6 months? ___________
4. What is the approximate ratio of Angelina's height at age 5 to her height at birth? ___________
5. Assuming her present growth pattern continues, estimate to the nearest inch how tall Angelina will be on her 10th birthday. ___________

   Hint: To extrapolate on a line graph:
   - Extend the graph by continuing the line in its same direction.
   - Read extrapolated data points from the extended line.

Reading a Circle Graph

A **circle graph** is drawn as a divided circle. Each **segment** (part) is given a name and value. The whole circle represents all (100%) of the data being displayed. Circle graphs are commonly used to display budgets for businesses and families.

- In the most common circle graph, like Graph A below, each segment is given a percent value. The sum of all segments adds up to 100%.
- In a second type, like Graph B below, each segment is given a number of cents as a value. Here the sum of segments adds up to $1.00.

Examples:

Graph A: MLX Corporation Sales
(Total Sales: $400,000)

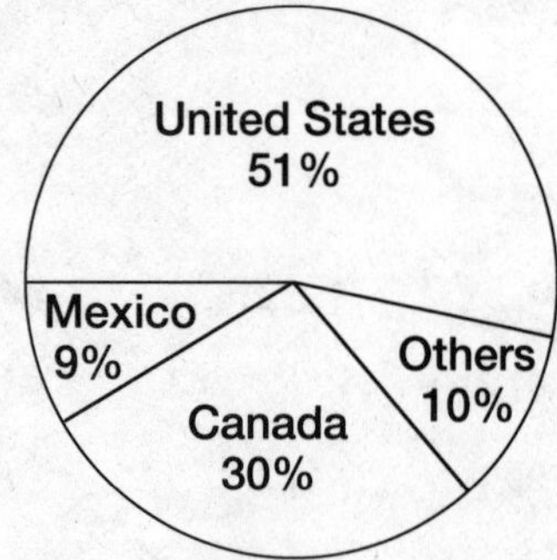

Breakdown per $1.00 of Sales

Graph B: Bly Company, Inc., Sales
(Total Sales: $750,000)

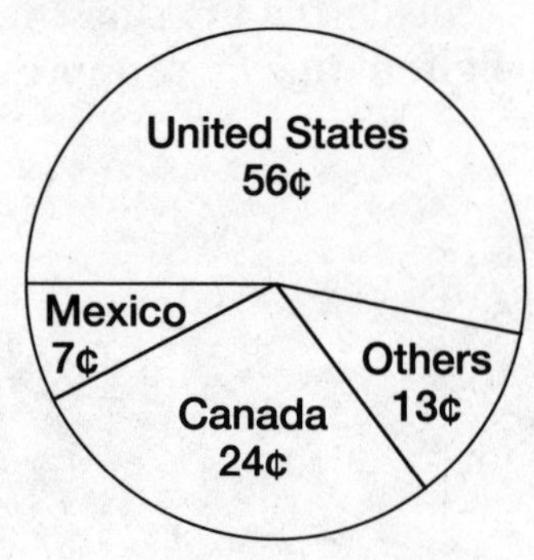

Questions about a circle graph usually ask you to find an amount of money, to find a percent, or to compare two or more values.

Sample Questions

Graph A

1. How much more of its sales (in percent) does MLX make in Canada than in Mexico?

2. What amount of money did MLX earn in sales in the United States?

Graph B

3. What percent of Bly Company's sales were made in Canada?

4. What dollar amount of sales was made in Canada?

Answers

Graph A

1. Subtract the Mexico percent (9%) from the Canada percent (30%).
Answer: 21%

2. To find the answer, compute 51% of $400,000.
Answer: $204,000

Graph B

3. See the segment labeled "Canada." 24¢ out of each sales dollar means that 24% of all sales were made in Canada.
Answer: 24%

4. Compute 24% of $750,000
Answer: $180,000

IN YOUR LIFE

Thinking about a Budget

Alison and Wendell Lewis are worried about money. They never seem to have any left over after paying their bills! After reading an article in a "Money Advice" column, they decided to take a closer look at their spending habits. As a guide, the article showed a "suggested" family budget. The article showed the following two graphs.

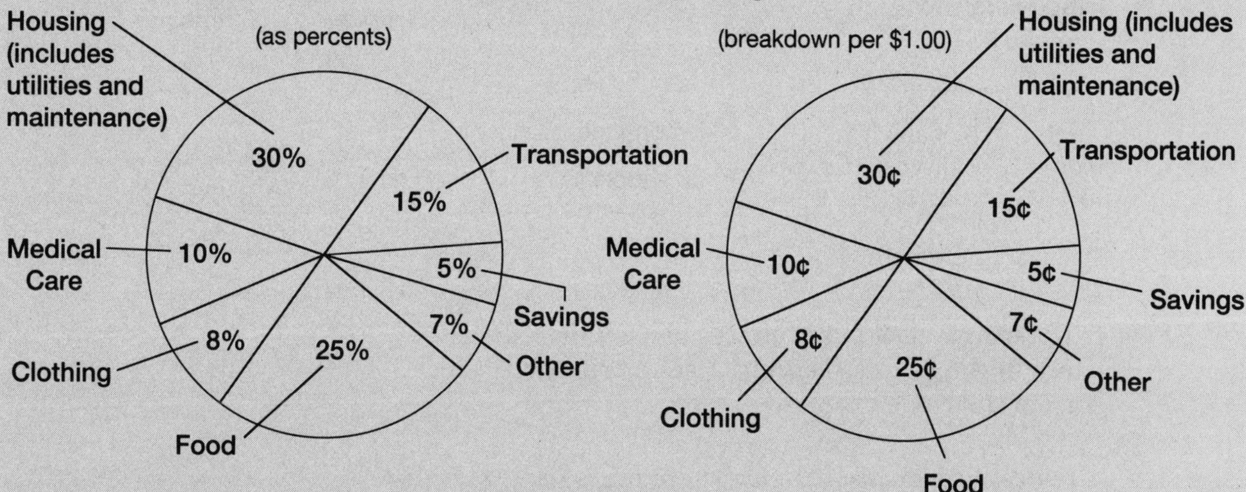

Alison and Wendell estimated the amount of money that they spent last year in each area identified on the graphs.

total spendable income:	$20,000	medical care:	$2,000
housing:	$5,000	clothing:	$3,000
transportation:	$2,500	savings:	0!
food:	$5,000	other:	$2,500

• "Other" includes entertainment and personal expenses.

▼ Practice

Use the graphs to help you answer the questions.

1. What percent of their income is spent in each area identified on the graphs?
housing: _____ % transportation: _____ % food: _____ % medical care: _____ %
clothing: _____ % savings: _____ % other: _____ %

2. a) In which two areas do Alison and Wendell spend more than the suggested percents ? _______________ and _______________

b) How much more (in dollars) do they spend each year in each of these two areas than would be recommended by the graphs?

__________ __________

Using More than One Data Source

Sometimes you may want to know something that you're not able to find on just one table or graph. In this case, you may need to take information from more than one data source.

Example: As a worker in a diet center, you've been asked, "How many calories are contained in an 8-ounce serving of party punch?"

Here's the information available to you:

Party Punch Recipe

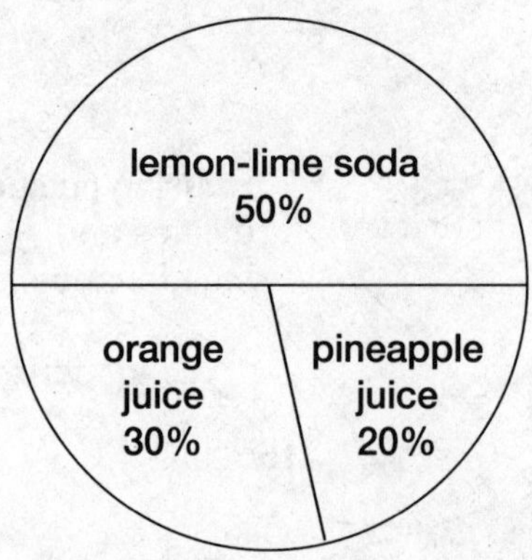

Nutrition Information

	Calories (per Ounce)	Carbohydrates (Grams per Ounce)
orange juice	14	3.5
lemon-lime soda	12	2.5
pineapple juice	17	4.3

Step 1. Determine how many ounces of each ingredient are in the 8-ounce serving. Use information from the circle graph to find out.

ounces of ingredient = *percent of ingredient* × *8 ounces*

<u>Amount</u> <u>of</u>:

orange juice = 30% × 8 = 2.4 ounces
lemon-lime soda = 50% × 8 = 4.0 ounces
pineapple juice = 20% × 8 = 1.6 ounces

Step 2. Using information from the table, compute the number of calories in the amount of each ingredient present in an 8-ounce serving.

number of calories = *calories per ounce* × *number of ounces*

<u>Calories</u> <u>of</u>:

orange juice = 14 × 2.4 = 33.6 calories
lemon-lime soda = 12 × 4.0 = 48.0 calories
pineapple juice = 17 × 1.6 = 27.2 calories

Answer: Total calories = 33.6 + 48.0 + 27.2 = 108.8 ≈ 109 calories.

▼ Practice

Use the graph and table on page 174 to solve problems 1–2.

1. Fill in the table at right as you answer the following questions.

   a) How many ounces of each ingredient are in a 12-ounce serving of party punch?

   b) How many calories of each ingredient are in a 12-ounce serving?

   c) How many total calories are in a 12-ounce serving?

12-Ounce Serving of Party Punch

Ingredient	Ounces	Calories
orange juice	______	______
lemon-lime soda	______	______
pineapple juice	______	______
	TOTAL CALORIES:	______

2. To the nearest $\frac{1}{10}$ gram, how many grams of *carbohydrates* are contained in a *10-ounce* serving of party punch?
   Hint: Write a table similar to the table in problem 1.

Now pretend you're working in a fitness center. You've taken heart-rate data on Fred Elling as shown on the bar graph. Using this bar graph and the line graph showing oxygen usage rate, solve problems 3–5.

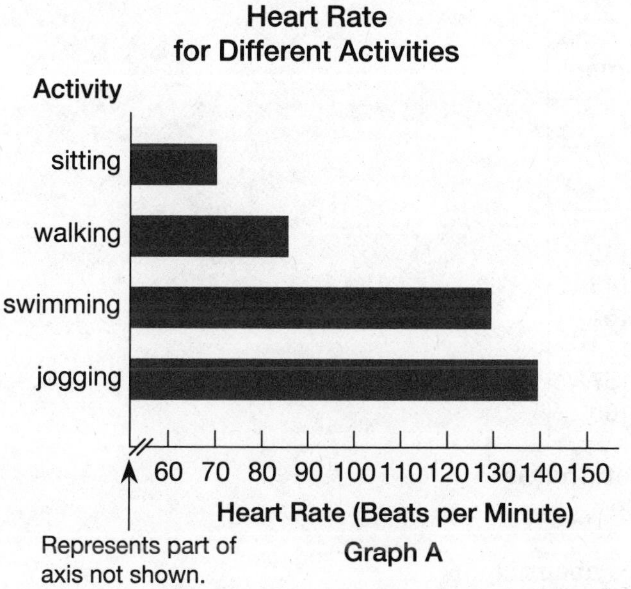

Graph A

Oxygen Usage Rate
(Measured for Different Heart Rates)

Oxygen Usage (Liters per Minute)
2.0 1.8 1.6 1.4 1.2 1.0 0.8 0.6 0.4 0.2
60 70 80 90 100 110 120 130 140 150
Heart Rate (beats per minute)

Graph B

3. To the nearest $\frac{1}{10}$ liter per minute, how much oxygen does Fred use as he does each activity?
   Hint: Find Fred's heart rate from the bar graph (A), then find his oxygen usage rate from the line graph (B).

Activity	Heart Rate (Graph A)	Oxygen Use (Graph B)
sitting	______	______
walking	______	______
swimming	______	______
jogging	______	______

4. What is the *ratio* of Fred's heart rate while jogging to his rate while sitting? __________

5. What is the *approximate ratio* of Fred's use of oxygen while jogging to his use while sitting? __________

Drawing Conclusions from Data

So far in this unit, you've practiced reading and analyzing data displayed on one or more tables and graphs. These are very important math skills.

An equally important skill is to be able to determine what conclusions can be drawn from the data you are given.

- When you **draw a conclusion** from data, you express an idea that is logically connected to that data.

At work, you may depend on data to tell you whether a product is well made or defective. Too many wrong conclusions here may cost you your job!

And in your personal life, just think who is most likely to show you data:

- someone who wants to sell you something;
- someone who wants to get you to think the way he or she thinks.

Example: Look at the following table.

Average Weights for Men and Women		
	Weight In Pounds	
Height	Women	Men
5'4"	124–138	135–145
5'5"	127–141	137–148
5'6"	130–144	139–151
5'7"	133–147	142–154
5'8"	136–150	145–157
5'9"	139–153	148–160

Which of the following statements is a conclusion that is supported by data in the table?

a) Between ages two and five, girls and boys are about equal in weight.
b) Women tend to do better on diets than do men.
c) Adult men tend to be heavier than adult women.

Statement a is true, but *is not supported* by data from the table. The table says nothing about comparative child sizes.

Statement b may or may not be true. However, the table gives no data that may help us decide either way.

Statement c is true and *is supported* by data on the table.

▼ Practice

Solve problem 1 based on the circle graph at right.

An author used this graph in an article about the value of recycling paper, metal, and glass.

Solid Waste Disposal in the United States

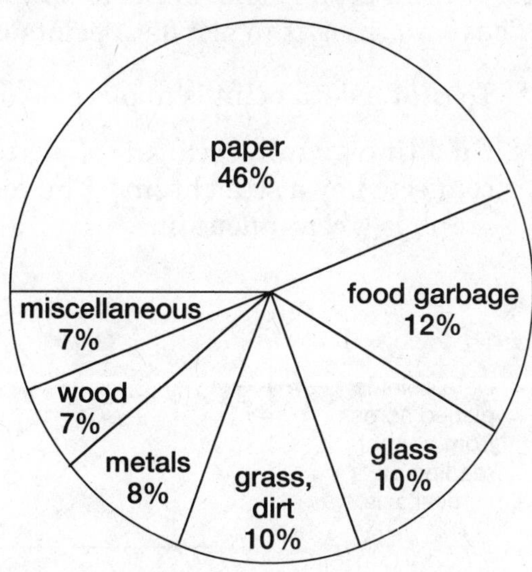

1. Which of the following statements is (are) supported by data on the graph? (More than 1 is possible.) Circle the letter of each choice.

   a) Paper and food together make up 58% of American solid waste.

   b) The United States is the world's leading user of paper products.

   c) 64% of American garbage consists of material that may be able to be recycled (paper, metal, and glass).

   d) Due to dirt, very little garbage can actually be recycled.

Solve problem 2 based on the line graphs below.

As part of a study of the causes and effects of lead pollution in the United States, the Environmental Protection Agency (EPA) compiled the data shown in the graphs below.

Graph A: Lead Used in Gasoline

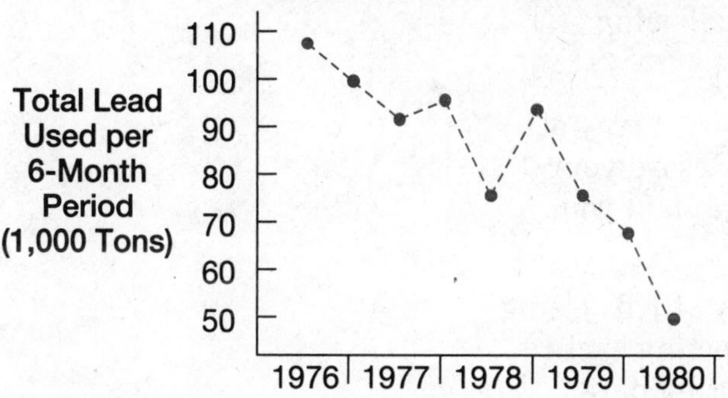

Graph B: Average Blood Lead Level in American Adults

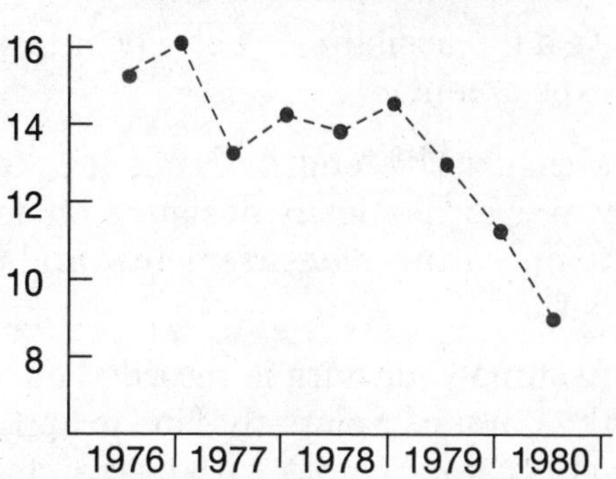

2. Which of the following statements is (are) a conclusion supported by data on the graphs? (More than 1 is possible.) Circle the letter of each choice.

   a) Lead is a dangerous pollutant present in leaded (regular) gasoline.

   b) Between 1976 and 1980, the amount of lead in the air decreased by more than one-half.

   c) By mid-1980, the amount of lead used in gasoline had decreased to less than half its 1976 value.

   d) The shapes of graphs A and B suggest that a relationship exists between the amount of lead used in gasoline and the blood lead level of American adults.

Drawing a Graph

On these final two pages, try something different. This time, *you* draw a line graph and a bar graph!

Drawing a graph is not difficult, as you'll see. In fact, it's fun. The main thing is to plot data points in the right place.

- To **plot** a data point is to place it correctly on a graph.

On a **line graph**, each pair of plotted points is connected by a straight line. The resulting graph is a continuous line.

On a **bar graph**, a plotted point takes the form of a short line that forms the top boundary of the bar. You then "fill in" the rest of the bar below.

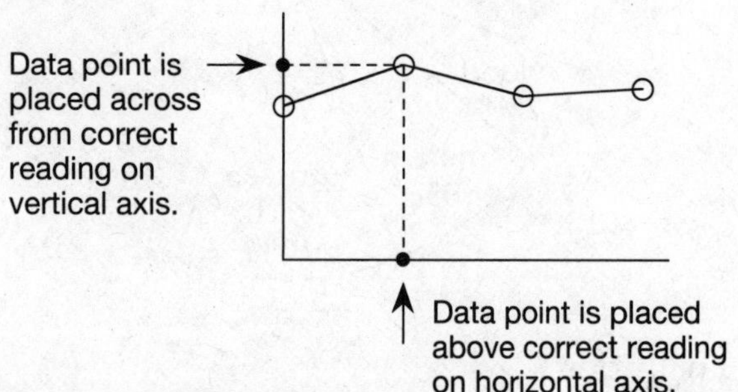
Data point is placed across from correct reading on vertical axis.
Data point is placed above correct reading on horizontal axis.

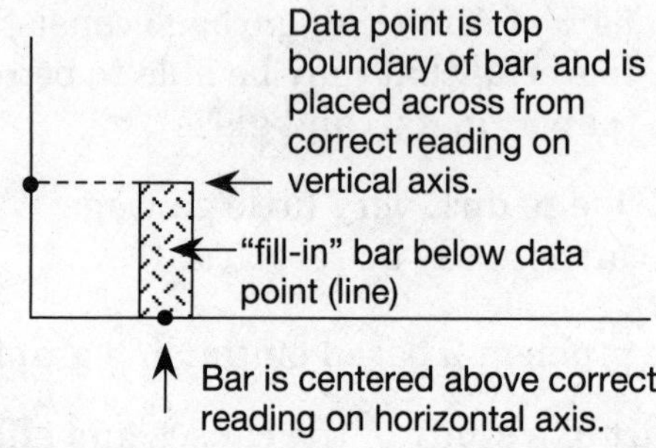
Data point is top boundary of bar, and is placed across from correct reading on vertical axis.
"fill-in" bar below data point (line)
Bar is centered above correct reading on horizontal axis.

▼ Practice

As a lab assistant, you've been asked to do the following experiment:

Measure the length of time it takes to freeze a size 4 tray of water in the newly designed Model 3A freezer. Record your temperature measurements, and make a line graph of your data.

Assume your data is recorded on the table below at left. Using the data, complete the line graph at right, connecting each pair of data points with a straight line. The starting data point and the 5-minute data point have been plotted as examples.

Time (min.)	Water Temperature (°F)
0 (start)	72
5	70
10	60
20	47
30	40
40	35
45	32 (5% ice)
50	32 (30% ice)
55	32 (60% ice)
60	32 (all ice)

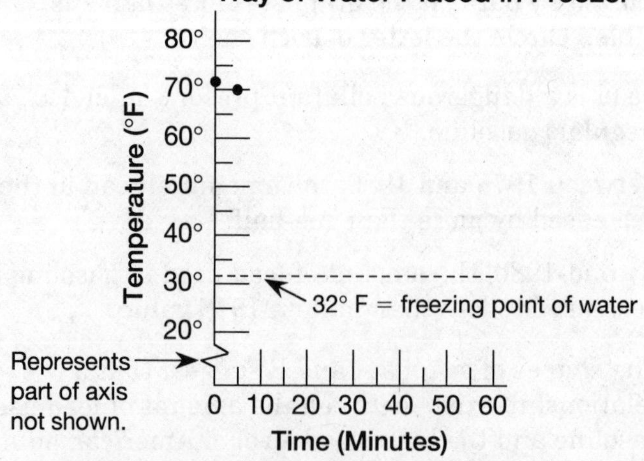
Tray of Water Placed in Freezer
80°
70°
60°
50°
40°
30°
20°
Temperature (°F)
32° F = freezing point of water
Represents part of axis not shown.
0 10 20 30 40 50 60
Time (Minutes)

ON THE JOB

Drawing a Bar Graph

You've been hired in the office at Roosevelt Elementary School. Part of your job responsibility is to keep a record of the number of students who are absent each day.

At the beginning of each new week, you're to draw a bar graph that visually displays the number of student absences on each day of the previous week. This gives the school principal a visual attendance record that's easy to read.

Each day, teachers give you a record of absences in their classes. You've found that the easiest thing for you to do is to keep a daily tally of all reported absences. For last week, your tally is written here.

Monday: 𝍸 𝍸 𝍸 𝍸 𝍸 𝍸 𝍸 𝍸 𝍸 ||||

Tuesday: 𝍸 𝍸 𝍸 𝍸 𝍸 𝍸 𝍸 ||

Wednesday: 𝍸 𝍸 𝍸 𝍸 𝍸 𝍸 𝍸

Thursday: 𝍸 𝍸 𝍸 𝍸 ||||

Friday: 𝍸 𝍸 𝍸 𝍸 𝍸 𝍸 𝍸 |

▼ MATH TIP

In a tally, each individual line / stands for a count of 1. A set of lines 𝍸 stands for 5.

Examples:

𝍸 || stands for 7.

𝍸 𝍸 𝍸 | stands for 16.

▼ Practice

Using the data from your tally, draw a bar graph below. The first bar is done as an example.

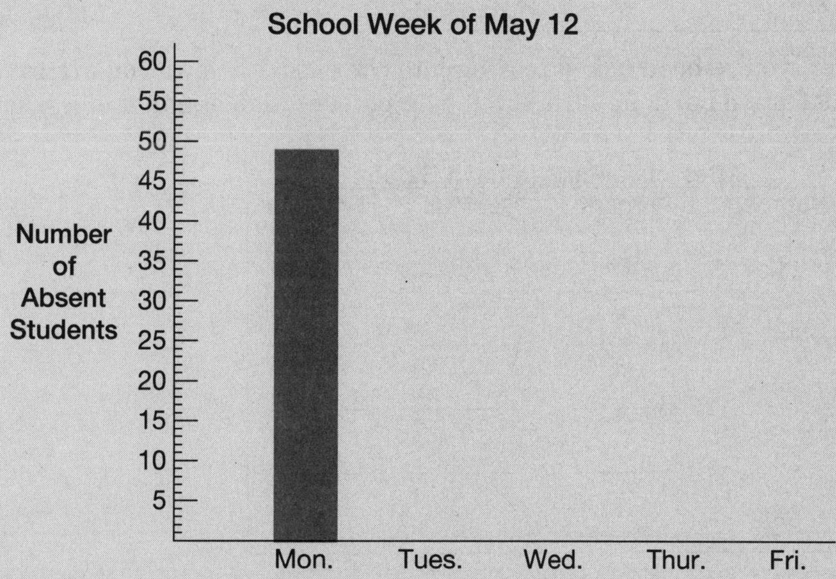

POST-TEST

Directions: The problems below represent many of the skills you've learned in *Math Skills That Work, Book Two*. Take your time and answer each question carefully. When you've finished, check your answers on page 199.

Unit One: Numbers Smaller than One (Pages 1–31)

1. The weights of the fish caught by the five top finishers in the Green Lake Fishing Contest are listed at right. Write the names in the order that they finished.

Name	Fish Weight
Tom	8.24 lb.
Louise	7.6 lb.
Tina	8.3 lb.
Enrico	7.47 lb.
Manny	8 lb.

______ First ______ Second ______ Third ______ Fourth ______ Fifth

heaviest ⟶ lightest

2. As a restaurant employee, you've been asked to total each amount of unopened spices listed below. Write each total both as an improper fraction and as a mixed number.

Spice	Container Size	Number of Containers	Improper Fraction	Mixed Number
Black pepper	$\frac{1}{2}$ lb.	11	**$\frac{11}{2}$ lb.**	**$5\frac{1}{2}$ lb.**
Red pepper	$\frac{1}{8}$ lb.	9	______	______
Chili powder	$\frac{1}{3}$ lb.	8	______	______
Powdered mustard	$\frac{1}{4}$ lb.	7	______	______
Garlic salt	$\frac{1}{5}$ lb.	12	______	______

3. As a production manager, you've been asked to complete the report below. You are to express the number of defective parts in each batch as a percent, a decimal, and a fraction.

Batch Number	Total Parts Tested	Defective Parts in Each Batch			
		Number	Percent	Decimal	Fraction
1	100	9	**9%**	**.09**	**$\frac{9}{100}$**
2	100	14	______	______	______
3	100	7	______	______	______
4	100	21	______	______	______
5	100	33	______	______	______

4. Cal works at a fruit and vegetable stand. He uses a calculator to find the price of each purchase. Five purchases are listed below.

Item	Weight (lb.)	Price (per lb.)	Estimate	Calculator Answer	Selling Price
Tomatoes	4.08	$1.92	______	7.8336	______
Broccoli	2.8	$.99	______	2.772	______
Grapes	6.19	$1.85	______	11.4515	______
Strawberries	5.2	$2.09	______	1.0868	______
Peaches	8.78	$1.04	______	9.1312	______

a) Write an estimate for the amount of each purchase. To estimate, round each amount to a whole number before multiplying.

b) Find each selling price by rounding the calculator answer to the nearest cent. Fill in the answers above.

c) Using your estimates as a guide, place an X through the one incorrect calculator answer. What do you think is wrong with the calculator answer?

5. At the store where you work, you've been asked to do the following:

a) Add each column to find the total amount of potatoes sold in each store.

b) Subtract each row to determine how many more pounds of potatoes Store A sold each day than Store B.

	Potatoes Sold in Store A (lb.)	Potatoes Sold in Store B (lb.)	Daily Difference (Store A – Store B)
Monday	147.96	118.6	______
Tuesday	135.7	102.94	______
Wednesday	107.68	92.59	______
Thursday	162.85	145	______
Friday	186	173.95	______
Week's total:	______	______	

6. As an employee of the payroll department, you've been asked to check the payroll figures shown below.

a) Multiply to find the amount that each of the following four employees earned last week:

Name	Hours Worked (a)	Hourly Pay Rate (b)	Total Earnings ($a \times b$)
Johnson	32	$7.50	______
Moore	40	$6.85	______
Peterson	24.5	$8.40	______
Zaneveld	38.75	$7.50	______

b) Divide to find the hourly rate these next four employees were paid for the earnings shown.

Name	Amount Earned (a)	Hours Worked (b)	Hourly Rate ($a \div b$)
Hanklin	$162.00	24	______
Jameson	$336.00	40	______
Nichols	$236.33	34.5	______
Wormsley	$273.75	36.5	______

Unit Three: Fractions (Pages 70–105)

7. The members of Sheldon Weight Loss Clinic have a bet on which group (women or men) can lose the most weight each month. Last month's results are shown below.

Women

Name	Weight Loss
Ardis	$3\frac{3}{4}$ lb.
Jeneanne	$2\frac{1}{4}$ lb.
Yolanda	$4\frac{1}{4}$ lb.
Mary Kay	$3\frac{3}{4}$ lb.
Total:	______

Men

Name	Weight Loss
Frank	$2\frac{1}{2}$ lb.
Robert	$3\frac{3}{4}$ lb.
Stuart	$2\frac{7}{8}$ lb.
Clayton	$4\frac{5}{8}$ lb.
Total:	______

a) Add to determine the two totals.

b) Which group (women or men) lost the most weight?

c) How much more weight did the winning group lose than the opposing group?

8. You're building a planter in the corner of your living room. For the front side of the planter, you've decided to use one of the two styles of brick shown below:

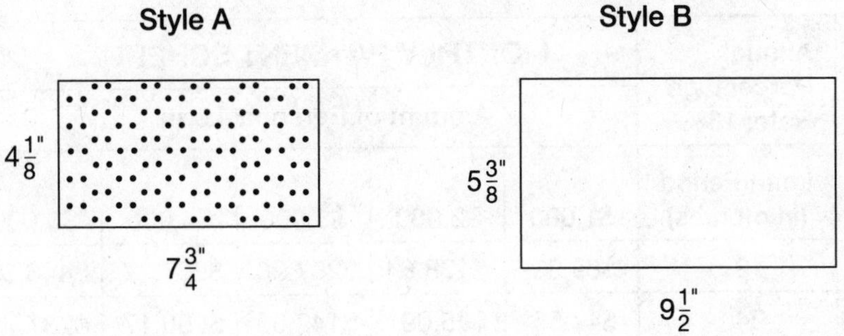

Style A — $4\frac{1}{8}$" by $7\frac{3}{4}$"

Style B — $5\frac{3}{8}$" by $9\frac{1}{2}$"

Front Side of Planter

length: 9 bricks; height: 5 bricks

As shown at right, you want the front side to be 9 bricks long and 5 bricks high.

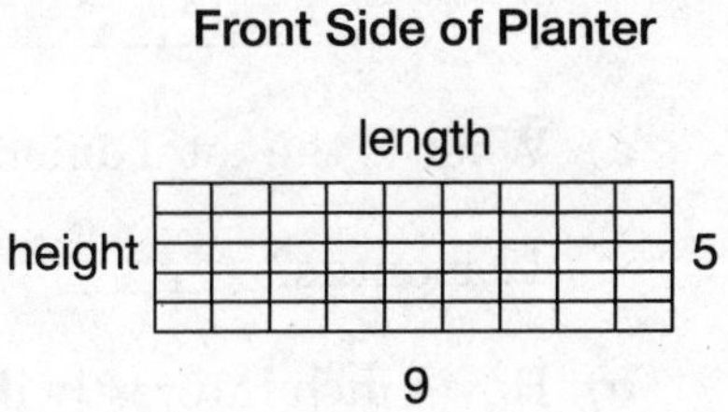

a) What will be the dimensions of the front side of the planter if you use Style A?

length: ________ height: ________

b) What will be the dimensions of the front side of the planter if you use Style B?

length: ________ height: ________

c) Suppose you decide to make the planter *exactly* $9\frac{1}{2}$ feet long instead. Can you span this length with a whole number of . . .

Style A bricks? ________ (yes or no) If yes, how many? ________

Style B bricks? ________ (yes or no) If yes, how many? ________

Hint: As a first step, change $9\frac{1}{2}$ feet to inches. Then divide by the length of each style.

Unit Four: Percents (Pages 106–139)

9. As a salesclerk, you would need to know how percent is used with sale items. For practice, fill in the blank in each box below.

a)
SHIRTS
Original Price
$26.00
Sale: 30% OFF
SALE PRICE: $ ________

b)
$35.00 Jackets
Now Only $28.00
SAVE ________ %

c)
PANTS
Originally $ ________
Now Only $32.50
SAVE 35%

d)
RUNNING SHOES
Were $42.00
Now $33\frac{1}{3}$% OFF
Pay Only $ ________

10. After receiving the following information, you decided to take out a $3,000 personal loan from your credit union.

Annual Percentage Rate: 13%	MONTHLY PAYMENT SCHEDULE				
	Amount of Personal Loan				
Loan Period (in months)	$1,000	$2,000	$3,000	$4,000	$5,000
12	$89.32	$178.64	$267.96	$357.27	$446.59
24	$47.55	$95.09	$142.63	$190.17	$237.71
36	$33.70	$67.39	$101.09	$134.78	$168.47

a) What is the total amount you will pay if you repay the loan in:

12 months? _______ 24 months? _______ 36 months? _______

b) How much interest will you pay if you repay the loan in:

12 months? _______ 24 months? _______ 36 months? _______

Unit Five: Topics in Measurement (Pages 140–159)

11. Determine the distance between each pair of towns shown at right. Round your answers to the nearest 10 miles. Write each answer next to the line joining the towns. (If you don't have a ruler, mark distances on a piece of paper, then measure each distance on the ruler below.)

Oak Ridge

Bly

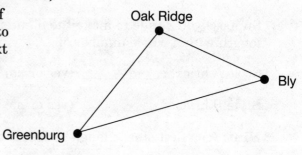

Greenburg

Scale: 1 inch = 50 miles

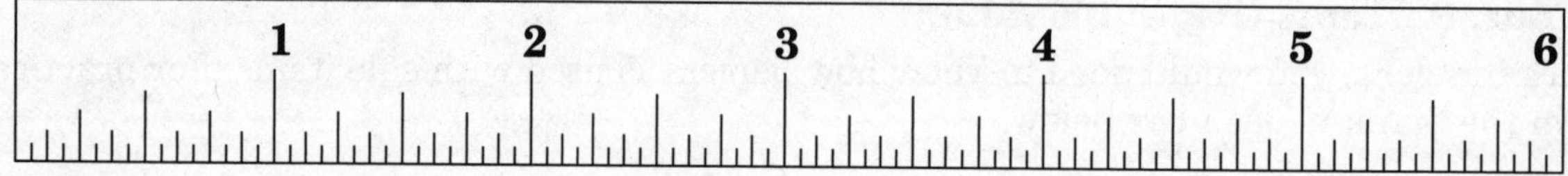

12. You've decided to carpet the living room shown at right.

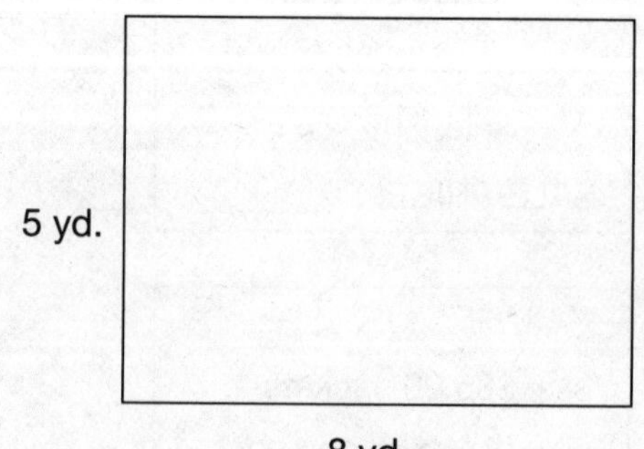

a) How many square yards of carpet do you need?

b) Paying $17.50 per square yard (including padding and installation), how much will your costs be?

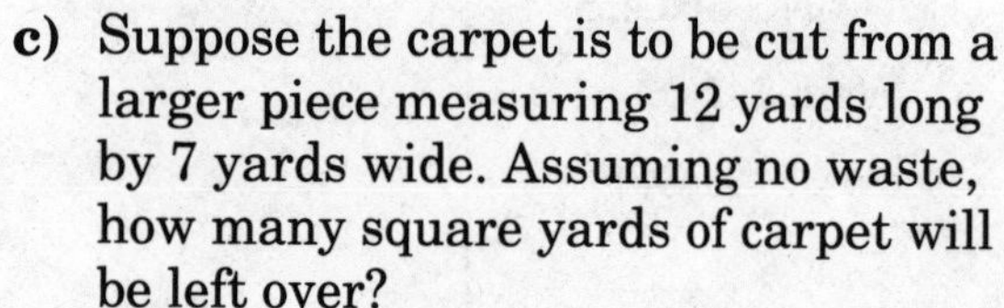

c) Suppose the carpet is to be cut from a larger piece measuring 12 yards long by 7 yards wide. Assuming no waste, how many square yards of carpet will be left over?

Unit Six: Data Analysis (Pages 160–179)

Problems 13–16 refer to the graph below. Circle each answer choice.

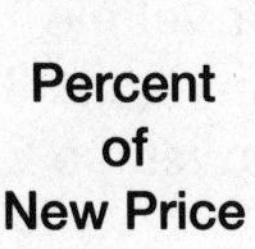

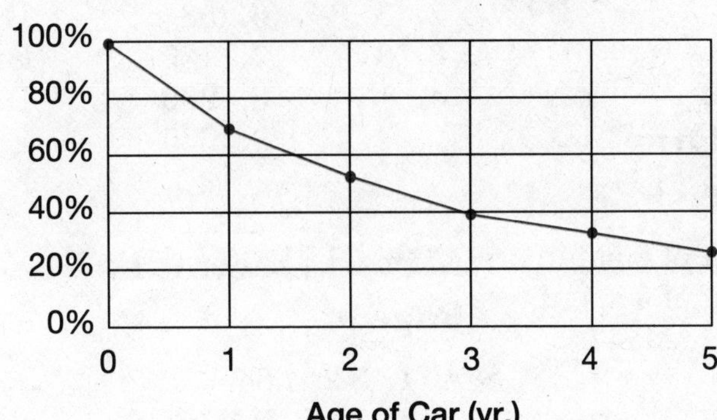

13. What is the approximate trade-in value of a $15,000 car after 3 years?

a) $4,000
b) $6,000
c) $9,000
d) $11,000

14. About how long does it take a new car to lose 20% of its new price if taken as a trade-in?

a) 3 months
b) 8 months
c) 12 months
d) 15 months

15. What is the approximate ratio of the trade-in value of a 3-year-old car to that of a 1-year-old car?

a) 4 to 7
b) 4 to 5
c) 4 to 3
d) 7 to 4

16. Which of the following conclusions is least supported by data on the graph?

a) The trade-in value of a car decreases to half of its new-car value in about $2\frac{1}{2}$ years.

b) The trade-in value of a 6-year-old car is most likely to be about 20% of its new value.

c) The trade-in value of a well-maintained car is higher than that of a poorly maintained car.

d) The trade-in value of a new car decreases most rapidly during the first year of ownership.

Answer Key

Unit One

Becoming Familiar with Numbers Smaller than One
Pages 2–3

A. **1.** 8 parts; 3 out of 8 left; 5 out of 8 eaten
2. 4 parts; 1 out of 4 left; 3 out of 4 spent
3. 100 parts; 53 out of 100 shaded; 47 out of 100 unshaded

B. **1.** twelve-hundredths, (inch)
2. two-thirds, (way)
3. half, (dollar)
4. fifteen percent, (original price)
5. quarter, (acre)
6. eight-tenths, (mile)
7. eighth, (teaspoon)
8. eighty percent, (math test)
9. half, (time)
10. ninety percent, (the price)

C.

1. half	**4.** fifth	**7.** eighth
2. third	**5.** sixth	**8.** ninth
3. fourth	**6.** seventh	**9.** tenth

Decimal Fractions
Page 5

1. .1, .01, .001
2. a) .1, .4, .9
b) .01, .06, .02
c) .001, .009, .005
3. a) .5
b) \$.09
c) .18
d) .182

Writing Zero as a Place Holder
Page 6

1. .05, .106, .007, .3~~0~~, .65~~0~~, .8~~00~~
2. .109, .048, .07~~0~~, .05~~0~~, .004, .097
3. \$.20; \$.50

Writing Decimal Fractions
Page 7

1. Type A: .048 inch; Type D: .2 inch; Type F: .015 inch; Type R: .125 inch; Type G: .05 inch; Type M: .4 inch
2. Johnson: .047 sec.; Whiteside: .3 sec.; Morris .31 sec.; Handly: .109 sec.; George: .07 sec.

Comparing Decimal Fractions
Page 8

1. .9
2. .3
3. .8
4. .13
5. .50
6. .53
7. .125
8. .200
9. .625
10. A: Envelope 2
B: Envelope 3
C: Envelope 1
D: Envelope 1
E: Envelope 3
F: Envelope 2

Mixed Decimals
Page 9

A. 1. 3.2, 4.84
2. 15.6, \$11.75
3. 6.008, \$26.05

B. Race #1: 1st = Brent; 2nd = Gary
Race #2: 1st = Ryan; 2nd = Patrick
Race #3: 1st = Harriet; 2nd = Meg
Race #4: 1st = Belinda; 2nd = Randy

Proper Fractions
Page 10

1. $\frac{6}{8}$
2. $\frac{3}{6}$
3. $\frac{2}{5}$
4. $\frac{2}{6}$
5. $\frac{8}{16}$
6.
7. 0 1
8. $\frac{85}{100}$

Writing Equivalent Fractions
Page 11

1. $\frac{1}{2} = \frac{3}{6}$
2. $\frac{3}{4} = \frac{6}{8}$
3. $\frac{2}{8} = \frac{1}{4}$
4. $\frac{1}{3} = \frac{2}{6}$
5. $\frac{1}{2} = \frac{4}{8}$
6. $\frac{5}{8} = \frac{10}{16}$

Simplifying Fractions
Page 12

1. $\frac{4}{12} = \frac{1}{3}, \frac{6}{8} = \frac{3}{4}, \frac{4}{6} = \frac{2}{3}, \frac{3}{9} = \frac{1}{3}, \frac{12}{16} = \frac{3}{4}$
2. $\frac{9}{15} = \frac{3}{5}, \frac{14}{16} = \frac{7}{8}, \frac{8}{32} = \frac{1}{4}, \frac{10}{24} = \frac{5}{12}, \frac{28}{64} = \frac{7}{16}$

On the Job
Page 13

1. C
2. F
3. B
4. A
5. G
6. E
7. D

Writing a Part as a Fraction of a Whole
Page 14

A. 1. $\frac{3}{4}$ foot **2.** $\frac{1}{2}$ foot **3.** $\frac{1}{3}$ yard

Writing a Part as a Fraction of a Whole

Page 14 (continued)

A. **4.** $\frac{2}{3}$ yard
5. $\frac{5}{6}$ yard
6. $\frac{1}{4}$ yard
7. $\frac{5}{6}$ foot

B. Monday: $\frac{1}{4}$ hour
Tuesday: $\frac{1}{3}$ hour
Wednesday: $\frac{3}{4}$ hour
Thursday: $\frac{5}{6}$ hour
Friday: $\frac{1}{2}$ hour

Raising Fractions to Higher Terms

Page 15

1. $\frac{4}{8}, \frac{2}{6}, \frac{2}{8}, \frac{6}{9}, \frac{9}{12}$
2. $\frac{4}{10}, \frac{6}{8}, \frac{4}{12}, \frac{10}{14}, \frac{5}{10}$
3. $\frac{5}{15}, \frac{12}{30}, \frac{10}{28}, \frac{22}{24}, \frac{24}{42}$

Comparing Proper Fractions

Page 17

A. **1.** $\frac{2}{3}$ $(\frac{8}{12})$, $\frac{2}{5}$ $(\frac{4}{10})$, $\frac{7}{8}$ $(\frac{14}{16})$, $\frac{4}{9}$
2. $\frac{10}{12}$, $\frac{6}{7}$ $(\frac{12}{14})$, $\frac{3}{8}$, $\frac{5}{8}$

B. **1.** $\frac{5}{32}$ inch, $\frac{3}{16}$ inch, $\frac{1}{4}$ inch, $\frac{5}{16}$ inch
2. $\frac{10}{32}$ inch, $\frac{3}{8}$ inch, $\frac{7}{16}$ inch, $\frac{1}{2}$ inch
3. $\frac{1}{2}$ inch, $\frac{9}{16}$ inch, $\frac{5}{8}$ inch, $\frac{3}{4}$ inch
4. $\frac{3}{4}$ inch, $\frac{7}{8}$ inch, $\frac{29}{32}$ inch, $\frac{15}{16}$ inch

Mixed Numbers and Improper Fractions

Page 19

A. Monday: $\frac{35}{8}$, $4\frac{3}{8}$
Tuesday: $\frac{20}{8}$, $2\frac{4}{8}$ $(2\frac{1}{2})$
Wednesday: $\frac{32}{8}$, 4
Thursday: $\frac{16}{8}$, 2
Friday: $\frac{27}{8}$, $3\frac{3}{8}$
Saturday: $\frac{19}{8}$, $2\frac{3}{8}$
Sunday: $\frac{8}{8}$, 1

B. **1.** $\frac{13}{4}$, $3\frac{1}{4}$
2. $\frac{20}{3}$, $6\frac{2}{3}$
3. $\frac{9}{2}$, $4\frac{1}{2}$
4. $\frac{21}{8}$, $2\frac{5}{8}$

Percent

Page 21

1. 40% shaded, 60% unshaded, 100% total
2. 40% shaded, 60% unshaded, 100% total
3. 75% shaded, 25% unshaded, 100% total

Percent

Page 21 (continued)

4. 20% shaded, 80% unshaded, 100% total
5. 300%
6. 500%
7. 200%
8. Gary: $30; Jesse: $25; Amy: $45
9. 50% unshaded
10. 55% unshaded
11. 40% unshaded

Writing Percent as a Decimal or a Fraction

Pages 22–23

1. $\frac{21}{100}$, .21, 21%
2. $\frac{53}{100}$, .53, 53%
3. $\frac{67}{100}$, .67, 67%
4. $\frac{11}{100}$, .11, 11%
5. $\frac{47}{100}$, .47, 47%
6. $\frac{83}{100}$, .83, 83%
7. **a)** $\frac{91}{100}$ meter
b) 30% of a meter
8. **a)** .350 (or .35) kilometer
b) $\frac{35}{100}$ (or $\frac{7}{20}$)
c) 35%
9. Monday: 89% present, 11% absent
Tuesday: 93% present, 7% absent
Wednesday: 96% present, 4% absent
Thursday: 86% present, 14% absent
Friday: 79% present, 21% absent
10. January: 17%, .17, $\frac{17}{100}$
February: 23%, .23, $\frac{23}{100}$
March: 26%, .26, $\frac{26}{100}$
April: 21%, .21, $\frac{21}{100}$
May: 16%, .16, $\frac{16}{100}$

Thinking about Decimals, Fractions, and Percents

Page 25

1. $.04, $\frac{4}{100}$, 4%
2. $.09, $\frac{9}{100}$, 9%
3. $.16, $\frac{16}{100}$, 16%
4. $.46, $\frac{46}{100}$, 46%
5. $.70, $\frac{70}{100}$, 70%
6. $.99, $\frac{99}{100}$, 99%

Thinking about Decimals, Fractions, and Percents

Page 25 (continued)

7. percent
8. decimal fraction
9. proper fraction
10. decimal fraction
11. proper fraction
12. percent

Thinking about Math Problems

Page 27

1. $218.46
2. $74.15
3. $53.53
4. 3 cookies
5. **a)** 86%
   b) 14% absent

Estimating: Your Most Important Math Tool

Page 29

1. estimate
2. exact number
3. estimate
4. exact number
5. estimate

Focus on Calculators

Page 31

Answers for 1 and 2 may vary. Most probable answers are given.

1. **a)** 8
   b) 99,999,999
2. Ⓒ
3. **a)** [0.47]
   b) [2.35]
   c) [187.]
   d) [2683.]

Unit Two

Estimating: Building Confidence with Decimals

Pages 35–36

1. **a)** 5 miles **b)** 3 meters **c)** 4 ounces
2. **a)** $8 **b)** 22 miles per gallon **c)** $12
3. **a)** 4 tons **b)** 12 pounds **c)** 12 inches
4. **a)** $7 **b)** $2 **c)** $25
5. $9 ($6 + $3), 9 (7 + 2), 11 (15 − 4)
6. 4 (12 − 8), $24 ($6 × 4), 36 (9 × 4)
7. $7 ($28 ÷ 4), 12 ($3\overline{)36}$)
8. $15
9. $27
10. $4
11. $10
12. $3
13. $12
14. TOTAL = $71
15. Yes, the estimate is less than $75.
16. c) 15.125 in.
17. a) $252.98

Estimating: Building Confidence with Decimals

Pages 35–36 (continued)

18. d) $1.98
19. b) $20.51
20. c) $338.18

Rounding Decimal Fractions to the Lead Digit

Page 37

1. .2, .5, .4, .9, .1, .3
2. .07, .02, .10 (or .1), .04, .04, .07
3. .006, .008, .007, .003, .007, .009

Rounding Numbers to a Chosen Place Value

Page 39

1. .7, .3, .7, .3, .5, .9
2. .46, .58, .82, .75, .51, .27
3. **a)** $4.48
   b) $13.23
   c) $1.58
   d) $3.30
   e) $11.50
   f) $7.67
   g) $6.77
   h) $16.71
   i) $4.16
   j) $1.58
   k) $10.99
4. **a)** .063 inch
   b) .078 inch
   c) .344 inch

Focus on Calculators

Page 41

1. 4.3, 5.795, 17.425, 1.1, 1.625, $5.42
2. $24.12
3. 7.5 in.
4. .385 in.
5. **a)** 44.25 hours
   b) 1.5 hours
   c) 5.75 hours
6. **a)** #1: difference is .006 in.
   #2: difference is .006 in.
   #3: difference is .006 in.
   b) The mechanism that tells the lathe how much to cut is off by .006 inch and needs to be reset or readjusted.

Page 43

1. $27.23, 63.2, 33.726, $13.28, 320
2. $63, $8.23, 20.25
3. turkey: $107.86; ham: $112.09; roast beef: $126.01
4. Jesse: $6.95; Ella: $7.49; Debbie: $8.60
5. **a)** terminating
   b) repeating
   c) repeating
   d) terminating

Adding Decimals

Page 45

1. .9, 1.29, $1.20, $9.20, 22.4, 6.625
2. .85, .85, 4.25, .637, $14.40, 18.425
3. .46, 1.14, 2.525, $7.28
4. 11.85, $8.05, 14.71
5. 4.52, 1.98, .94, 3.04
6. gallons: 50.4; amount spent: $74.11
7. a) turkey: 48 lb.; roast beef: 59 lb.; ham: 47 lb.
b) turkey: 48.3 lb.; roast beef: 58.43 lb.; ham: 46.43 lb.

Subtracting Decimals

Page 47

1. .4, .72, $2.19, 8.3, $1.72, 1.75
2. .39, .272, .15, .177, 2.95, 3.625
3. .15, 1.15, .204, $2.25
4. $1.63, 3.725, 4.55, $7.72
5. .4, .5, .2, 1.6
6. a) Barton: 1.95 sec.; Clancy: 2.35 sec.; Ewa: 1.225 sec.; Hanson: .84 sec.; McDougal: 3.45 sec.
b) slowest − fastest = 53.1 − 50.49 = 2.61 sec.
7. a) Estimate is .1 in.; exact is .075 in.
b) Estimate is .1 in.; exact is .085 in.
c) Estimate is 2 in.; exact is 1.425 in.
d) Estimate is 2 in.; exact is 2.102 in.

In Your Life

Pages 48–49

A. 1. 94° F to 105° F
2. 33° C to 43° C
3. 98.6° F or 37° C
B. 4. Put arrow above 98.6° F.
5. a) 101.6° F
b) 103.2° F
6. a) 3.9° F (103.2° F − 99.3° F)
b) .7° F (99.3° F − 98.6° F)
C. 7. Put arrow above 37° C.
8. a) 39.3° C
b) 2.3° C
9. a) 1.4° C
b) .9° C

Multiplying Decimals

Pages 50–53

1. 5.40, 2.35, 112.5, 1.950
2. 17.1, 4.92, 58.8, 14, 1.84

Multiplying Decimals

Pages 50–53 (continued)

3. $1.90, 6.15, $19.25, .22, $55.17
4. 1.4, .9, 27.3, 17.3, .1
5. .686, 3.76, 1.7860, .37410
6. .413, .215, 3.42, .273, 4.55
7. .02, $8.60, 2.04, .05, $12.10
8. 1.8 (2 × .9), $10 ($5 × 2), 3.6 (.9 × 4), .36 (.4 × .9)
9. .09, .045, .0048, .035
10. .08, .3, .42, .028, .027
11. .072, .015, .00024, .045, .15
12. Franklin: $44.60; Garland: $41.42; NAD Co. $676.48; ALU Inc.: $625.74
13. c) $3.93
14. b) 63
15. a) 170.1
16. d) $14.34
17. b) 0.027122
18. d) 3.8

Multiplying By 10, 100, or 1,000

Page 54

1. 3.5; 4; 2,090
2. Box A: 41.5 pounds; Box B: 32 pounds; Box C: 30 pounds; Box D: 11 pounds; Box E: 20 pounds; Box F: 27 pounds

On the Job

Page 55

1.

Last Name	Total Hours	Base Rate (1st 40 Hours)	Overtime Rate (1.5 × Base) (A)	Regular Earnings (B)	Overtime Earnings (C)	Total Earnings (D)
Amberg	43.75	$6.80	$10.20	$272.00	$38.25	$310.25
Heiden	41.5	$6.40	$9.60	$256.00	$14.40	$270.40
Loude	44.25	$7.20	$10.80	$288.00	$45.90	$333.90
Varley	42.5	$10.00	$15.00	$400.00	$37.50	$437.50
Waxman	43	$7.60	$11.40	$304.00	$34.20	$338.20

2. .5 hour

3. 43 hours

Dividing a Decimal by a Whole Number

Pages 56–57

1. 2.32, .124, 8.3, .826, .292
2. 2.12, 9.1, .34, 10.2, .135
3. $7.86, 6.6, $.14, $1.18, .206
4. 8 (5)40), .3 (3).9), $36 (7)$252), .2 (4).8), 1 (9)9)
5. .062, .071, .064, .053, .09
6. .081, .032, .0012, .07, .083
7. .033, .0129, .085, .0021, .0126
8. .05, .008, .0005
9. .05, .05, .05, .06, .02

On the Job

Page 58

1. .067 m	**3.** .128 m	**5.** .2085 m
2. .092 m	**4.** .104 m	**6.** .2415 m

Dividing a Larger Whole Number into a Smaller Whole Number

Page 59

1. .5, .75, .375
2. .25, .25, .4, .75, .875
3. .5, .8, .75, .8, .3125
4. .75, .6, .625, .1875, .25

On the Job

Page 60

1. Shift A: .5; Shift B: .6; Shift C: .667;
Shift D: .625; Shift E: .7; Shift F: .833
2. Part-time: Shift A
Full-time: Shift D
3. a) The least efficient shift is Shift F.
b) Shift F is least efficient most probably because employees get tired when working 12 straight hours and tend to make more mistakes.

In Your Life

Page 61

1. .09 inch
2. #3; the other bits would make holes that are too small
3. $\frac{1}{4}$", $\frac{5}{16}$", $\frac{21}{64}$", $\frac{11}{32}$"

On the Job

Page 63

1.

Fraction in Words	Proper Fraction		Decimal Equivalent	Acceptable Range
one-fourth (one-quarter)	$\frac{1}{4}$		.25	.15–.35
one-third	$\frac{1}{3}$	≈	.33	.23–.43
one-half	$\frac{1}{2}$		.5	.4–.6
two-thirds	$\frac{2}{3}$	≈	.67	.57–.77
three-fourths (three-quarters)	$\frac{3}{4}$		.75	.65–.85

On the Job

Page 63 (continued)

2. 3.9 pounds to 4.1 pounds
3. B, E, D, F, C, A

Dividing by a Decimal

Pages 64–65

1. 52, 4.6, 12, 5.2, 2.3
2. 70, 3, .31, 3,254, 603
3. .23, 15,240, 23.2, 5.2, 6.5
4. 20, 500, 200
5. 30, 13, 2,340, 1,100, 12
6. 200, 2,100, 20
7. 300, 300, 210, 200, 210

In Your Life

Page 66

1. 10/10: 25.1 (300 ÷ 11.95)
10/17: 17.0 (219.4 ÷ 12.9)
10/24: 18.2 (181.8 ÷ 10)
2. The spark plug most likely broke during the week of 10/17. The clue is the otherwise unexplained drop in gas mileage from about 25 to about 17.

Dividing by 10, 100, or 1,000

Page 67

1. .82, .0085, .0456
2. jackets: $25.08
dress shirts: $12.89
pairs of socks: $2.45
raincoats: $37.59
watches: $24.78

Skill Review

Page 69

1. 6 hours and 12 minutes
2. a) 107 miles **b)** 53.5 miles per hour
3. a) 157.5 miles **b)** 76.5 miles **c)** No
4. About 41 minutes

Unit Three

Estimating: Building Confidence with Fractions

Pages 73–75

1. 5 acres, 4 pieces, 4 pints
2. 7 pounds, 2 feet, 8 crates

Estimating: Building Confidence with Fractions
Pages 73–75 (continued)

3. 6 cups
4. 2 yards
5. 32 pounds
6. 6 strips
7. $2\frac{1}{2}$, $2\frac{1}{2}$, $1\frac{1}{2}$, $1\frac{1}{2}$, 2
8. estimate 7; answer c) $6\frac{19}{24}$
9. estimate \$18; answer b) \$17.70
10. estimate 8; answer c) 9
11. estimate $1\frac{1}{2}$; answer a) $1\frac{11}{24}$
12. estimate 1; answer b) $1\frac{7}{24}$

Focus on Calculators
Page 77

1. a) $8\frac{5}{24}$
2. b) $5\frac{1}{30}$
3. b) $69\frac{1}{8}$
4. c) $2\frac{7}{16}$
5. \$5.67
6. \$.73 per pound
7. Abbott: 23 weeks
   Foote: 34 weeks
   Hughes: 17 weeks
   Riker: 64 weeks

Adding Like Fractions
Pages 78–80

1. $\frac{2}{3}$, $\frac{7}{8}$, $\frac{3}{4}$, $\frac{4}{5}$, $\frac{11}{12}$
2. $\frac{1}{2}$ $(\frac{4}{8})$, $\frac{1}{3}$ $(\frac{3}{9})$, $\frac{3}{4}$ $(\frac{6}{8})$, $\frac{1}{2}$ $(\frac{2}{4})$, $\frac{2}{3}$ $(\frac{8}{12})$
3. $\frac{3}{4}$ $(\frac{6}{8})$, $\frac{2}{3}$ $(\frac{6}{9})$, $\frac{3}{5}$ $(\frac{6}{10})$, $\frac{2}{3}$ $(\frac{4}{6})$, $\frac{3}{4}$ $(\frac{9}{12})$
4. $1(\frac{6}{6})$, $1(\frac{8}{8})$, $1(\frac{4}{4})$, $1(\frac{3}{3})$, $1(\frac{16}{16})$
5. $2(\frac{8}{4})$, $2(\frac{6}{3})$, $3(\frac{24}{8})$
6. $1\frac{1}{4}$, $1\frac{3}{8}$, $1\frac{1}{6}$, $1\frac{5}{12}$, $1\frac{1}{3}$
7. $1\frac{1}{2}$, $1\frac{1}{4}$, $1\frac{1}{3}$, $1\frac{1}{5}$, $1\frac{1}{6}$
8. $6\frac{1}{2}$, $6\frac{1}{3}$, $2\frac{1}{2}$, $11\frac{1}{4}$, 7
9. $8\frac{1}{3}$, $12\frac{2}{3}$, $3\frac{1}{4}$, $5\frac{3}{4}$, $16\frac{1}{2}$
10. cotton: $6\frac{1}{4}$; flannel: $9\frac{1}{2}$; corduroy: $4\frac{1}{3}$; wool: $5\frac{1}{4}$; polyester: $5\frac{3}{4}$
11. Frankle: $2(\frac{8}{4})$; Hall: 5; Lewis: 3 Moore: 5

Subtracting Like Fractions
Pages 81–82

1. $\frac{1}{4}$, $\frac{3}{8}$, $\frac{2}{5}$, $\frac{2}{9}$, $\frac{3}{10}$
2. $\frac{1}{4}$ $(\frac{2}{8})$, $\frac{2}{3}$ $(\frac{6}{9})$, $\frac{2}{3}$ $(\frac{8}{12})$, $\frac{1}{4}$ $(\frac{4}{16})$, $\frac{1}{2}$ $(\frac{2}{4})$
3. $5\frac{1}{2}$, $6\frac{1}{2}$, $4\frac{2}{3}$, $2\frac{3}{5}$, $7\frac{7}{12}$
4. $2\frac{1}{2}$, $4\frac{3}{4}$, $1\frac{2}{3}$, $3\frac{5}{8}$, $7\frac{1}{6}$
5. $\frac{1}{3}$, $\frac{1}{2}$ $(\frac{4}{8})$, $\frac{1}{3}$ $(\frac{3}{9})$, $\frac{5}{16}$, $\frac{1}{4}$

Subtracting Like Fractions
Pages 81–82 (continued)

6. Roll A: $3\frac{1}{2}$; Roll B: $4\frac{1}{3}$; Roll C: $1\frac{1}{2}$; Roll D: $12\frac{1}{4}$; Roll E: $\frac{7}{18}$
7. $1\frac{1}{2}$ miles $(7\frac{3}{4} - 6\frac{1}{4})$

Subtracting Fractions from Whole Numbers
Page 83

1. $5\frac{3}{3}$, $2\frac{4}{4}$, $4\frac{2}{2}$, $1\frac{8}{8}$, $3\frac{16}{16}$
2. $3\frac{1}{2}$, $4\frac{1}{4}$, $6\frac{5}{8}$, $1\frac{7}{16}$,
3. $3\frac{1}{3}$, $1\frac{3}{4}$, $2\frac{7}{8}$, $5\frac{1}{4}$, $6\frac{3}{10}$
4. $6\frac{2}{5}$, $7\frac{11}{16}$, $1\frac{5}{8}$, $5\frac{5}{12}$, $8\frac{2}{3}$

Subtracting Mixed Numbers by Borrowing
Page 84

1. $1\frac{1}{2}$ $(1\frac{2}{4})$, $2\frac{2}{3}$
2. $3\frac{3}{4}$, $1\frac{4}{5}$, $4\frac{2}{3}$, $1\frac{3}{4}$, $\frac{3}{4}$

In Your Life
Page 85

1. 31 inches
2. $5\frac{1}{4}$ inches $(36\frac{1}{4} - 31)$
3. $34\frac{3}{4}$ inches $(36\frac{1}{4} - \frac{3}{4} - \frac{3}{4})$
4. $5\frac{7}{16}$ inches $(13 - 7\frac{9}{16})$
5. a) $13\frac{7}{8}$ inches b) $12\frac{1}{8}$ inches
6. $11\frac{1}{4}$ inches $(\frac{5}{8} + 10\frac{5}{8})$

Adding and Subtracting Unlike Fractions
Page 87

1. $\frac{6}{8} + \frac{1}{8} = \frac{7}{8}$
2. $1 - \frac{3}{4} = \frac{1}{4}$
3. $\frac{2}{6}$, $\frac{4}{8}$, $\frac{6}{9}$, $\frac{6}{8}$, $\frac{8}{12}$
4. $\frac{6}{10}$, $\frac{9}{12}$, $\frac{2}{8}$, $\frac{14}{16}$, $\frac{12}{16}$
5. $\frac{5}{6}$, $\frac{3}{10}$, $\frac{1}{8}$, $1\frac{1}{8}$ $(\frac{9}{8})$, 2 $(\frac{24}{12})$
6. $\frac{2}{3}$, $\frac{1}{2}$, $1\frac{1}{4}$, $\frac{1}{6}$, $\frac{1}{8}$
7. $\frac{11}{14}$, $\frac{1}{9}$, $1\frac{2}{3}$, $\frac{1}{4}$
8. $\frac{5}{6}$, $1\frac{3}{8}$, $\frac{7}{10}$, $1\frac{5}{8}$, $1\frac{1}{2}$

Choosing a Common Denominator
Page 88

1. $\frac{1}{6}$, $\frac{11}{12}$, $\frac{1}{20}$, $1\frac{1}{30}$, $1\frac{11}{12}$
2. $1\frac{1}{6}$, $\frac{3}{10}$, $\frac{5}{12}$, $1\frac{1}{12}$, $1\frac{17}{30}$

On the Job
Page 89

1. Monday: $2\frac{1}{8}$; Tuesday $1\frac{7}{8}$;
   Wednesday: $1\frac{5}{8}$; Thursday: $2\frac{1}{4}$;
   Friday: $2\frac{3}{8}$
2. $\frac{3}{8}$ cubic yard
3. $\frac{1}{12}$ cubic yard
4. $3\frac{1}{4}$ cubic yards
5. $\frac{3}{4}$ $(\frac{6}{8})$ cubic yard

Adding and Subtracting Mixed Numbers
Pages 90-91

1. $3\frac{7}{8}$, $7\frac{1}{6}$, $10\frac{1}{2}$, $9\frac{3}{4}$
2. $4\frac{5}{8}$, $4\frac{1}{2}$, $8\frac{2}{3}$, $6\frac{7}{8}$, $12\frac{5}{6}$
3. Tuesday: $19\frac{1}{12}$; Wednesday: $20\frac{11}{12}$;
   Thursday: $18\frac{3}{4}$; Friday: $16\frac{5}{12}$
4. $3\frac{5}{12}$, $4\frac{7}{16}$, $2\frac{19}{20}$
5. $3\frac{1}{12}$, $3\frac{1}{9}$, $4\frac{11}{20}$, $1\frac{1}{12}$, $2\frac{1}{10}$
6. $2\frac{3}{4}$, $3\frac{15}{16}$, $1\frac{17}{20}$, $2\frac{23}{24}$, $4\frac{5}{6}$
7. **a)** Style A: length = $13\frac{5}{8}$ in.;
   width = 11 in.
   Style B: length = 17 in.;
   width = $13\frac{3}{8}$ in.
   b) length difference = $3\frac{3}{8}$ in.
   width difference = $2\frac{3}{8}$ in.

In Your Life
Page 92

1. Bobby: 27 pounds; Matthew: $24\frac{1}{4}$ pounds;
   Timothy: $24\frac{1}{2}$ pounds; Jimmy: $24\frac{1}{4}$ pounds
2. **a)** Bobby leaves 5 lb.; Matthew leaves $2\frac{1}{4}$ lb.; Timothy leaves $2\frac{1}{2}$ lb. Jimmy leaves $2\frac{1}{4}$ lb.
   b) 12 pounds total
   c) Bobby: $10\frac{3}{4}$ pounds; Matthew: $12\frac{1}{4}$ pounds; Timothy: $11\frac{1}{4}$ pounds; Jimmy: 12 pounds
   d) $46\frac{1}{4}$ pounds

On the Job
Page 93

1.

	First Year	Second Year
Marnie Casper	$2\frac{3}{8}$"	$2\frac{5}{8}$"
James Lynde	$2\frac{1}{8}$"	$1\frac{1}{2}$"
Susan Moore	$2\frac{1}{8}$"	$2\frac{5}{8}$"
Isabel Gonzalez	$1\frac{15}{16}$"	$2\frac{7}{16}$"
Alonso White	$1\frac{15}{16}$"	$1\frac{13}{16}$"

2. first year: Marnie Casper; second year: Marnie Casper and Susan Moore

Multiplying Fractions
Pages 94–96

1. $\frac{1}{6}$, $\frac{2}{15}$, $\frac{3}{12}$, $\frac{4}{45}$, $\frac{3}{16}$
2. $\frac{2}{21}$, $\frac{1}{4}$, $\frac{8}{15}$, $\frac{9}{70}$, $\frac{15}{24}$
3. $\frac{1}{10}$, $\frac{1}{4}$, $\frac{4}{5}$
4. $\frac{5}{8}$, $\frac{10}{21}$, 1, 1
5. $\frac{5}{8}$, $\frac{3}{10}$, $\frac{4}{27}$, $1\frac{2}{7}$
6. 2, $\frac{1}{12}$, $1\frac{2}{3}$, $\frac{2}{9}$
7. $1\frac{2}{3}$, $1\frac{1}{2}$, $5\frac{1}{7}$, $7\frac{1}{3}$
8. $4\frac{4}{5}$, $6\frac{1}{8}$, 9, $2\frac{1}{2}$, $9\frac{3}{4}$
9.

Cooking Time

	Style		
Weight	**Rare**	**Medium**	**Well Done**
per pound	$\frac{1}{2}$ hr.	$\frac{5}{8}$ hr.	$\frac{3}{4}$ hr.
3 lb.	$1\frac{1}{2}$	$1\frac{7}{8}$	$2\frac{1}{4}$
4 lb.	2	$2\frac{1}{2}$	3
5 lb.	$2\frac{1}{2}$	$3\frac{1}{8}$	$3\frac{3}{4}$
6 lb.	3	$3\frac{3}{4}$	$4\frac{1}{2}$

Multiplying with Mixed Numbers
Page 97

1. $6\frac{2}{3}$, $18\frac{3}{4}$, $2\frac{7}{10}$, $8\frac{3}{4}$
2. $\frac{15}{16}$, $13\frac{1}{2}$, $10\frac{9}{20}$, $11\frac{11}{12}$, $25\frac{1}{3}$

In Your Life
Page 98

1. Project #1: Length of support A is $34\frac{9}{16}$".
2. Project #2: Width of partial strip is $\frac{3}{4}$'.

On the Job
Page 99

1.

RECIPE FOR SPLIT-PEA SOUP

Ingredients	Amount of Each Ingredient Needed: To Feed 6 (as Given)	To Feed 30 (× 5)	To Feed 48 (× 8)
green split peas	$2\frac{1}{4}$ cups	$11\frac{1}{4}$	18
broth	$2\frac{5}{8}$ cups	$13\frac{1}{8}$	21
sliced onion	$1\frac{2}{3}$ cups	$8\frac{1}{3}$	$13\frac{1}{3}$
salt	1 teaspoon	5	8
pepper	$\frac{1}{2}$ teaspoon	$2\frac{1}{2}$	4
dried marjoram	$\frac{1}{4}$ teaspoon	$1\frac{1}{4}$	2
diced celery	$1\frac{1}{8}$ cups	$5\frac{5}{8}$	9
diced carrot	$\frac{7}{8}$ cup	$4\frac{3}{8}$	7

Dividing Fractions
Pages 101–103

1. $\frac{4}{3}$, $\frac{8}{7}$, $\frac{2}{1}$, $\frac{16}{9}$, $\frac{3}{2}$
2. $\frac{3}{5}$, $\frac{8}{11}$, $\frac{2}{5}$, $\frac{3}{7}$, $\frac{16}{21}$
3. $\frac{1}{3}$, $\frac{1}{2}$, $\frac{1}{5}$, $\frac{1}{12}$, $\frac{1}{16}$
4. $\frac{2}{7}$, $\frac{3}{14}$, $\frac{4}{7}$, $\frac{8}{19}$, $\frac{16}{25}$
5. $\frac{2}{3}$, 1, $2\frac{1}{4}$
6. $1\frac{1}{3}$, $1\frac{1}{8}$, $\frac{8}{9}$, $1\frac{3}{4}$, $2\frac{1}{16}$
7. 1, $\frac{15}{32}$, 8, $1\frac{1}{2}$, 1
8. $\frac{5}{16}$, $1\frac{5}{6}$, $\frac{5}{16}$
9. $\frac{1}{8}$, $\frac{7}{32}$, $\frac{9}{50}$, $\frac{7}{12}$, $1\frac{1}{3}$
10. $\frac{3}{5}$, $2\frac{1}{6}$, $\frac{2}{3}$, $\frac{1}{2}$, $\frac{9}{15}$
11. 15, 8, 9
12. $10\frac{1}{2}$, 12, 16, 9, 10
13. 2, $1\frac{1}{2}$, $1\frac{3}{7}$, $\frac{18}{85}$
14. 4, $2\frac{1}{3}$, $1\frac{5}{13}$, $\frac{23}{25}$, $2\frac{16}{19}$

Skill Review
Pages 104–105

1. $2\frac{3}{8}$ yards
2. $5\frac{3}{8}$ yards **3.** $\frac{3}{8}$ of a yard more is needed.
4. **a)** $8\frac{5}{8}$ yards **b)** 9 yards **c)** $5\frac{1}{4}$ yards
5. $9\frac{1}{4}$ yards left over
6. 5 size 10 jumpers **7.** 10 size 8 jumpers
8. **a)** 3 **b)** 3 **c)** 3 **d)** 4 **e)** 3

Unit Four

Identifying Numbers in Percent Problems
Page 108

1. part = 75, percent = 25%, whole = 300
2. part = 54, percent = 60%, whole = 90
3. **c)** whole **4. b)** percent

The Percent Circle
Page 109

1. P = 75, % = 20%, W = 375
2. P = 255, % = 85%, W = 300
3. %
4. P
5. W
6. %

Using the Percent Circle
Page 111

1. . . . multiply the percent by the whole.
2. . . . divide the part by the whole.
3. . . . divide the part by the percent.
4. %, division
5. W, division
6. W, division
7. %, division
8. P, multiplication

P
% × W

Focus on Calculators
Pages 112–115

A. 1. $88 3. $9.90 5. $.95
2. 7.6 4. 61.5 lb. 6. $3,480

B. 1. 20% 3. 5% 5. 8%
2. 16.67% 4. 37.5% 6. 40%

C. 1. 90 3. 800 5. $800
2. 200 4. $7.04 6. $1,025

D. 1. **a)** $105.99 **b)** $271.43 **c)** $58.16 **d)** $74.97 **e)** $90.48
2. **a)** 9.5% **b)** 24.6% **c)** 6.5% **d)** 6.1% **e)** 5.4%
3. **a)** $15.00 **b)** $62.00 **c)** $65.00

Increasing or Decreasing an Amount
Page 117

1. $210 **4.** 253 pounds **7.** $10.35
2. $1,185.60 **5.** $14.99 **8.** $19.22
3. 875 miles **6.** $41.60

On the Job
Page 119

a) $.25/$1, $\frac{1}{4}$ **c)** $.15/$1, $\frac{3}{20}$ **e)** $.40/$1, $\frac{2}{5}$
b) $.35/$1, $\frac{7}{20}$ **d)** $.10/$1, $\frac{1}{10}$ **f)** $.50/$1, $\frac{1}{2}$

Changing Fractions to Percents
Page 120

1. 50%, 60%, $62\frac{1}{2}$%, 90%, $83\frac{1}{3}$%

2. a) 20% off **c)** 25% off
b) $33\frac{1}{3}$% off **d)** $66\frac{2}{3}$% off

Commonly Used Percents, Decimals, and Fractions
Page 121

1.

Percent	Decimal	Fraction
10%	.1	$\frac{1}{10}$
20%	**.2**	$\frac{1}{5}$
25%	.25	$\frac{1}{4}$
30%	.3	$\frac{3}{10}$
$33\frac{1}{3}$%	$.33\frac{1}{3}$	$\frac{1}{3}$
40%	**.4**	$\frac{2}{5}$
50%	.5	$\frac{1}{2}$

Percent	Decimal	Fraction
60%	.6	$\frac{3}{5}$
$66\frac{2}{3}$%	**$.66\frac{2}{3}$**	$\frac{2}{3}$
70%	.7	$\frac{7}{10}$
75%	.75	$\frac{3}{4}$
80%	**.8**	$\frac{4}{5}$
90%	.9	$\frac{9}{10}$

2. a) 10% = $.10
b) 25% = $.25
c) $\$.33\frac{1}{3}$
d) $.75
e) $.90
f) $.20
g) $66\frac{2}{3}\% = \$.66\frac{2}{3}$
h) 50% = $.50

Finding the Part
Pages 122–123

1.

	75%	40%	5%	$66\frac{2}{3}$%	$33\frac{1}{3}$%
Decimal	.75	.4	.05	$.66\frac{2}{3}$	$.33\frac{1}{3}$
Fraction	$\frac{3}{4}$	$\frac{2}{5}$	$\frac{1}{20}$	$\frac{2}{3}$	$\frac{1}{3}$

2.

Item	Regular Price	Discount Rate	Discount (a)	Sale Price (b)
sport shirt	$12.90	20%	**$ 2.58**	**$10.32**
dress pants	$32.60	15%	$ 4.89	$27.71
dress shoes	$49.96	25%	$12.49	$37.47
bathrobe	$24.00	$33\frac{1}{3}$%	$ 8.00	$16.00
tie	$6.60	50%	$ 3.30	$ 3.30
ring	$19.80	$66\frac{2}{3}$%	$13.20	$ 6.60

3.

Item	Price	Sales Tax Rate	Sales Tax (a)	Total Purchase Price (b)
houseplant	$16.95	6%	**$1.02**	**$17.97**
restaurant meal	$23.75	8%	$ 1.90	$ 25.65
coffee table	$84.90	5%	$ 4.25	$ 89.15
microwave oven	$279.00	4%	$11.16	$ 290.16
lawn mower	$189.50	7.5%	$14.21	$ 203.71
used car	$999.00	5.5%	$54.95	$1,053.95

Finding the Percent
Pages 124–125

1. 20% **2.** 25% **3.** 25% **4.** $12\frac{1}{2}$%

5.

Item	Regular Price	Savings Bonus	Percent of Savings (Nearest 1%) (a)	Sale Price (b)
gloves	$20	$4	**20%**	**$16**
purse	$35	$5	14%	$30
coat	$117	$39	33%	$78
sweater	$40	$10	25%	$30
shoes	$47	$14	30%	$33
scarf	$12.50	$1.25	10%	$11.25

Finding the Percent
Pages 124–125 (continued)

6.

Measure Number	Number of Responses	"Yes" Responses	"No" Responses	Percent "Yes" (a)	Percent "No" (b)	Percent "Undecided" (c)
1	200	50	125	**25%**	**63%**	**12%**
2	400	150	225	38%	56%	6%
3	300	50	175	17%	58%	25%
4	300	150	100	50%	33%	17%
5	500	175	230	35%	46%	19%

Finding the Whole
Pages 126–127

1. 38 **2.** $36 **3.** $47 **4.** 375

5. a) $54
b) $23.75
c) $10
d) $50
e) $84

6. a) $285
b) $300
c) $277
d) $683.75
e) $263.49

7. a) 450 miles
b) 400 miles
c) 372 miles
d) 300 miles

On the Job
Page 128

1. a) $15.96
b) $ 1.47
c) $39.45
d) $ 5.96
e) $77.34

2. a) $200
b) $140.18
c) $340.18
d) 41%

3. $1,799

In Your Life
Page 129

1. $4.80
2. 20%
3. $40
4. $11.00
5. $33\frac{1}{3}$%, $30
6. $75, $60

Understanding Simple Interest
Page 131

1. a) $20
b) $75
c) $65
d) $180
e) $360
f) $300

2. $165

3. a) $91
b) $791

4. $1,062.50

5. a) $1,350
b) $5,850

On the Job
Page 133

1. $\frac{1}{4}$ year, $\frac{2}{3}$ year, $\frac{5}{6}$ year

2. a) .5 year, .25 year, .75 year
b) .33 year, .67 year, .92 year

On the Job
Page 133 (continued)

3. Johnson: $7.50
Laurence: $26
Murphy: $131.25

4. Burkle: $40, $540
Hanks: $104.85, $803.85
White: $7.47, $256.47

In Your Life
Page 134

1. a) $15 **b)** $18.75

2. $2.50; $37.50 − 2(17.50) = $37.50 − $35 = $2.50

In Your Life
Page 135

1. March: $4.50
April: $8.25
May: $1.88

2. a) $376
b) $2,376

In Your Life
Page 137

1. a) 12%
b) 24 months: $353
36 months: $249
48 months: $197
c) 24 months: $8,472
36 months: $8,964
48 months: $9,456
d) 24 months: $972
36 months: $1,464
48 months: $1,956

2. a) 10%
b) $1,668
c) $288 ($1,956 − $1,668)

3. On new-car and used-car loans, the credit union or bank holds the title of the car until the loan is totally repaid. In the case of default—where the borrower stops making payments—the lender has the right to sell the car to pay off the loan. A new car is easier for a lender to sell than a used car. Thus, a new-car loan is less risky. A signature loan is the most risky loan of all, because the bank holds no title during the loan repayment period. Banks and credit unions follow a general rule: the greater the risk, the higher the APR.

Skill Review
Page 139

1. a) \$375
   b) \$653.33
2. a) 19" set: \$15 b) 19" set: \$285
   26" set: \$24.50 26" set: \$465.50
3. a) 19" set: \$60
   26" set: \$98
   b) 19" Set:

Principal:	\$240.00
Interest:	64.80
Total:	\$304.80

26" Set:

Principal:	\$392.00
Interest:	105.84
Total:	\$497.84

4. a) 19" set: \$30
   26" set: \$49
   b) Total = \$30 + 12(\$24.75) = \$327
   c) Total = \$49 + 24(\$23.75) = \$619
   Interest = \$619 − \$490 = \$129

Unit Five

Introducing Measurement
Page 143

1. longer
2. heavier
3. larger
4. less
5. km
6. m
7. mm
8. m
9. kg
10. mg
11. kg
12. g
13. l
14. ml
15. ml
16. l

Measuring with an English Ruler
Pages 144–145

1. $\frac{1}{2}$ inch
2. $\frac{3}{4}$ inch
3. $\frac{3}{8}$ inch
4. $\frac{9}{16}$ inch
5. $\frac{13}{16}$ inch
6. $1\frac{3}{8}$ inches
7. $2\frac{1}{2}$ inches
8. $3\frac{1}{4}$ inches
9. $4\frac{11}{16}$ inches
10. a) $4\frac{3}{8}$ inches
11. b) $4\frac{3}{8}$ inches
12. b) $4\frac{1}{2}$ inches

In Your Life
Page 146

1. a) 1,050 miles ($600 \times 1\frac{3}{4}$)
   b) 900 miles ($600 \times 1\frac{1}{2}$)
   c) 1,200 miles (600×2)
   d) 600 miles (600×1)
2. a) 3,900 miles ($600 \times 3\frac{1}{4} \times 2$)
   b) 7 hours ($3{,}900 \div 550$)

Measuring with a Centimeter Ruler
Page 147

1. 13 mm or 1.3 cm
2. 6 cm
3. 7 cm 7 mm or 7.7 cm

On the Job
Page 148

1. 5 mm, 7 mm, 9 mm, 12 mm, 19 mm
2. a) 3 mm b) 6 mm c) 11 mm
3. 1 foot = 304.8 mm

In Your Life
Page 149

1. B: $\frac{3}{4}$ lb. or 12 oz.; C: $2\frac{1}{2}$ lb. or 2 lb. 8 oz.;
   D: $3\frac{1}{4}$ lb. or 3 lb. 4 oz.;
   E: $3\frac{3}{4}$ lb. or 3 lb. 12 oz.
2. a) Estimate: 4 lb. × \$1 = \$4
   b) Estimate: 5 lb. × \$2 = \$10

On the Job
Page 150

Customer Billing Amounts

Item	Cost (a)	Weight	Postage (b)	Total Cost (a + b)
a) mechanical pencil	\$3.89	**$1\frac{3}{4}$ oz.**	**\$.52**	**\$4.41**
b) pocket watch	\$15.99	5 oz.	\$1.21	\$17.20
c) hand calculator	\$7.29	$7\frac{1}{2}$ oz.	\$1.33	\$8.62
d) French perfume	\$18.75	$10\frac{1}{4}$ oz.	\$1.56	\$20.31
e) pocket dictionary	\$12.50	$13\frac{3}{4}$ oz.	\$1.67	\$14.17

On the Job
Page 151

1. B: 3.2 kg or 3 kg 200 g;
   C: 4.1 kg or 4 kg 100 g;
   D: 4.9 kg or 4 kg 900 g;
   E: .5 kg or 500 g
2. \$19.20 (\$3.49 × 5.5 kg)

In Your Life
Page 152

1. 450 grams
2. A: 3 oz. or 84 grams;
   B: $8\frac{1}{2}$ oz. or 240 grams;
   C: $11\frac{1}{2}$ oz. or 325 grams
3. 618 calories

Reading a Weather Thermometer
Page 153

1. 75° F **3.** 71° F **5.** 1° C
2. 88° F **4.** 0° C **6.** 212° F

On the Job
Page 155

1. About 5.3 quarts (5 × 1.06)
2. About 19.5 gallons (75 × .26)
3. 500 ml is about $16\frac{2}{3}$ ounces (500 ÷ 30)
4. $1.50 per quart ($1.59 ÷ 1.06)
5. $1.43 per gallon ($.38 × 4 = $1.52; $1.52 ÷ 1.06 = $1.43)

Becoming Familiar with Area
Page 156

1. 8 sq. ft. **2.** 15 m^2 **3.** 5 sq. yd.

In Your Life
Page 157

1. a) 120 sq. ft. (12 × 10)
b) 120 tiles
c) $130.80 (120 × $1.09)
2. a) 180 sq. ft. (12 × 15)
b) 320 tiles (180 ÷ $\frac{9}{16}$)
c) $313.60 (320 × $.98)

Becoming Familiar with Volume
Page 158

1. 16 cu. yd. **2.** 18 m^3 **3.** 15 cu. in.

In Your Life
Page 159

1.

left side yard	$3\frac{5}{9}$	cubic yards
right side yard	$6\frac{2}{9}$	cubic yards
front yard	$13\frac{3}{9}$	cubic yards
backyard	15	cubic yards

Total: $37\frac{10}{9} = 38\frac{1}{9}$ cubic yards

2. $343 ($9 × $38\frac{1}{9}$)

Unit Six

Numerical Data
Page 163

1. 151 pounds
2. 158 pounds (halfway between 154 and 162)

Numerical Data
Page 163 (continued)

3. 5'4" to 6'4"
4. 183 pounds (170 + 13 or 175 + 8)
5. 139 pounds
6. 112 pounds (halfway between 109 and 115)
7. 5'0" to 6'0"
8. 176 pounds (166 + 10)

On the Job
Page 164

1. a) regular **b)** size 14
2. Size 12, regular. The sleeve length is too short in the petite size.

The Language of Data Analysis
Pages 165–167

A. 1. Frank: 102.5° F (102.45° F rounded to nearest tenth)
Janessa: 100.7° F
Stacey: 102.3° F (102.25° F rounded to nearest tenth)
Bill: 102.6° F
2. 101.5° F (102.4° F − .9° F)
3. 99.6° F (100.8° F − 1.2° F)

B. 1. math: 30
science: 35
social studies: 40
English: $39\frac{1}{2}$
2. a) math: 33.8
science: 37.25
social studies: 40.6
English: 40.75
b) The median is a better indication of how most students are doing on the test. One high set of scores, such as Louise's, puts the average up high but does not affect the median. For example, the average math score of 33.8 is higher than every student's score except Louise's.

C. 1. A: $20.00; B: $16.00; C: $14.00; D: $15.00; E: $12.00
2. average profit = $15.40
3. median profit = $15.00
4. ratio = $\frac{\$60}{\$52} = \frac{15}{13}$ or 15:13
5. ratio = $\frac{\$16}{\$12} = \frac{4}{3}$ or 4:3
6. ratio = $\frac{\$20}{\$12} = \frac{5}{3}$ or 5:3

On the Job
Page 169

1. \$135,000 (\$1,625,000 ÷ 12)
2. best month: \$350,000;
   worst month: \$25,000
3. \$250,000 (divide the sum of \$200,000 + \$350,000 + \$200,000 by 3)
4. Christmas season: December;
   summer season: June
5. ratio = $\frac{350}{175} = \frac{2}{1}$ or 2:1
6. median monthly sales = \$112,500
   (The median is the average of \$100,000 and \$125,000—even though two months have sales of \$100,000.)

In Your Life
Page 171

1. 52 inches
2. 28 inches (48 − 20)
3. 26 inches
4. $\frac{46}{20} = \frac{23}{10}$ or about 2:1
5. About 56 inches

In Your Life
Page 173

1. housing: 25%; transportation: 12.5%;
   food: 25%; medical care: 10%;
   clothing: 15%; savings: 0%; other: 12.5%
2. **a)** clothing and other
   b) clothing: \$1,400 more (\$3,000 − \$1,600)
   other: \$1,100 more (\$2,500 − \$1,400)

Using More than One Data Source
Page 175

1. a), b), and c):

Ingredient	Ounces	Calories
orange juice	3.6	50.4 (14 × 3.6)
lemon-lime soda	6	72 (12 × 6)
pineapple juice	2.4	40.8 (17 × 2.4)

TOTAL CALORIES: 163.2

2.

Ingredient	Ounces	Carbohydrates
orange juice	3	10.5 grams (3.5 × 3)
lemon-lime soda	5	12.5 grams (2.5 × 5)
pineapple juice	2	8.6 grams (4.3 × 2)

TOTAL CARBOHYDRATES: 31.6 grams

Using More than One Data Source
Page 175 (continued)

3.

Activity	Heart Rate	Oxygen Use
sitting	70	.2 liters per min.
walking	85	.6 liters per min.
swimming	130	1.6 liters per min.
jogging	140	1.8 liters per min.

4. ratio = $\frac{140}{70} = \frac{2}{1}$ or 2:1
5. ratio = $\frac{1.8}{.2} = \frac{9}{1}$ or 9:1

Drawing Conclusions from Data
Page 177

1. Statements a) and c) are supported by data on the graph. In contrast, b) and d) may or may not be true, but the graph gives us no direct information on these statements.
2. Both c) and d) are supported by information in the graphs. Choosing d) is correct because the shapes of the two graphs are similar, which does *suggest* a relationship exists, even though the nature of that relationship is not indicated.

Drawing a Graph
Page 178

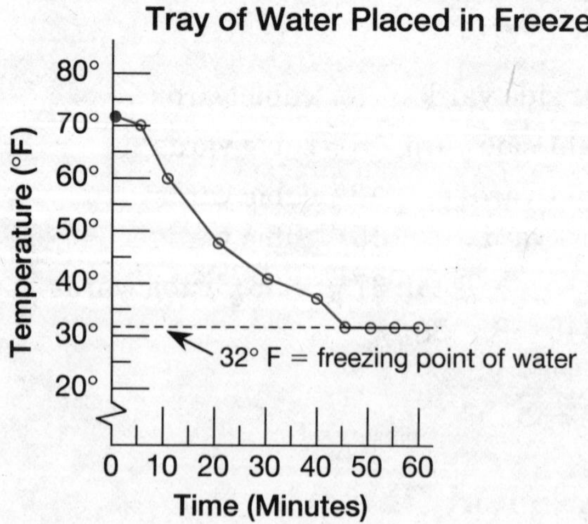

On the Job
Page 179

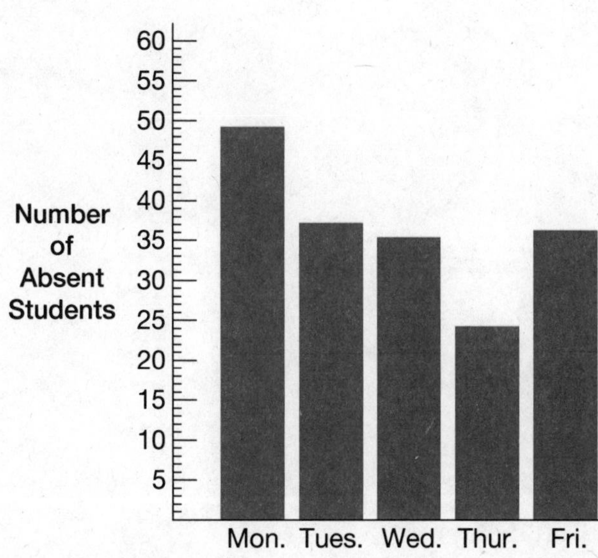

Post-Test

Pages 180–185

1. first: Tina; second: Tom; third: Manny; fourth: Louise; fifth: Enrico
2. Black pepper: $\frac{11}{2}$ lb., $5\frac{1}{2}$ lb.

   Red pepper: $\frac{9}{8}$ lb., $1\frac{1}{8}$ lb.

   Chili powder: $\frac{8}{3}$ lb., $2\frac{2}{3}$ lb.

   Powdered mustard: $\frac{7}{4}$ lb., $1\frac{3}{4}$ lb.

   Garlic salt: $\frac{12}{5}$ lb., $2\frac{2}{5}$ lb.
3. Batch 1: 9%, .09, $\frac{9}{100}$

   Batch 2: 14%, .14, $\frac{14}{100} = \frac{7}{50}$

   Batch 3: 7%, .07, $\frac{7}{100}$

   Batch 4: 21%, .21, $\frac{21}{100}$

   Batch 5: 33%, .33, $\frac{33}{100}$
4. **a) & b)**

	Estimate	Selling Price
Tomatoes	$8.00	$7.83
Broccoli	$3.00	$2.77
Grapes	$12.00	$11.45
Strawberries	$10.00	~~$1.09~~
Peaches	$9.00	$9.13

   c) The selling price of strawberries is incorrectly calculated. That answer should be $10.87. Cal probably entered the decimal point on the calculator in the wrong place.

Post-Test
Pages 180–185 (continued)

5. **a) & b)**

	Potatoes Sold in Store A	Potatoes Sold in Store B	Daily Difference
Monday	147.96	118.6	29.36
Tuesday	135.7	102.94	32.76
Wednesday	107.68	92.59	15.09
Thursday	162.85	145	17.85
Friday	186	173.95	12.05
Week's total:	740.19	633.08	

6. **a)** Johnson: $240.00
Moore: $274.00
Peterson: $205.80
Zaneveld: $290.63

   b) Hanklin: $6.75
Jameson: $8.40
Nichols: $6.85
Wormsley: $7.50
7. **a)** Women's total: $12\frac{8}{4} = $ 14 lb.

   Men's total: $11\frac{22}{8} = 13\frac{6}{8} = 13\frac{3}{4}$ lb.

   b) The women lost the most weight.

   c) The women lost $\frac{1}{4}$ pound more than the men.
8. **a)** length: $7\frac{3}{4}'' \times 9 = 69\frac{3}{4}''$

   height: $4\frac{1}{8}'' \times 5 = 20\frac{5}{8}''$

   b) length: $9\frac{1}{2}'' \times 9 = 85\frac{1}{2}''$

   height: $5\frac{3}{8}'' \times 5 = 26\frac{7}{8}''$

   c) Change $9\frac{1}{2}$ feet to inches:

   $9\frac{1}{2}$ feet $= 12 \times 9\frac{1}{2} = 114''$

   Style A bricks: $114 \div 7\frac{3}{4} = 14\frac{22}{33}$

   No, the length can't be spanned with a whole number of Style A bricks.

   Style B bricks: $114 \div 9\frac{1}{2} = 12$

   Yes, the length can be spanned with exactly 12 Style B bricks.
9. **a)** Sale Price: $18.20 ($26.00 − $7.80)

   b) Save 20% ($7.00 ÷ $35.00)

   c) Originally $50.00 ($32.50 ÷ 65%)

   d) Pay Only $28.00 ($42.00 − $14.00)
10. **a)** 12 months: $3,215.52 ($267.96 × 12)

    24 months: $3,423.12 ($142.63 × 24)

    36 months: $3,639.24 ($101.09 × 36)

    b) 12 months: $215.52 ($3,215.52 − $3,000.00)

    24 months: $423.12 ($3,423.12 − $3,000.00)

    36 months: $639.24 ($3,639.24 − $3,000.00)

Post-Test
Pages 180–185 (continued)

11. Greenburg to Oak Ridge: $1\frac{1}{2}$ inches = 75 miles ≈ 80 miles

Greenburg to Bly: $2\frac{1}{8}$ inches = 106.25 miles ≈ 110 miles

Oak Ridge to Bly: $1\frac{1}{4}$ inches = 62.5 miles ≈ 60 miles

12. a) 40 sq. yd. (5 yd. × 8 yd.)

b) $700 ($17.50 × 40)

c) 44 sq. yd. left over (84 sq. yd. − 40 sq. yd.)

13. b) $6,000 ($15,000 × 40%)

14. b) 8 months (The line drops to the 80% level in about $\frac{2}{3}$ of the first year. $\frac{2}{3}$ of a year is 8 months.)

15. a) 4 to 7 (You calculate this ratio by taking the ratio of percents. A 3-year-old car is worth 40% of its new price, while a 1-year-old car is worth about 70% of its new price.

Ratio $= \frac{40\%}{70\%} = \frac{4}{7}$, or 4 : 7.)

16. c) The trade-in value of a well-maintained car is higher than that of a poorly maintained car.

(This statement is a fact, but the graph contains no information that could be used to support it.)